The
CLOCK
BOOK

An Overview of

HEIRLOOM and CONTEMPORARY
CLOCKS
in American Homes

With 144 Line Drawings by the Author

Philip E. Balcomb
Star Fellow
National Association of Watch and Clock Collectors

Author of
The Clock Repair PRIMER
The Clock Repair FIRST READER

Library of Congress Catalog Card No. 96-090257

Balcomb, Philip E.

The CLOCK BOOK
    An Overview of Heirloom and Contemporary
Clocks in American Homes

    Bibliography
        Index
Source Reference

First Printing September, 1996

ISBN No. 0-9620456-3-2

TEMPUS PRESS
P. O. Box 235, 104 Geneva Drive
Tell City, IN 47586-0235

Manufactured in The United States of America

FOREWORD

In almost forty years of repairing clocks, first those in my own collection, then for friends and folks they referred to me, it has been my good fortune to have seen a great many interesting specimens. I have had hands-on experience with most of those in this book. Over the years, I have been pleasantly surprised at the great variety and quality of clocks that are retained as treasured objects in homes from the most humble to the very affluent.

Over these years, I have accumulated a modest library of books on clocks of all kinds, but none that present a broad picture of the basic styles among the thousands of individual case designs produced by a great many manufacturers. This is similar to the situation that existed when I first looked for basic books on clock repair and found none.

The Clock Repair PRIMER and *The Clock Repair FIRST READER* were an attempt to fill that gap. Since the *PRIMER* was first published some ten years ago, more than thirty thousand copies have been sold. The continuing sale of these books is most gratifying and indicates that a perceived need has existed and at least to some extent fulfilled.

People with even a casual interest in clocks who would like to know more about them have had to accumulate information from a great many sources. *The CLOCK Book* is intended to perform as a broad beginner's guide to more specific areas of interest. Of necessity, it touches only the high spots. I hope it will encourage readers to home in on particular aspects of this fascinating subject.

A Bibliography is provided in the back of the book on page 179. It lists a number of books on specific horological subjects. Some are out of print, but most are available from book sellers specializing in books on clocks. A list of some of these is also included on page 181 of this book.

It is my hope that *The CLOCK BOOK* will stimulate the reader's interest to the point where clock collecting, even of a few clocks, will become the stimulating and rewarding hobby it has been for me.

Philip E. Balcomb
August 9. 1996

DEDICATION

Throughout the arduous task of creating this book and two life-threatening situations resulting in major surgery and difficult recovery, my family has been a bulwark of strength and encouragement. Without them, it would never have been completed.

It is with grateful thanks that I dedicate this book to my wife, Virginia, my daughters, Judy Wente and Pam Herring and my son-in-law Ted Herring.

They have each generously provided much needed encouragement and support over a stressful period of almost five years. Not only have they helped me deal with infirmities, they have consistently reinforced my determination to complete this project, which has given me an invaluable sense of purpose.

I also acknowledge the indirect support of the thousands of readers of my clock repair books who have been most generous in expressing their appreciation.

Philip E. Balcomb
Tell City, IN
August 10, 1996

TABLE of CONTENTS

x

CHAPTER ONE

The Fascination of Clocks

ALMOST EVERYONE has some appreciation for clocks, particularly those that have an audible tick and announce the hours by sounds of various kinds. They seem almost alive. Clocks appeal not only to the senses of sight and hearing, they invite the viewer to touch them. The owner of a fine clock nearly always develops a very personal relationship with it.

This interaction is strongest in the case of clocks that require winding to restore the power they need to function. During the latter part of the nineteenth century the low price of mass produced clocks made it possible for millions of ordinary people to own them. For maximum economy in manufacturing, these clocks ran for only 30 hours. Such clocks were common well into the twentieth century with 30 hour alarm clocks.

This short running time meant that people had to wind their clocks every day. It was routine for most people to "wind the clock and throw out the cat !" This routine was a common ritual. Often, because the family clock was a highly prized possession, the head of the house frequently appointed himself the sole caretaker of that treasure. Every night, before going to bed, he would wind the clock and set it by another valued timepiece, his pocket watch. Before watches became common, the chime of tower clocks, or the shriek of a factory whistle was relied on.

This close association of a man and a mechanical object became an important element in his life and that of the entire family. Many people alive today can recall this procedure as a time of reverent observation when they, as children, stood and listened to the scratching sound of the ratchets as father wound the clock. For anyone else to touch, much less tinker with any aspect of the family clock was unthinkable.

In a sincere effort to take the best possible care of their clocks, many owners used well intentioned practices that were actually damaging to the movements. The most common of these, dunking the movements in *Coal Oil* (kerosene made from coal) left a film that attracted and held dust which acted as an abrasive, causing excessive wear. Modern petroleum kerosene behaves the same way with respect to clocks. Improper lubricating is still one of the most common clock problems.

A small tin, used by pharmacists as a container for salves and ointments, was frequently placed in the bottom of the clock case and filled with coal oil. It was assumed that the vapor given off by the coal oil would continuously lubricate the movement. This vapor created a sticky varnish-like coating that attracted dust. This coating accumulated and in time literally *gummed up the works*.

I have seen many clock movements encrusted with heavy accumulations of dust and dirt collected by the coal oil residue. Almost invariably, severe wear had resulted. The interiors of these clocks frequently retain a strong odor of kerosene that assails one's nostrils whenever the door is opened.

Overoiling of clock movements can have the same harmful results. Some spots require only minute quantities of oil, others should never be oiled. Lubrication should only be done by experienced clock repairers. Periodic inspection, adjustment and lubrication by qualified people can reduce wear and significantly extend the useful life of a clock.

Nearly every one of the thousands of people who have brought clocks to me for repair has expressed some deep feeling about their clock. Often, I am told that the clock has been in the family for many years. Many people honestly believe their clock is much older that it is.. There is no harm in this, but a more accurate estimate of age can actually enhance the pleasure one derives from the certainty of his knowledge.

Among other things, this book will give you some clues to the relative age of many clocks, with an inkling of some of the fascinating history behind them. Inevitably, the question of value will arise and we will address that.

While beauty is truly in the eye of the beholder, with respect to clocks, the estimation of beauty is colored by the personal relationship between the owner and the clock. One owned by a forebear or close relative or a dear friend, takes on the aura of the memory of that person. This association may

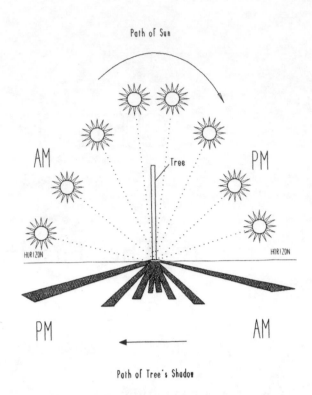

Figure 1 Sun and Shadow Show Passage of Time

transform a very ordinary clock from an almost ugly duckling to a treasured heirloom. It is especially true of clocks that "*Beauty is in the eye of the beholder.*"

For many centuries, clock movements whose function is to tell time have commonly been housed in cases intended to be viewed as fine pieces of furniture, or as objects of art. Case styles range from the almost primitive simplicity of the Shakers, to elegant Louis XIV sculptural ormolu, the ornate Victorian, Classic Roman, Rustic Mission, Art Nouveau, and countless other variations.

Like fashions in other areas of life, certain families of design were popular during different periods of history. While there have been faddish styles that have risen and fallen rapidly, a few with particular uniqueness or integrity of design have endured for centuries.

Oddly, among this group is what might otherwise be classed as a novelty, the Cuckoo Clock. These clocks of German origin, especially older ones, are family treasures today.

The design of clock cases has, to a large extent, been the result of changes and improvements in the design of clock movements. A most important factor is the gradual reduction in movement size.

HOW IT ALL STARTED

All animals relate to time. The lives of most are deeply affected by the obvious sequence of night following day. Some are active in daylight, while others are at their best in darkness. In addition to the obvious difference between night and day, early man discovered a regularity in the movement of the sun and the shadow of a tree, from morning to night. This led to the development of the Sun Dial. This is a simple method of making visible the precisely timed movement of the earth about the sun. Thus, high noon could be determined with reasonable accuracy, using a large sun dial. This was true only when the sun shone, however.

The performance of religious rituals and ceremonies have long been related to time. At first, elaborate, but crude structures such as Stonehenge, were built to make use of the movement of heavenly bodies. They provided a remarkably accurate means of dividing Years, Days and eventually Hours, into usable segments. Later, more elaborate and sophisticated structures served the same purposes more efficiently.

Such time oriented devices were typical of nearly all early civilizations.

Over the centuries, the design of sun dials was refined. In early times, sun dials were used to set clocks. Water clocks that measured the flow of water through a restricted passage, candles marked to show the passage of time and countless other devices served as crude timekeepers. There were countless devices for keeping track of time.

Those who understood the mysteries of time and were able to predict eclipses and other natural phenomena were considered extremely wise and had great power over the lower orders. How they

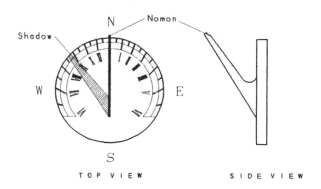

Figure 2 Sun Dial

determined these phenomena was held as a closely guarded secret by the priests or officials privy to the knowledge..

Sand Glasses

Perhaps the most ingeniously simple among ancient devices used for measuring time is the sand glass, or hour glass. These instruments consist of two funnel shaped glass bubbles joined at their small ends, with a tiny hole between them. A hole in the large end of one bubble allows sand to be introduced. With the end containing the sand up, all of the sand must pass through the opening into the lower bubble in the predetermined period of time. By varying the quantity of sand, the period measured could be adjusted. After the correct amount of sand was arrived at, the opening in the upper glass bubble was heated and sealed. The completed sand glass was then mounted in a protective case of wood or metal. These cases varied from very simple to elaborately ornate.

At best, sand glasses provided only a near estimate of the time period they were intended to define, yet some were remarkably accurate.

For untold centuries, hourglasses were used to measure time on land and at sea. For maximum accuracy, it was necessary to have a sharp-eyed person watch the passage of the last grain of sandand then to immediately invert the glass so the

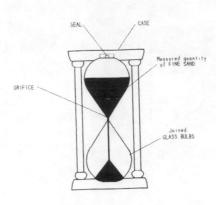

Figure 3 Sand Glass or Hour Glass

sand ran in the opposite direction. An audible signal, such as a bell, was frequently sounded to announce the end of the measured period of time.

Nautical Time

On ships, sand glasses measured half hours.

As a seaman turned the glass upside down, he also rang a bell. Each watch, or time on duty for a part of the crew, lasted four hours. Thus, the bell was sounded eight times during a watch.

The first half hour was marked by a single stroke on the bell. A stroke was added at each following half hour, with a pause between each pair of strokes. At two hours, the bell was struck four times, at two and a half hours, five times. At the end of the watch, the bell was struck eight times. The four pairs of strokes indicated the passage of four hours.

This system of periodically announcing the time by striking bells is still in use at sea. Time is kept by much more accurate self-striking clocks. For navigation, much more sophisticated timekeepers are now in use. Even they have been largely supplanted by radio navigation utilizing orbiting satellites.

Even when the sand in the glass passed from one chamber to another in precisely an hour, failure to turn the glass at the precise moment of the last grain passing resulted in cumulative error.

The interval measured by individual sand glasses might be many seconds to several minutes more or less than their nominal time period. Each was, however, quite consistent in the duration of the period it did measure. Sand glasses measuring roughly three minutes are readily available and quite commonly used today for timing the cooking of boiled eggs

MECHANICAL CLOCKS

The desire for a means of producing smaller and more accurate divisions of time led to the development of the mechanical clock. The essence of time keeping is the measurement of the duration of a repeated motion. A mechanical device showing the passage of time must have a source of power and a means of generating such motion. Devices to produce this intermittent conversion of power to motion, allowing the power to escape in predictable increments, are known as *escapements*.

In all probability, the first clock maker, noticed that the twisted ropes of a child's swing caused rotation in first one direction, then the other, repeatedly until all energy was expended. Using this principle, he devised a means of establishing short time intervals.

It was found that an arm, suspended on a cord, like the ropes of a child's swing, at its center, would oscillate at a constant rate when a very slight rotating impulse was applied.

A person, by assisting the motion of each twist of the cord could sustain the action for a limited period, but a clock requires a continuous source of power. This was provided by a rope attached to a drum to which a heavy weight was attached.

When the drum was wound to wrap the rope around it, the weight was pulled up, storing power.

A gear at the end of the drum transferred that power to drive a series of gears in a train that formed the clock movement. The final element of this train was the escape wheel.

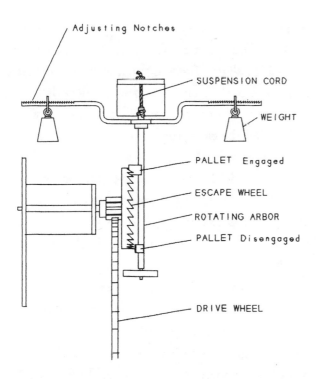

Figure 4 Foliot Clock Escapement

A brief impulse of power was supplied at the end of each oscillation, pushing the arm in the opposite direction. On the shaft supporting the rotating arm, two flat ears called *pallets* alternately received a tiny push from the tips of teeth on a wheel powered by the movement. This released the power of the weights at a fairly uniform rate.

In this way, the oscillating motion of the rotating arm was maintained. Varying the distance of a weight from the shaft on each side of the bar increased or decreased the rate of oscillation. This provided a means of adjustment, to cause the clock to run faster or slower.

This device to control the rate of escape of power is known as the *Foliot (folio) Escapement.*

The earliest clocks, powered by large weights, required that the movements be mounted high on a wall shelf to provide enough distance for the weights to fall while powering the clock for 24 hours.

When clock cases that enclosed the weights were made, they had to be tall. Until the poem "Grand-father's Clock" became popular, they were called simply *Tall Clocks.* The correct term is still TALL Clock, although *Grandfather* is common.

The sheer size and usually excellent cabinet work of most tall clocks sets them apart. Before the start of mass production manufacturing, all clocks were made by hand, using primitive methods and tools.

Since the art of coiled flat spring making was also primitive and comparatively unreliable, most clocks used weights for power. Unlike springs, weights have the advantage of providing exactly the same power throughout their travel. A few master clock makers did use carefully made and selected springs for power in small table clocks.

The first mechanical clocks were probably developed in England in the late 1200's. Later, there was sporadic clock making activity in the courts of other European countries. About 1550, in the German principalities, metal working skills had advanced to the point where complicated mechanical devices conceived by inventive minds were produced by a few master craftsmen.

Crude flat coil springs became available to provide a power source adequate for mechanical toys. However, their performance was so unpredictable that they were not usable as a source of power for time keeping.

Most of the spring driven clocks of the period from 1550 to about 1560 were actually elaborately decorated automated clockwork toys that incidentally incorporated a clock. Human and animal figures that moved were common and there were tiny multi-pipe organs and other operating instruments simulating trumpeters or a small orchestra. Some included marvelously intricate orrerys that reproduced the movement of the planets in their orbits.

In addition, the entire apparatus was frequently mounted on a wheeled carriage, powered by the spring, to carry it the length of a formal banquet table, while it performed for the assembled guests. Some even carried food. The intricacy of the animation and sound generation of some of these artifacts rival those of Disney *audio animatronics* in the electronic age, more than 400 years later.

While woefully unreliable as time keepers, the non-horological aspects of these spring powered devices encouraged the refinement of the mechanical skills and equipment for making movement parts that later contributed significantly to the production of much more accurate clocks.

DISCOVERY of the PENDULUM

A frenzy of exploration was started by Christopher Columbus in the 15th Century. There was an urgent need for improved precision in navigation, requiring much more precise timekeeping. This ultimately led to the development of the first accurate time pieces.

In 1657, Christian Huygens, a Dutch scientist, discovered the principle of the pendulum. He found that a suspended body swung in a constant arc and oscillated at the same rate, regardless of the length of the arc. He also noted that the greater the distance from the suspension point to the suspended body, the slower the rate of oscillation.

When applied to clock movements, the pendulum provided a much more accurate means of controlling the rate of the escape of power than was possible with the ancient foliot escapement. Many clocks were converted from foliot to pendulum and some of these have survived.

This new development was picked up quickly by English clock makers. It took on the order of a hundred years for clock makers in other parts of Europe to adopt it.

ADJUSTING for ACCURATE TIME

Using the principle that the rate of oscillation of a pendulum is a direct function of its length, a means of adjusting that length would make possible more accurate control. To achieve this a heavy weight, or *bob,* is commonly located at the bottom of the pendulum rod and is supported by a nut on a threaded shaft. Raising the bob by screwing the nut upward shortens the effective length of the pendulum and results in slightly faster swings. This makes the clock run faster. Lowering the bob causes the clock to run slower.

Another device has a means of raising or lowering a fork that fits over the suspension spring, to change the point at which the suspension spring bends. This also changes the effective length of the pendulum.

Even though such devices can provide close adjustment, other factors, notably temperature and humidity, can alter the length of the pendulum rod, thus changing its rate of oscillation. These variables, while apparently not of great magnitude, can result in gain or loss of several seconds per day, minutes per month.

Temperature affects nearly all materials. Humidity has an effect on woods, which expand as humidity increases, but little or none on metals. Some woods are far more prone to expansion or contraction resulting from changes in humidity than others. Those commonly used for pendulum rods are the least affected.

TEMPERATURE COMPENSATION

Nearly all materials, especially metals, expand noticeably when heated and contract when cooled. Wood is affected only minimally by variations in temperature. This is one of the reasons it is used extensively for pendulum rods.

The rate of expansion of solids, expressed in inches per degree of change is called the *coefficient* of expansion. The coefficient of expansion of some metals is much greater than that of others. Brass, commonly used in pendulum assemblies, has a coefficient of 0.00001" (one one hundred thousandth of an inch) per degree Fahrenheit. The coefficient of steel is 0.000006", much less than

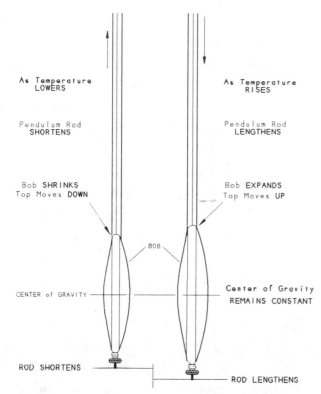

Figure 5 Pendulum Temperature Compensation

brass, while lead's is almost three times that, or 0.000016"

Steel which is much less affected by temperature than brass, is a more desirable material for pendulum rods. However, where the pendulum is exposed to view, the attractiveness of brass argues for its use.

Pendulum rods, whatever the material, become longer or shorter with changes in the temperature of the air surrounding them. This alters the rate of their oscillation or beat and the accuracy of the clock. This problem could be minimized by maintaining a precisely constant temperature around the pendulum, or by developing devices capable of *compensating* for temperature changes.

The earliest and simplest solution to this problem was a large pendulum bob made of brass, sometimes with a lead filling and a steel pendulum rod. Increased temperature causes the rod to lengthen downward.

The same temperature increase causes the bob to expand upward, from its support point, the nut on the pendulum rod. This raises the center of gravity of the bob. The brass and lead of the bob expands at a greater rate than the steel of the rod. As the steel rod lengthens, the center of the bob rises. In principle, the center of the bob maintains its distance from the pendulum suspension point. This compensation is only approximate, but does help.

Mercury, while liquid at normal temperatures, is a metal. Its volume increases much faster than other metals with increases in temperature. This accounts for its use in thermometers.

Some of the earliest precision time keepers employed mercury encased in metal or glass tubes as the bob of the pendulum. Using a large steel rod and several pounds of mercury, it is practical to design a combination that produces very good compensation. Because mercury increases significantly in volume as temperature rises, it expands in the tube. This raises the center of gravity of the tube and compensates for the lengthening of the steel rod caused by the temperature rise. As temperatures fall, the process is reversed.

In the not too distant past, temperature in homes and other buildings varied widely, making temperature compensation an important consideration for clock makers. Lead and brass bobs are common in mass produced and some other clocks. This is not because the weight is necessary to the function of the movement, but because their relatively high rates of expansion and contraction compensate, to some degree, for temperature changes.

CLOCK MAKING

Before mass production manufacturing, England and France were the world leaders in clock making. While their output was the product of individual craftsmen, it was significant because each master had a number of apprentices working under his close direction. The master closely supervised the work and the finished clock bore his name.

Most wealthy families around the world owned one or more clocks. They were indeed a status symbol. Clocks made by skilled English craftsmen were common among the nobility of most nations.

The Craft Guilds of the time, developing and refining the apprentice system, made it possible for a journeyman clock maker to oversee the work of many apprentices in training, He would routinely incorporate their work into finished products that he signed as his own. This multiplied the number of clocks each journeyman could produce. The cost, however, was high and only the wealthy could afford to purchase clocks. Most were made to order, a practice that led to innovations, especially in case design, to suit the whims of the prospective owner.

The development and refinement of tools for cutting teeth, drilling and polishing pivot holes, making and hardening pivots and many other operations necessary to clock making is a fascinating subject for many hobbyists.

Some craftsmen developed special tools, or became especially proficient in producing particular elements of clocks. Such experts commonly produced and sold their output to other clock makers, who incorporated it into the finished product.

Clocks are usually identified by the makers of their movements. Usually, all other parts including the case, dial and decoration were made by specialists in those elements. This remained true, even after the introduction of mass production.

Clock Making in the United States

In the colonies that became the United States, clocks were imported in the early stages of settlement. It wasn't long until clock makers trained in England or Holland migrated with their knowledge and tools and began making clock movements. They used mostly imported materials and sometimes finished parts from England. Such supplies were very expensive.

Among the many grievances of the colonies with the mother country, England, was an embargo on the importation of brass, the commonly used material for most clock movement parts. As an alternative material, American clock makers designed and constructed movements made almost entirely of wood.

The earliest clocks to be made in quantity were the Pillar and Scroll case style made by Eli Terry, Silas Hoadley and Seth Thomas in the early 1800's. They were fitted with wood weight driven movements.

Wood movements continued to be manufactured in quantity until about 1840.

While bulky and not very pretty, these movements performed remarkably well and a surprising number of them are still operative today.

With reasonable care and the air-conditioned atmosphere and uniform temperature in most modern homes, they can be expected to last almost indefinitely.

Clocks with wood movements are highly prized by many collectors, especially the original Pillar and Scroll style.

When brass became available and a process for economically rolling it into sheets was invented around 1850, punch presses and dies perfected and reliable steel coil springs could be obtained, mass-production movement making became a major industry.

Millions of clocks were manufactured each year and the United States quickly became the largest producer in the world. Clock manufacturing in other countries was seriously affected and America continued to dominate the market for almost a hundred years.

Electric Clocks

In the 1930's, clock movements consisting of an extremely simple and inexpensive electric motor and a few small gears were introduced. These are called *synchronous motors* because they operate in synchronization with the current cycles produced by electric generators. The power companies had developed methods of very accurately producing 60 alternating cycles per second in their production of power. Using this consistent measurement, corrected periodically by the power companies, time keeping of an accuracy far better than that of most mechanical clocks became commonplace. Millions are in use today.

These very good timekeepers eliminate the need for winding, divorcing the owner from his clock. Electric clocks are, however, locked into the power system and require a nearby outlet. Worst of all, they stop completely when there is an interruption of power and, when power is restored, they blatantly show the wrong time.

Synchronous clocks quickly displaced mechanical ones, many of which, unfortunately were consigned to the trash dump and lost forever. It is somewhat remarkable that so many have survived.

With the arrival of the space age and the exploration of exotic electrical and electronic concepts, there was a spinoff in time keeping.

The first product was a battery operated movement, developed in Japan. It was self-contained and used a C-size battery which powered it for about a year. Again, as with synchronous clocks, no winding was necessary. Batteries did run out of power and the clock stopped.

Interestingly, many of these clocks employ a miniaturized mechanical balance wheel movement, with a very small spring which is wound periodically by a tiny motor driven by the battery. Some more sophisticated movements have chimes which are powered by the battery. The chime train is connected to the spring winding arbor and the spring is wound a little each time the chime is activated. There are many variations of this kind of system.

The most revolutionary breakthrough in electrical timekeeping employs a once exotic device resulting from space research, the *quartz chip*. When electric current is applied, these chips oscillate at a very precise rate. With proper circuitry, they make possible a time keeping mechanism which is extremely small and reliable. A single AA size alkaline battery will power a quartz movement for a year or more.

Clocks, from tiny alarms to cheaply cased decorative ones with very large faces use these movements. Because of their low prices, they are probably the most popular timekeepers sold today. Unfortunately, the interface with humans is almost nonexistent. These clocks depend on their owner only to replace a battery every year.

It is unlikely that quartz clocks will ever become family heirlooms. They are a good example of the use and throw away attitudes common today.

At this writing, there is an ongoing contest between digital time readouts and the traditional dial and hands. In at least one model of wrist watch, both are visible at the same time.

CLOCKS as HEIRLOOMS

Until the introduction of electric timekeeping, clocks were among the most prized possessions of the average family. Clock movements, with reasonable care, last a very long time. When trouble does develop, it can nearly always be overcome by a competent repairman.

Many families today proudly possess one or more timepieces handed down from their forebears. Many of these are true antiques, more than a hundred years old. They are heirlooms in every sense of the word.

CLOCKS as OBJECTS of BEAUTY

The appearance of the case of a clock generally mirrors the tastes of the time in which it was made.. Popular furniture styles were often mirrored in clock case design.

As we will see in some detail later in this book, tastes changed and the design of clock cases changed as well. Regardless of when they were created, every clock case was intended to appeal to a prospective owner. They invariably reflected the tastes of their time.

The very earliest clock cases were made for the nobility and privileged classes of society. We can safely assume that they were designed to represent the most sophisticated tastes of their time.

As clocks became available to the common man, most cases were designed to please him. They represented the collective tastes of a much larger segment of society than when clocks were custom made.

The cases in which mechanical clock movements are housed generally were made with great care by highly skilled craftsmen. They were intended to last a very long time. Materials were carefully selected and shaped, then assembled and finished. Especially during the 19th Century, this was true even of mass produced clocks that were manufactured in the millions.

Wood Cases

Wood is by far the most common material chosen for clock cases. It is readily available and can be easily worked into various shapes. Its color and grain can be most attractive. Wood has another enviable property; it shows its age gracefully and with added beauty.

From the Gothic elegance of early tall clocks to the simplicity of Shaker designs to the ornate carved, turned and pressed decoration of the Victorian era, wood cases have preserved the standards of beauty of their era.

Stone Cases

Polished stone is beautiful to almost everyone. Whether the jet black of obsidian, or the variegated colors of onyx and marble, stone has a depth unmatched by other materials. A major drawback, however, is that it is also very heavy.

In European courts, especially France, the cases housing clock movements were much more important than the time keeper. Each was first an *object d'art* and only secondarily a clock. This is most evident when small dials appear in large cases.

French clock makers to the nobility, hundreds of years ago, utilized the sculptural qualities of stone. Sculptors commissioned by clock makers to produce clock cases often signed their handiwork as they did their pure artistic sculptural works.

Around 1890, French clock makers began using simpler cases made of onyx and other stone to house their movements. Many of these clocks were exported and examples can be found in the United States today. These were high quality clocks and most of the cases were classically attractive. Often, they were accompanied by matching sidepieces, candelabra or vases.

Some American clock manufacturers, noting the growing popularity of these clocks, had stone cases made in Europe. They were shipped to the United States where American movements were installed and sold as American clocks.

Stone is very heavy and the costs were high. Stone cased clocks were comparatively expensive.

Cast Iron Adamantine-Finished Cases

Enterprising American clock manufacturers designed a case along the lines of many French onyx clocks. It was typically rectangular in shape with a base and flat top extending over the front and sides.

The front corners are supported by claw feet made of pot metal, with simpler feet at the rear. Classic half columns with pot metal capitals and pediments are attached on either side of the clock bezel.

These cases were made of thin sections of cast iron and finished with a thick jet-black paint made with natural asphalt. This paint, about which little is known, had the ability to fill the pitted surface left by the sand of the molds. At the same time it produced a glossy and very durable surface finish, though it was soft and easily scratched.

Derived from *adamant*, unyielding, the dictionary definition of *adamantine* is "hard, unbreakable". In the eyes of the makers, their cases undoubtedly had these qualities. The word was adopted as a generic identification.

These clocks were heavy and expensive to manufacture and ship. In a short time, the designs were adapted to wood construction and the era of the "Beautiful Black" clock emerged.

Millions of these wood clocks were made over a period of several decades

Marbleized Finish Cases

Marbleized or simulated marble finishes were developed and used extensively in the later stages of production of the "Black" or flat-top style case. These finishes were also advertised as "*Adamantine*". The use of this word for this application is even more inappropriate than it was for the black iron cases, since the finish was perhaps even softer and more subject to damage.

I am not aware of the details of these finishes, but they were made up of a celluloid-like material with colors swirled to simulate a marble pattern. The resultant product was a thin celluloid-like sheet film which was laminated to the wood.

The overall appearance of these marbleized finish clocks is rich and colorful. Their primary weakness is their susceptibility to scratching and other surface damage. The finish is quite soft and repair is almost impossible, except for very small irregularities.

Flat-top clocks by all major clock manufacturers used marbleized finishes. Like natural marble, the dominant color varied from red to green to light ivory and tan.

Wood Veneer Cases

Veneer is very thin wood, usually of a rare or exotic variety with unusually attractive grain patterns. By slicing the logs of these expensive woods into thin sheets and laminating them to common woods, their beauty can be spread over a much greater number of cases.

Some of the finest furniture ever made has employed veneer. In addition to efficiently utilizing rare woods, veneering allows the cabinet maker to select grain patterns. Using sheets on either side of a cut, he can create a mirrored pattern. This is called book matching, like opening the pages of a book. He can select attractive patterns and reject less desirable ones.

Veneers in contrasting colors or shades can easily be incorporated in a single surface. Elaborate inlay patterns can be created.

The substructure of high quality veneered furniture is made of the most stable and strongest wood readily available, regardless of its surface appearance. This assures a strong case which, when covered with veneer and finished, is also a beautiful one. Conversely, solid wood cases are like the substructure of a veneer case, but the surface pattern can vary widely.

The earliest tall clock cases, made in England, were commonly made of pine, veneered with other species. Sometimes the veneer was made from local oak and walnut. The primary reason for the use of veneer in these cases was to create pleasing grain pattern.

Case *Decoration*

To enhance the attractiveness of clock cases, many forms of solid embellishment have been used. Inlays of wood veneer, pewter, brass, mother-of-pearl, ivory, bone and other materials had their day. Among the most common attachments are finials made of wood or brass, full and half columns, turned balls and spindles and carved decorations. Statuettes were or added to many clock cases.

Hand painting of dials was sometimes quite elaborate and colorful. Now almost a lost art, reverse painting on glass tablets enriched the appearance of a clock immeasurably.

Reverse painting, in which illustrations were painted in reverse on the back of the glass, was used extensively, especially in early banjo and triple decker clocks. This was a uniquely American application of an ancient art. Later, it was replaced by mass produced transfers, stencils and decals.

Some tall clock cases were painted black and painted with designs of oriental nature. This style was especially popular in England.

CLOCK SOUNDS

Much of the fascination of mechanical clocks stems from the sounds made by their movements as they perform their function of moving the clock hands in accurate progression.

From the almost inaudible ticking of a fine carriage clock, to the rich chimes of a grandfather clock, to the stentorian tolling of Big Ben as it counts the hours, each clock has its own characteristic voice.

The BEAT

The earliest rhythm known to man was the beating of his own heart. Since this was discovered, we have been generating sounds at regular intervals, notably with drums, to produce audible rhythms. Such rhythms, in turn, stimulate a desire to react by tapping toes, moving hands, or dancing.

The beat of most clocks is nothing like that made by drums, or bass guitars. It is much quieter, yet sharp and very uniform. To most people it is a very soothing sound.

The characteristic ticking of clocks is produced by the impact of a single tooth of a rotating escape wheel as it is stopped by contact with a pallet of an oscillating verge. This may sound complicated, but this escape mechanism simply stops and releases the teeth of a wheel. It is the means of controlling the *rate* at which power is released from springs or weights. It establishes and regulates the time keeping function of the clock.

Watches and many very small clocks have a *balance wheel* escapement. This is a small wheel with a tiny hair spring that rotates back and forth at a regular rate. It controls the motion of the pallets, and the rate at which power is released. Balance wheels oscillate rather rapidly, producing a beat with a very short interval. The sound is a quick *tick, tick, tick, tick, tick.* It is almost inaudible unless the clock is held very close to the ear.

Most larger clocks have movements controlled by a pendulum that swings back and forth. The longer the pendulum, the slower the rate of oscillation.

Most Tall (Grandfather) clocks have what is called a "*Seconds Beat*" pendulum. This is usually a little more than a yard long and takes a second to swing from one side to the other. These movements are larger than those in smaller clocks and the sound produced by the escape mechanism is usually louder. Regardless of the size of the movement, the beat should be an even

tick .... tick .... tick........tick.......tick

not

tick .. tock .... tick .. tock.

In the days before radio and television, homes were typically quiet, except for human noises. The ticking and striking of a clock was the only sound to be heard continuously, all day and all night. This provided a reassuring continuity to life. Even today, it is a common practice to place a ticking clock in a new puppy's sleeping place.

SOUND QUALITY

In many respects, striking and chiming clocks are like musical instruments. All sounds are produced by vibrations generating waves in the air. The frequency of these waves determines the pitch and the depth the amplitude of the sound.

An electronic synthesizer is capable of generating sounds of any specific frequency, producing a "pure" tone.

Musical instruments on the other hand, create not only a basic tone, or note, but *overtones* in addition. It is these overtones that are responsible for the richness of sound of particularly fine instruments, like a Stradivarius violin. The mix of overtones varies with each instrument, depending largely on the characteristics of the case.

The sound of a violin is produced by the vibration of a string at a designated frequency. This vibration is transmitted to the body, or case, of the instrument by the bridge, causing it to sympathetically vibrate and amplify the sound generated by the string. In doing so, the thin wood of the body vibrates and the sound generated bounces back and forth inside the uniquely shaped case, producing overtones. This is called *resonance*, or *timbre*.

Experts have put forth many theories on why a Stradivarius violin produces its unique and wonderful sound. These include the type of wood used in the case and its aging or curing, the precise shape and thickness of each of the elements, the type of glue and technique of applying it, the final finishing of the wood and the character of the varnish used. Nobody has ever been able to truly duplicate the tone quality of a Stradivarius.

The quality of the sound generated by clocks, whether simply for announcing the hours, or for producing elaborate melodies, has always been of concern to most clock makers and certainly to clock owners who live with them. Richness of tone is a characteristic of the finest clocks.

The earliest clock sound makers were probably bells made of cast iron. The discovery of bronze bell-metal and the development of the now typical bell shape made it possible to produce large bells for tower clocks that had remarkable resonance. They continue to vibrate long after they have been struck.

When clocks were made smaller and adapted to indoor use, a bowl-shaped bell of cast iron announced the hours. Later, as metallurgy progressed, other types of metal were used, notably brass, bronze and nickel-silver.

Rarely, leaded glass bells may be found in old clocks.

In addition to bells of various shapes, tubes, bars and coils of various metals found favor as striking and chiming elements.

CLOCK CASES and SOUND

Not many common clock cases were designed primarily to improve the sound of their striking or chiming elements. An exception is the Seth Thomas line of *Sonora* clocks which have a unique resonating box made of thin wood inside the case, on which bells are mounted. Sonora chimes have unusual clarity and resonance.

Early on it was discovered that mounting a coil gong on the thin back board of a wood case amplified and improved the tonal quality of the sound.

Later, it became common practice to mount the gong on a metal stand firmly attached to a thin base board forming the bottom of the case. It is essential that all elements of this arrangement be firmly connected for maximum resonance.

The overall character of the case has a great influence on the quality of the sound produced by a clock. In general, because there is more surface area, larger cases resonate more than smaller ones, producing a richer sound.

Details of case construction also affect sound quality. Any loose elements can produce annoying rattling noises. This also happens if a key or other object is left on the bottom of a case. As with the Stradivarius violins, many unknown elements affect sound quality. Variations in these elements result in each clock having its own set of overtones and overall sound which are apparent to the trained ear.

Perhaps the most significant thing affecting sound quality is the adjustment of the impacting hammer. While the dimensions will vary from clock to clock, the hammer should strike the bell or gong sharply, then instantly move back to barely clear the vibrating sound maker.

Most American clocks have hammers consisting of a thick round piece of brass crimped on a wire arm. When it strikes a large coiled steel gong, as is usually the case, this often produces a very loud sharp noise. The variety of steel alloys used in coil gongs produces varying tone quality.

Many hammers, especially in chiming clocks, are cylindrical, with a leather or plastic insert that becomes the striking face. This slightly cushions the impact and usually results in a softer, less metallic and more pleasing tone.

At best, large coil gongs struck by a brass hammer tend to produce a loud and rather jarring note. This can be modified a bit by adjusting the hammer arm so that the hammer barely touches the gong on impact. Sometimes, the hammer is wrapped in leather to produce a softer tone.

CHIMES and CHIME MELODIES

For centuries, certain English churches have been equipped with tuned bells hung in the belfry. Originally, each bell had to be swung by a man pulling a rope attached to the bell mount, causing it to strike a clapper hung inside.

Traditionally, the bell ringer would pull the ropes in a set sequence, producing an atonal sound called *changes*. Eventually a system of levers was developed to enable the ringer to lift and drop individual clappers against the outside of the bells. This made it possible to play simple tunes.

The bell ringers of some of these churches developed easily recognized melodies that became identified with that church, i.e., *St. Michael's*

The most popular of these tunes used in clocks today is known as *Westminster*, since it is the one played by the Westminster Great Clock, whose huge bell, named *Big Ben* chimes the hours for all of London.

These tunes are in four parts, one of which is played at each successive quarter hour. Some modern chiming clocks can play any one of several melodies, as selected by moving a lever on the face of the dial. Cuckoo clocks, in addition to a gong strike, use whistles to announce the hours and sometimes, quarter hours.

There a few rare clocks that have small pipe organs that play one or several melodies. Others have music box type mechanisms. A few even have tiny mechanical orchestras.

Clock works power music boxes, simple and complex. The better ones have long playing times capable of reproducing complete melodies and use interchangeable discs to activate the tines of the steel comb that creates the tones. Rarely, such musical movements have been used in tall clocks.

In recent years, battery powered quartz clock movements have been made by the millions. Some are provided with electronic sound generators that produce classic chime melodies which are recognizable but of inferior quality as compared to conventional chimes.

CHAPTER TWO

CLOCKS In GENERAL
An OvervIew

CLOCKS ARE UTILITARIAN, in the sense that they are used to tell time. Traditionally, clocks are displayed in full view of people and are a prominent element in the decor of a room. If large, like a tall clock, they become a form of furniture. Even smaller clocks often reflect the furniture styles of the period in which they were made. Their designers have tried to make them as attractive as possible.

When first seeing an individual clock, most viewers will make an instant judgment as to its appearance. Some will be considered beautiful, while others may seem ugly. That judgment is strictly subjective and will vary widely between individuals.

Each clock is made up of several basic visible elements whose appearance can be varied almost infinitely. A few of these are strictly functional, but most are adapted in one way or another to be pleasing to the eye.

Essential features of every clock are a movement to provide its time keeping ability, a case to house the movement and hands or other means of showing the time. In its simplest form, this is a box with hands. Even without numbers on a dial, the relative position of the hands makes it possible to tell the time reasonably accurately. In its simplest form, a clock is a box with hands.

. The simplest dials use only dots or other symbols, but no numerals, at the hour points. Some, as in Mission style clocks, may have no markings at all, depending on the observer's familiarity with clock hand positions to tell time.

Particularly during the early centuries of clock making by hand, clocks were very expensive. They were always prominently displayed by their proud owners who wanted this significant possession to be as attractive as possible.

The first decoration of a clock was probably by blacksmiths in England, when they stamped a time track and numerals on an iron dial. When more easily worked brass became the material of choice for clock movements that functioned without cases, the exposed brass plates of the movement were elaborately engraved.

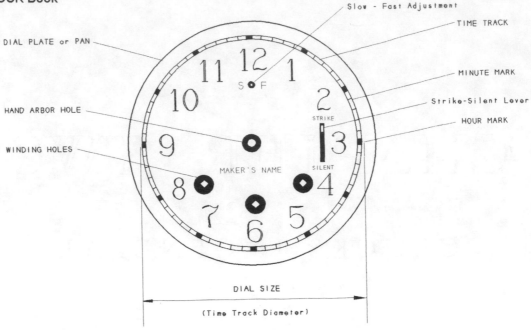

Figure 6 Elements of a Typical Clock Dial

Early European clock cases were made of cast and hammered brass sheets and were intended primarily to protect the movement from the dirt, smoke and cooking greases common in most homes equipped with fireplaces. These cases were sometimes decorated with engraving. Shaped like lanterns of the time, among collectors they are now called *Lantern* clocks.

IDENTIFYING the ELEMENTS of CLOCKS

Since each clock is the sum of its parts, identifying it and assessing its authenticity is dependent on an evaluation of each of its elements and their relationship to each other.

Marriages, the mixing of elements from different clocks, sometimes even those of different makers, is not uncommon, particularly in older clocks.

The resulting assembly, while it might outwardly appear genuine, will not be authentic and will have lost much of its value. Unfortunately, many old movements have been thrown away and replaced with modern quartz movements

In this book, we will try to provide a good basic introduction to the fundamental characteristics of *families* of clock designs. Because of the almost infinite variety of details found in clocks, a careful in-depth study of all the elements of a particular style or model by an expert may be necessary to determine its authenticity.

We will go into mechanical details only superficially and will confine our observations to those elements that can be readily seen. This may sometimes require that a door be opened so you can see elements inside the case, such as pendulums, maker's labels, etc.

For an introduction to how clocks work, see *The Clock Repair PRIMER.* and *The Clock Repair FIRST READER*, by the author of this book.

CASE DESIGN

The case is the largest and most obvious element of most clocks. Many mass production clock manufacturers attached a name to each of their case designs. This name identifies the entire clock.

Case size and design and the materials from which it is made are a clock's most prominent features.

As a timekeeper, a clock must have a means of visually showing the time. This is usually a dial and hands that frequently form the major visual element of a clock.

In some clocks, the dial is the *only* visible element, so large it completely covers the case that houses the movement.

Extra dials and hands may be added to show a variety of time associated events, such as seconds, phases of the moon and tide rise and fall. In addition to the essential case and dial, most clocks have purely decorative elements. Some add features that can be both utilitarian and decorative, such as a bezel and glass to protect the hands and dial.

This chapter, will provide brief historical background information and will broadly discuss the visible elements of clocks. Even among professional horologists (*experts on timekeepers*), clocks are generally identified by the design of their cases. We will touch on the early evolution of case design, how it reflects the tastes of the period in which it was made and how it relates to and is dependent on the characteristics of the specific movement it houses.

Later in this book, you will find a number of illustrations of clock case designs, both domestic and foreign, that are found in American homes today. An understanding of basic clock elements will prove useful there.

DIAL COMPONENTS

The Dial Plate

Most clock dials consist of a plate, made of metal or wood. Visual details, such as numerals are usually painted over a base coat or are printed on paper that is then glued to the plate surface.

Many very old clocks and some more recent higher quality clocks have polished metal dials. The details may be engraved, etched or stamped in the metal.

Old metal dials and those of better quality made in recent years are usually made of brass. Sometimes they are silver plated with black enamel or shellac filling incised or engraved numerals. Recently made dials of this type commonly employ aluminum which is sometimes anodized to a gold color to simulate higher quality dials.

Comparatively few dials, notably Viennese and French, are made of copper with porcelain faces. They are extremely durable and many which are well over a hundred years old are still in fine condition.

A few clocks have dial plates of glass, with the numerals and decoration printed or painted in reverse on the back side. Some, like old French *"picture frame"* clocks, have glass or porcelain dial plates with the numerals carried on elaborate individual medallions of porcelain on cast brass attached to the face.

Cast iron cased clocks often have dials of the same material, or of cast bronze, with raised numerals and decorative elements.

The Time Track

As an instrument for measuring and displaying the passage of time, clocks usually have a scale on the dial, divided into time units. This is called the *Time Track*. It is made up of two concentric circles placed close together.

Radial lines are placed between the circles at intervals of six degrees, for a total of 60, each representing one minute. Usually, every fifth mark is widened or a diamond or circle inserted, to emphasize the hour as well as five minute interval points, which are the same.

Time tracks may be simple circles with or without minute increments and/or five minute markers. Some are elaborately decorated. Some dials have *no* time track.

Dial sizes are determined by the outside diameter of the largest circle of the time track, with no regard to the size of the plate on which the dial is displayed. If the time track has a radius of three inches, it will be classed as a six inch dial.

Holes are provided in dials to permit manual operation of various essential movement functions. These include one for the hand arbor to pass through, one or more to allow engaging the key on a winding arbor and slots for control levers Most important is the winding of the springs that power the time, chime and strike trains.

1. Hand Arbor and Winding Arbor Holes

There is always a hole at the center of the dial, through which the hand shaft or arbor passes. This hole may be just a little larger than the shaft, or it may be large enough to pass an alarm setting disc. This hole on some early American clocks is much larger than the shaft and may be scalloped. Especially in weight-driven and Kitchen clocks, an alarm setting dial may be located in this opening.

Usually, except with rope or chain pull up weight drives, there is a hole in the dial for the winding arbor of the time train. If there is a strike train, there will be a second hole.

When there is a chime train, a third hole will be provided for its winding arbor. The square end of each arbor is visible just behind the dial. Winding arbor holes are usually just large enough in diameter to admit the winding key or crank.

A few early American wood movement clocks had rope pull up drives. Sometimes dummy winding holes and arbors were painted on the dial to make it look like a wind-up type.

3. Slow-Fast Adjustment

Many clocks made during the late 19th and early 20th century have a small round hole, usually directly above the numeral 12. A small square ended shaft centered in this hole may be turned to adjust the timekeepking of the clock.

Keys for this type of clock have two ends, one with a small square hole to match this arbor, the other mating with the larger spring winding arbors.

The letters S and F are usually found on either side of this hole. Turning the key counter-clockwise, toward the S, causes the clock to run *slower*, toward the F *faster*.

4. Strike and/or Chime Control

Some clocks have a slot, usually on the right side, near the edge of the dial plate. In this slot is a lever that may be moved up or down to select the chime tune to be played or to silence the chime and/or strike. The words *Strike* and *Silent* at either end of the slot on the dial indicate the position of the lever to control these functions.

Many newer tall clocks are capable of announcing the quarter hours with any one of three chime melodies. A slot in the dial with a lever, similar to the one described above carries the names of the various tunes. Usually *St. Michael's, Whittington, or Westminster.* The tunes may be selected by moving the lever to the printed name of the tune desired.

In rare clocks with organ pipes, bells, or other means of generating musical notes, a choice of melodies to be played can be selected by any one of various means, depending on the ingenuity of the maker.

All of the notes for these melodies are generated by pins on a cylinder driven by the movement. Each pin activates a specific note whether the notes are by chime, whistle, bells, organ or other means .

Figure 7   Clock Dial with Roman Numerals

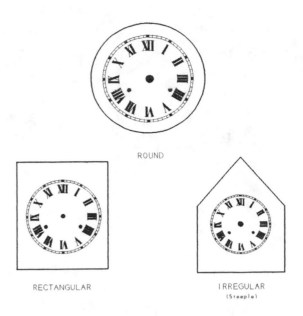

Figure 8   Some Dial Plate Shapes

Dial Numerals

Both Arabic and Roman numerals are commonly found on clock dials. The styles of each type vary almost infinitely, reflecting the artistic tastes of the times and the maker.

Arabic numerals are almost always placed in a horizontal position at each hour mark, so they are read normally. They may, however be oriented radially. In this case, the 12 and 6 are upright and the bottoms of the 9, 10, 11, 1, 2 and 3 are toward the center, while the tops of the 4, 5, 7 and 8 are oriented to the center. Roman numerals are positioned radially, so that those from IIII to VIII are inverted.

Most people are unaware of an interesting anomaly in clock dials. The Roman numeral for 4 is normally written IV. Clock dials almost invariably use IIII. The reason for this is that the four elements provide a better visual balance with the four elements of the normally written VIII on the opposite side, as shown here:

VIII   IV

VIII   IIII

Applied Numerals and Markers

Early in the 20th century, with the Mission and Art Nouveau styles then popular, clock dials frequently consisted simply of the case material, usually wood, with metal numerals arranged where the hour marks would be. There was no time track or other marking. Sometimes there were no numerals at all, simply geometric figures made of metal or another material applied to the face.

Where foreign alphabets or characters were used, the numerals of clocks made for those markets frequently employed the prevailing local style. It is interesting, however, that in some cases the numerals were Arabic or Roman, while all other markings were in the local alphabet, i.e., Japanese, Chinese, Cyrillic, etc.

CONVEX TIME TRACK   CONVEX CENTER   FULL CONCAVE

Figure 9 Examples of Embossed Dial Plates

Dial Plate Shapes

The plate on which the dial of a clock is printed, painted or engraved can be of any shape. The one usually used is that which best suits the particular case style and construction. The plate for the Steeple clock dial is a good example of this. This is generally true, regardless of the material or materials employed.

Porcelain dials are nearly always round, because the stresses caused by the intense heat involved in melting and cooling the minerals that form the porcelain matrix is more evenly distributed. This minimizes undesirable checking and cracking.

Irregular dial shapes usually fit the door or bezel opening of specific case designs. A pointed dial plate for an American Sharp Gothic Steeple clock is shown in Figure 8.

More complex shapes will be found in tall or Grandfather clock dials. In almost every case, the dial plate shape follows that of the case in which it is mounted.

Especially in Tall Clock dials, a cut-out for a moving moon face at the top of the dial was very common

Embossed Dial Plates

Especially during the mid-nineteenth century, most American clock dial plates were made of *sheet zinc*. This is a very malleable material and is comparatively easy to form by pressing between dies.

Many clock manufacturers developed dial plates that had raised or depressed areas as shown in Figure 9. This technique is called *embossing*.

The Ogee style of case, introduced around 1830, along with the later half-column and column and cornice clocks and many shelf clock styles were commonly equipped with painted zinc dials. Millions of these clocks had embossed dials. The sheet zinc is soft, very thin and easily bent. Embossing made these flimsy sheets much stiffer.

Embossed dials were painted and decorated in the same manner as flat ones. They usually had Roman numerals and colorful designs in the corners and, sometimes, in the center section of the dial. They were subject to deterioration of the paint, just like flat dials. In addition to the simple embossed zinc dials shown in Figure 9, some very fine dials, usually made of brass, were embossed with very intricate decorative designs.

Painted Metal Plate Dials

The white paint used on metal clock dial plates, especially those made of zinc, is subject to checking, cracking and flaking. While most such clocks are more than 100 years old, this damage is not caused simply by age.

Variations in temperature cause the zinc of the dial plate and the paint to expand and contract. The *rate* of expansion of the zinc is much greater than that of the paint. When the zinc expands, the paint coat is stretched beyond the limits of its tensile strength and it fails, cracking and forming an alligator pattern.

The bond between the paint and metal is weakened and eventually the paint will separate from the metal. Repeated cycles of such differential expansion and contraction almost completely destroy the bond between paint and metal and the paint falls away in flakes.

The homes in which these dials existed for most of their lives were subject to radical variations in temperature, from highs of around 100° to lows well below freezing.

Temperature differentials of more than 30° *in a day* were not uncommon. This accelerated the deterioration of the paint. While almost all the paint is missing from some metal dials, many have lost only a few flakes. Some, notably those made of iron and found in old English tall clocks remain essentially intact. This is because the iron and paint expand and contract at more nearly the same rate.

The much more even temperatures made possible by thermostatically controlled central heating and air conditioning common in homes today would have almost eliminated this problem.

Significant advances in paint formulation now provide paint films that are much more flexible and have better adhesion to metals. If modern paints had been available 200 years ago, flaking would have been much less of a problem.

Figure 10 Typical Simple Calendar Dial

Printed Paper Dials

A few printed paper dials were applied by their makers to the wood dial plates of clocks with wood movements made about 1820. In the early 20th century, paper dials became common, notably on millions of American alarm clocks.

While there are artists today who repaint old dials, this is time consuming and expensive. Excellent dials printed on paper of a color similar to that of the paint on old dials are available. It has become common practice to paste paper dials on metal plates that were originally painted.

Calendar Dials

Many simple calendar clocks show only the date, indicated by a single slender hand, usually painted red. A ring of numerals, from 1 through 31, is provided, outside the time track. This type is shown in Figure 10 Typically, a long hand indicates the date.

More complex calendar mechanisms indicate the day of the week as well as the date. Some, as the

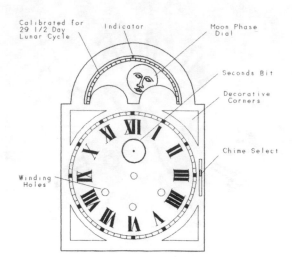

Figure 11   Triple Chime Moon Phase Dial

Fashion, made by Southern Calendar Clock Co. and others, automatically adjust for the irregular number of days in months and even for Leap Year. A separate dial with cylinder indicators for this information is located below the time dial. Such mechanisms are known as *perpetual* calendars.

These clocks have a separate device, made up of wheels and levers, mounted at the bottom of the case. It is activated around midnight each day by the clock movement and advances the wheels and hands to show information appropriate for that function on that day.

There are a number of other calendar clocks with similar devices, most of which were made only in limited numbers.

Seconds Bits

Perhaps the earliest addition to dials reading minutes and hours was the seconds bit. This is a small circle *(Time Track)* with 60 divisions for seconds and a hand that makes one revolution per minute. Seconds bits are sometimes quite small, but some are rather large.

Tall Clocks, with pendulums that beat once each second, were easily adapted to indicate seconds. A few English and Scottish tall clocks have long seconds hands using the standard time track. When long seconds hands are used, numerals are usually placed at five second intervals *outside* the time track. They may be oriented radially, or horizontally.

Complex Dials

The occurrence of time related events, other than the passage of seconds, minutes and hours are of great importance to people by whom they are affected. Those involved in agricultural pursuits use the movement of the moon as a guide to planting, harvesting and other activities.

Particularly in tall clocks, the dials reflect the more complex movements many of them contain. The earliest and most common, especially in recent years, shows the *phases of the moon* and its progression through its 29 ½ day cycle.

For mariners and those living near the sea shore, the motion of the tides is most important. The *tide cycle* is the same as the moon's, 29 ½ days; a tide dial indicates the days of the cycle and the occurrence of high and low tides.

A few clocks, referred to as *complicated*, have several dials indicating a wide variety of activities, from the movements of the planets around the sun, to the times of religious ceremonies. Such clocks will often have more than one dial, with each dial indicating a specific time-related event.

Many complex dials are elaborately decorated. Complicated French clocks typically combine fire gilt ormolu decoration with decorated porcelain dials and elaborate case decoration.

Program clocks for regulating factory operations by activating audible signals such as bells or whistles at specific preset times, became common in the early 1900s.

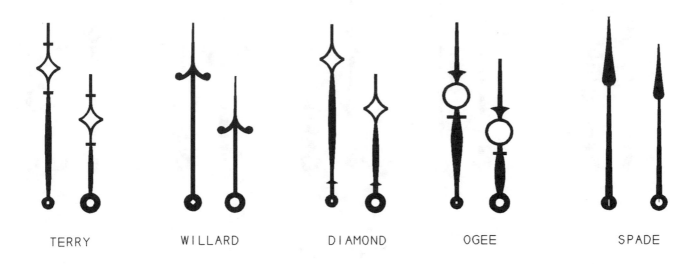

TERRY   WILLARD   DIAMOND   OGEE   SPADE

Figure 12 Representative Early American Clock Hands

CLOCK HAND STYLES

In addition to their utilitarian function of indicating the time, the hands of clocks have always been an important element of their design.

A particular design may be identified with a specific maker, or with a case style produced by many makers. In some cases, general characteristics are associated with a country or geographic area.

During the many centuries when all clock parts were individually crafted, no two were ever quite alike. Each maker undoubtedly had patterns for the designs he used, but the piercing, cutting out and filing of each hand made it unique. With the advent of mass production, identical hands were produced by the millions.

Materials Used for Hands

The ideal material for clock hands would be strong, hard and stiff. The stronger the material, the more delicate the hand can be without danger of bending when it is moved to set the time. The earliest hands were made of cast or wrought iron and were far from delicate. When brass came into common use for clock movements, it wasn't long until the hands were also made of this material. Some brass alloys are comparatively strong, but are also easily worked. Craftsmen with artistic ability began to design and make elaborate hands that were highly prized and often bought by other makers.

There was no production of brass in America in the late 1700s. When supplies from overseas were embargoed by the King, the only brass available was obtained by melting down old articles made of this material. American clock makers were able to obtain only very limited quantities of brass for movements, so they made movements of wood and sometimes made hands of cast pewter. This is a very soft metal and, even though the hands were quite thick, they were easily bent and broken during setting of the hands.

Steel of the proper formulation can be worked in a comparatively soft state and then hardened. It is an almost ideal material for clock hands which can be delicate in appearance, yet very strong. In addition, proper heat treatment permanently colors the surface of the metal to a deep blue, almost black. For more than a hundred years, steel has been the material of choice for clock hands.

MALTESE   MOON   SPEAR   TREFOIL   VIENNA

F R E N C H

Figure 13 American and European Clock Hands

In recent years, replacement hands and even those on some new clocks have been made of very soft thin aluminum, painted black. They are very easily bent.

Hand Size and Shape

Hands are moving parts of a clock. Their rotation is the result of the movement's work. They move in a vertical plane and the minute hand in particular has a long lever arm. The heavier the outer end of the hand, the more power is consumed to overcome gravity in raising it from the six to the twelve position. Gravity, on the other hand, adds to the power available as the hand falls from twelve to six. The finer the movement, the more significant the extra weight becomes.

This effect introduces a potentially undesirable variable into the time keeping accuracy of a clock, so it was felt necessary to keep the outer end of the hands as light as possible. At the same time there was an urge to make highly decorative designs. The result was extremely delicate tracery. This is particularly noticeable in the hands of French and Viennese clocks. Such hands were only practical because there were steel makers who had developed closely guarded formulas for producing steel of high strength.

Some minute hands were provided with a counter-balancing tail opposite the pointing portion. Usually, its design is tastefully integrated with that of the rest of the hand.

The length of the minute hand, measured from the center of the hole fitting the minute arbor to its tip, is usually equal to the radius of the outer circle of the time track.

The hour hand is shorter than the minute hand. Its tip usually overlaps the inside of the numerals on the dial. Most often, if not identical and when individually they may appear quite different, there is a recognizable similarity between the shape of the two hands of a given style.

The difference in length between the hour and minute hand in a pair varies widely, but usually it is comparatively small.

Early American clock hands followed the English tradition, were usually made of brass, and were comparatively elaborate. Some were made of cast pewter in an effort to eliminate laborious hand filing. A notable exception to this was the delicate arrow head design developed and used by the Willards for their banjo clocks.

Standardized Hand Styles

There is an almost infinite variety of clock hand styles. A few basic designs were adopted by many manufacturers and became what might be called industry standards. While details might vary, the similarity is evident. Some hand styles were introduced and used to such an extent by their originators that they are known by that individual's name.

In one case, the maker's initials were part of the design and were not duplicated by others, i.e., *S* as part of the head of the minute hand and *T*, as part of the head of the hour hand, standing for *Seth Thomas*.

There are countless variations of the styles shown here. While the basic style of each variant is easily recognized, proportions and minor details will change. We have selected those most likely to be found on clocks in American homes today. Broken or lost hands have frequently been replaced with substitutes unlike the originals..

Early American Hand Styles

Two of the most creative and innovative clock makers in early nineteenth century America were Eli Terry and Simon Willard. Terry is credited with designing the *Pillar and Scroll* clock and Willard, the *Banjo*. Each is uniquely American. Even the hands used on these clocks were original in design.

Produced in limited numbers by these makers, these clocks are highly prized by collectors.

Willard and Terry not only created new case styles, they designed new movements and hands. Terry and Willard hands were both unique and remarkably simple as compared to the traditional elaborate tall clock hands employed by most clock makers of the time.

Most hands of the Terry style were made of steel or wrought iron in the design shown in Figure 11 and, for a very short period, in a heavier, but similar style, in cast pewter.

Pewter hands were easily bent and broken, so few original ones have survived. In addition, they were comparatively heavy and imposed an unnecessary additional load on the movement.

Willard hands are made of relatively thick steel, because of the thinness of the body shape. True Willard and early Terry hands were laboriously cut from sheet steel, pierced and carefully filed to shape. They are remarkably graceful, yet quite utilitarian.

Terry and Willard produced limited numbers of these hands, but the Terry style was adopted and used by Seth Thomas when he acquired the rights to manufacture Terry's Pillar and Scroll.

Most hands of the Terry style were made of steel or wrought iron in the design shown in Figure 12 and, for a very short period, in a heavier, but similar style, in cast pewter.

Pewter hands were easily bent and broken, so few original ones have survived. In addition, they were comparatively heavy and imposed an unnecessary additional load on the movement. However, they were used on wood movements that were basically over powered.

Willard hands were cut to shape and polished, then heated to a blue color and tempered by cooling. They are remarkably graceful, yet quite strong.

In spite of the trend toward standardization, hand design variation continued to proliferate, some hand styles were tried and quickly dropped. There have been almost infinite variations over the years. A few remained popular for many years.

Even today, with the tremendous number of cheap quartz movement clocks, new styles appear.

It is a good idea to apply only a little force when setting the hands on any clock, to avoid possible damage. This is especially true of any hands that are delicate in appearance.

Diamond Pattern Hands

These are a simplified modification of the Terry hand. The basic design may even have existed prior to Terry's use of it on the Pillar and Scroll clock. The style has been used off and on for a wide variety of clocks by many manufacturers. Made of steel, these are sturdy but graceful, easily seen and attractive hands. Diamond pattern hands were used by many manufacturers and are suitable to any dial design.

Ogee Hands

This style, characterized by a large circle beneath and inverted spear, was used by many manufacturers. It was produced off and on for at least a hundred years. While used primarily on Ogee clocks, this design is found on other case styles as well. While still recognizable as of this basic style, there were many variations.

Spade Hands

These hands are found on clocks made in nearly all corners of the earth. They are simple, sturdy and attractive, easy to manufacture and, above all, strong. There are probably more hands of spade design than any other.

Nearly all spade hands are made of steel, heated to develop a blue color, then quenched to temper them. This provides color and additional strength.

Maltese Hands

Based on the classic Maltese cross, these hands bear only a passing resemblance to that symbol. They are attractive and enjoyed sporadic popularity on a variety of clocks, especially American Kitchen clocks. Details of the design were highly varied. Some variations of Maltese hands are extremely delicate, while others are almost coarse in appearance.

Maltese hands were used on a wide variety of clocks, both large and small.

Moon Hands

Moon hands have a circle at the outer end, pierced by another non-concentric circle. This gives the appearance of a new moon. Similar designs have both circles concentric. Some moon hands are almost delicate in appearance while others are heavy looking.

FRENCH CLOCK HANDS

Even before precision mass production techniques, French hands were among the most delicate to be found anywhere. Usually made of steel, hardened and tempered, they are strong, but must be treated carefully to avoid damage. As in England and America, there was great variety among those that were hand made.

Only because of the unusually well made movements produced by French clock makers were such delicate hands practical. The design of the movements made it possible to move the hands with very little resistance with almost no force required. The friction inherent in an ordinary movement would result in severe damage by bending to such delicate hands.

Spear Hands

Spear hands provide an example of a notably different design between the minute and hour hands. The basic tip of both hands is the same, but that of the minute hand is embellished with a pair of arc and circle scrolls. This makes the hour hand so obviously different from the minute hand that it can be easily distinguished. For this reason, there is frequently little difference in their lengths, the difference in design making it easy to see the difference between them.

While widely used on clocks of French manufacture, spear hands, or variations of this design are occasionally found on other clocks.

Trefoil Hands

Typically French in their elegance of design and very high quality, trefoil hands were not copied to any significant extent in other clock making countries. This may by due to the difficulty of fabricating their extremely delicate shape.

Trefoil hands are among the most intricately beautiful ever mass produced. They have been used extensively on many styles of French Clocks over a period of many years.

French Comtoise or Morbiere Clock Hands

In the Franche-Comte region of France, large shelf mounted, wall and other styles of clocks were produced. The best known have elaborate brass repousse' shields behind a porcelain dial and equally ornate pendulums.

The hands of these clocks are usually of brass with elaborate designs, often stamped or engraved, like those of early English clocks.

VIENNESE HANDS

Viennese clocks are characteristically of high quality. Their hands are among the finest ever made on a mass production basis.

Shown in Figure 13 is only one representative pair of Vienna wall clock hands. They are typically delicate and of very high quality.

These hands are made of thin high strength steel, polished, heat blued, hardened and tempered.

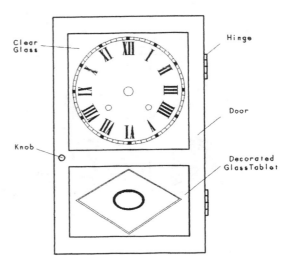

Figure 14 Early American Clock Door

HAND and DIAL PROTECTION

Glazed Doors

The dial and hands of the earliest domestic clocks were completely unprotected. It became evident that protecting the movement from grease and grime resulting from cooking and open fires would improve a clock's performance and life. When cases were added, dial and hands remained unprotected.

To protect the hands from damage and the dial against dirt, a glass cover was provided on even some of the earliest cases. In wood tall clock cases, this was simply a sheet of glass mounted in a door attached to the hood. Such doors have remained a feature of tall clocks to this day.

With the American introduction of Pillar and Scroll and Banjo cases, with their reverse painted glass became a major form of decoration. Fig. 14 illustrates a door of a Pillar and Scroll clock case. The lower glass, or *tablet* is decorated with a reverse painted design.

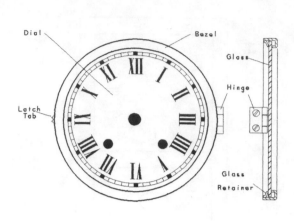

Figure 15 Typical Sheet Brass Bezel

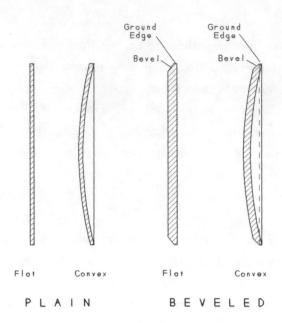

Figure 16 Types of Bezel Glasses

The lower glass panel, referred to as a *tablet*, was often decorated with elaborate reverse painting, usually illustrating an outstanding building. An elaborate border featured the use of gold leaf, as well as color. American clock manufacturers continued to use decoration applied to the back of glass door panels very extensively until around the end of the nineteenth century.

Early in this period, a method of transferring printed images, similar to decals, from paper to glass, was developed and was widely used as a replacement for hand painting on glasses.

Clock Bezels

When it was desired to cover only the dial with a glass door, a round frame with hinges, carrying a circle of glass was used, as in the top door of a Banjo clock. Early bezels were usually made of cast brass, machined and polished. Later ones were formed of very thin brass sheet.

A formed thin brass bezel is shown in Figure 15. It is shaped so that the circle of glass rests against a shoulder formed near the front. Small metal clips

are soldered to the sides of the bezel to hold the glass in place.

A single hinge is usually soldered to the rim of the bezel, but rivets are sometimes found. The hinge is then attached to the case, or to the dial plate, with screws.

The bezel hinge may be attached to the case in several ways, commonly to the metal pan on which the dial is mounted. It is sometimes soldered to a separate ring that is then screwed to the case. The strength of the hinge varies with the overall quality of the clock.

Very slight interference between the dial pan or metal ring and the bezel serves to hold the bezel in position when closed. A small metal tab is sometimes attached to the outside of the bezel rim, opposite the hinge and is used to open the bezel door. Many bezels have a small knob made of wood or metal to assist in opening them.

A purely decorative ring fitting around the dial and frequently attached to or an integral part of the dial, is also known as a bezel. A conventional hinged bezel and glass is usually provided to cover the dial and its bezel.

CLOCK GLASSES

Until about the middle of the nineteenth century, flat glass was produced by glass blowers who created a large thin bubble of molten glass, then cut and spun it to form a sheet. Such glass, known as *bubble glass* is full of irregularities in thickness and small bubble inclusions are common. This was the only glass available for window glazing as well as clock making. Looking through the glass in the windows of old buildings gives a distorted image.

The original glass in very old clockswas bubble glass, with all of its imperfections. Later manufactured glass, made by rolling it in a molten state between rollers, was smoother.

Very smooth, flat glass can be made by the tedious process of grinding and polishing. Using glass melted to temperatures providing maximum fluidity, it is poured onto hot plates and then insulated to permit very slow cooling. This minimizes cooling stresses and cracking.

Grinding and polishing with very fine abrasives is a long and demanding process. The *plate glass* thus produced is very expensive and its use limited, mostly to large store windows.

Plate Glass is sometimes used in high quality tall (*Grandfather*) clocks. Individual panes are commonly ground to a bevel on all sides and then polished.. This is referred to as *bevel* glass.

Glass in most clocks is the same as that once used for glazing windows and is comparatively thin. Present day glass suppliers usually replace original glasses with the thicker *double strength* glass commonly used in single glazed windows today. This is more durable, but it is thicker and significantly heavier. The extra weight may cause hinge screws to pull out of the case.

Before mass production methods were introduced, glass was very expensive and was only available in smaller sizes. Most windows before that time were made of small panes.

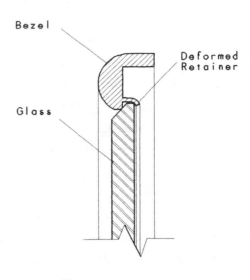

Figure 17 Beveled Glass Secured in Bezel

This is evident in the windows of Colonial homes and public buildings, such as Independence Hall.

Made from large bubbles of blown molten glass, cut and flattened, these panes and those used in clock cases of the time had irregular surfaces and small air bubbles are frequently seen.

Glass for Clock Bezels and Tablets

Bezel glass is usually ordinary flat window glass. Some makers, however, used convex shaped glasses. Originally, these were cut from pieces of large blown glass bubbles. Later, they were made by heating and forming disks of flat glass.

Mechanically polished plate glass, both flat and convex, is found in some bezel glasses. Because of its cost, its use has generally been limited to more expensive clocks.

More than twice as thick as window glass, plate glass is cut to size and then the edges of each piece are precisely bevel ground and polished. Beveled bezel glass must be very closely fitted to the bezel.

Comparatively recently, *float glass*. made by pouring molten glass on a pool of mercury, has been introduced. It is comparable to plate glass, at much lower cost.

As shown in Figure 16, the glass is placed against a shoulder in the face of the bezel and the edge of the bezel is then very carefully rolled over to secure the glass. Sometimes, beveled glass is retained with clips, like ordinary glass.

Not all bezels are made of metal. Many, particularly those on many types of American wall clocks, were made of wood. A simple shoulder was turned on the inside of the bezel, the glass placed against it and secured with glazier's points.

Simple round wood bezels were a feature of several shelf or mantel clocks.

CLOCK CASE STYLES

The overall style of a clock case is the product of many elements. The physical limitations imposed by the size and space requirements of the movement are basic. The importance of its time telling function must be considered.

Where viewing by people at a distance is expected, a large dial and hands are required. The largest cases are the towers of buildings, the smallest little short of watches. The movements of clocks with even very large dials are often quite small in comparison with the dial.

TOWER CLOCKS

The earliest known mechanical clocks were made by blacksmiths for churches. Such a movement, made in 1386, while not operating, is preserved at the Cathedral of Salisbury, England. It is over 600 years old! The craftsmanship of the blacksmith who made it is remarkable.

Figure 18 Colonial American Church Tower Clock

Tower clocks derive their name from the fact that tower clocks were located in the most visible place in the church property, its tower.

Whether church towers existed before clocks in English towns is a moot question. Structures of some kind were undoubtedly built to support bells used in religious rites. For many centuries church towers have been designed and built specifically to hold clocks and their bells.

For hundreds of years, tower clocks were the only timepieces available to millions of people.

In continental Europe, rather elaborate public clocks appeared in the early sixteenth century. The dials were usually mounted on the walls of buildings and often featured animated allegorical figures.

American Tower and other Public Clocks

Tower clocks are part of the earliest history of America. Even small New England towns boasted

Figure 19 American Street Clock

a clock in the tower of a church or town hall. The one in Independence Hall in Philadelphia is part of a National Treasure. Many have survived and continue to tell time for the community, even though almost everyone has a wristwatch.

Outside of New England, tower clocks became an integral part of the towns that sprouted up as settlement expanded westward.

Rural America is still dotted with churches, court houses and other public buildings with a public clock. Unfortunately, the movements of many have been discarded and sometimes replaced with electrically driven movements. Some have been stored, but the fate of many is unknown.

Around the 1890-1920 period, another form of American public clock became common, even in small towns in the United States. Businesses installed clocks on their buildings or on sidewalks in front of them. The cast iron cases of these clocks, some very elaborately decorated, had two or more dials. Some were mounted on the corners of

buildings and had four dials. Many were mounted on the sides of buildings and had two dials.

The dials of street clocks were commonly two to three feet in diameter. The cast iron box displaying the dials rested on a cast iron post about eight feet in length. Advances in the art of iron casting made possible the intricate detail found in many street clock cases.

Street Clock movements were usually similar to those used in tower clocks, but somewhat smaller. They were nearly always weight driven and, while ruggedly built, using iron castings, were generally of high quality.

Street clock movements were sometimes located inside the building and powered a system of shafts and gears to move the hands. Some movements were contained in the case of the clock. Because of the significant weight and friction of the mechanism, they were ruggedly built.

The hand drive shafts for many post mounted street clocks ran through a pipe or tunnel under the sidewalk. The shafts for clocks mounted on buildings went through a hole in the wall.

CLOCK CASE DESIGN TRANSITION

In many instances, there is a traceable transition of refinements that results in a particular case style. One of these is the Classic English Long Case or Tall Case clock.

The earliest English Clocks for domestic use were made around the year 1600. They were supported on wall brackets and powered by weights hung on ropes and wrapped around drums in the movement. The ropes were not attached to the drum, but simply wrapped several times around it. The friction of several wraps was sufficient to prevent slippage. A small weight at the end opposite the large powering weight insured that the rope remained in firm contact with the drum. Pulling on the small weight wound the clock.

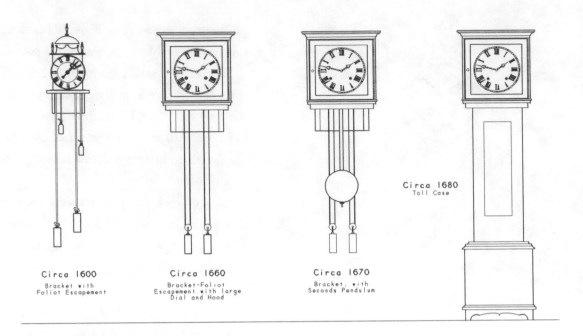

Figure 20   Evolution of the English Long Case Clock (ca.1600-1700)

Originally, these clocks had foliot escapements, but around 1670 pendulums and anchor escapements were introduced. Early bracket clocks had only an hour hand. Minutes were estimated by the position of the hand between hours.

Around 1660 a minute hand was added and hoods were installed to protect the movement from the soot, grease and dirt common in homes relying on open fireplaces for heating.

The movement was made mostly of iron, with square corner posts. A simple case of brass sheets attached to the corner posts enclosed the movement. An iron bell on top sounded the hours.

Because its shape resembled the candle lanterns in common use at that time, that name has been arbitrarily applied to this style of clock.

This was the beginning of a long period during which clock movements were commonly enclosed in cases made of wood and other materials.

A major change occurred about 1670 with the adoption of the Huygens pendulum by most English clock makers. While at first the pendulum

assembly consisted of a very short rod with a marble-sized bob, contained within the lantern case, the long seconds beat pendulum quickly became standard.

English tall clocks had very simple, functional pendulums, usually plain iron rods with a cast iron bob. They were not very attractive. Largely for aesthetic reasons, a long supporting case replaced the bracket and the long case clock was born. The style continues right up to the present.

The pendulum was hidden from view behind a door in the waist of the clock case. American tall case clocks made in the past hundred years have glass panels in the front and side of the waist.

ENGLISH PENDULUM BRACKET CLOCKS

The name *Bracket* attached to this style of clock infers that it was intended to be supported on a wall bracket, like the lantern or hooded clocks. Sometimes they were mounted on a shelf or bracket, but more often they were located on

Robert Seignior
ca 1670

Joseph Knibb.
ca 1680

Thomas Tompion
ca 1705

John Jullian
ca.1730

Figure 21 Representative English Bracket Clock Styles (ca. 1700)

a mantle, table or other piece of sturdy furniture, frequently a large, heavy table.

First made around 1670, bracket clocks are notable for the fact that they were the first reasonably successful spring-driven clocks made in England.

Bracket clocks have been made for over three hundred years with minor changes, but adhering to the basic style. They vary in size from about a foot high to almost two feet. The earliest cases were ebony veneer or painted wood.

The chapter ring, a metal ring carrying the time track and numerals, or dial and the corner escutcheons were frequently mounted on blue or red velvet covering a brass plate.

Later bracket clock cases were made of a wide variety of materials, including ebony and tortoiseshell. Case embellishment varied from simple columns to sometimes very ornate ormolu or gilt decoration.

The earliest bracket clock cases were classed as *architectural* in style, with roof-like pediment tops.

Around 1670, other forms of top design developed. It became common to have a brass or gilt handle mounted on the top.

While the handle appears to be primarily a decorative device, it made it easier to move these comparatively heavy clocks from place to place.

A large door at the back of the case allows access to the movement. The short pendulum is suspended behind the back plate, which is frequently elaborately engraved, sometimes including the name of the maker and the year of manufacture.

Some old bracket clocks are quite large, some almost two feet tall. A few have very complicated chiming mechanisms, playing one or more melodies on bells. Even fewer are equipped with mechanically operated air pumps to produce tunes on pipes or whistles.

English bracket style clocks of essentially traditional design have been produced almost continuously since their inception.

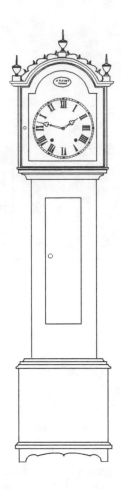

Figure 22 Simon Willard Whales Tail Tall Clock (ca. 1790)

AMERICAN ORIGINAL CLOCK CASES

Distinctive American Tall Clock Designs

While all American clock makers adhered to the English tradition, gradual changes were introduced. This was consistent with the history of English clock making, but some very distinctly American case designs emerged. Among these was a more delicate treatment of the top splat. Fine fretwork created by scroll sawing thin slabs of wood, marked the work of certain makers and was sometimes adopted with little change by others.

One of the most popular of these distinctive patterns is known as *Whales Tail* (Figure 22) It was used by Simon Willard and others on tall clocks as

shown in Figure 22. Other designs were equally delicate. There were many excellent clock movement and case makers active in New England before the Revolutionary War. They worked as individuals, with possibly one or two apprentices.

When not making or repairing clocks, they often engaged in other pursuits requiring fine craftsmanship, notably making and repairing nautical and surveying instruments. In Colonial America, these pursuits were essential and the instruments they used required constant maintenance to provide the necessary accuracy.

During this period, a spring driven device for turning a suspended roast in front of a fireplace was called a Roasting Jack. It was developed and made by various clock makers. Its design is sometimes attributed to the American patriot and silversmith, Paul Revere.

The Willard Banjo

There were a number of journeyman clock makers in America at the time of the Revolution. A majority of them had been trained in the English tradition and made long case clocks with movements of brass from England. Their workmanship was a tribute to the masters under whom they were apprenticed. Some were members of the second or third generation in the colony.

A few American clock makers at the beginning of the nineteenth century were remarkably innovative. There was a near frenzy to develop new and different movements and cases for clocks. One of the most notable achievements was the small eight day, time only, weight driven clock movement developed by Simon Willard and that was used in his banjo and Massachusetts shelf clocks.

This movement was simple in design and of very high quality. It was small, requiring a minimum of brass. It used a system of pulleys that, with a heavy weight, powered it for a full eight days.

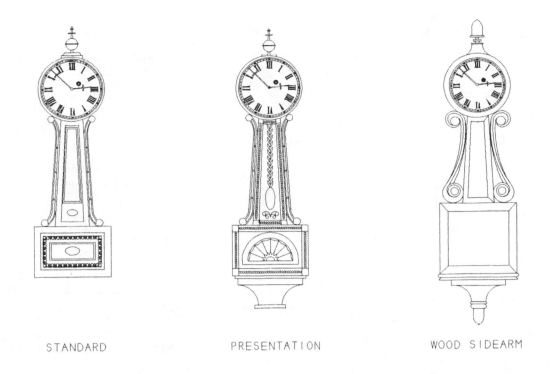

STANDARD   PRESENTATION   WOOD SIDEARM

Figure 23 Representative American Wall Clock Styles (ca. 1820)

The small size of this movement and the short fall of the weight led to Willard's design of the *Improved Patent Timepiece* case, now known as the *Banjo* style. Willard's banjo case designs are consistent in quality with his fine tall clocks. Featuring elegant reverse painted glasses, with lavish use of gold leaf, the Willard Patent Timepiece achieved quick recognition among the wealthier citizens of the infant United States.

In spite of Willard's patent, other clock makers made similar movements and cases. Willard and his sons made both banjo and tall case clocks by hand for many years, varying the details of decoration, but adhering generally to the original banjo case design.

Simon Willard and his sons continued to make both banjo and tall case clocks for many years, but finally were unable to compete with the much cheaper mass produced clocks made by the many clock factories then in business..

For almost two hundred years, the banjo clock design has been copied, off and on, in almost pure Willard style and in countless variations, by many manufacturers. While remaining popular in the United States, it has met with less favor abroad.

Among replicas sought by collectors are those by Waltham, Elmer Stennes and, currently, Foster Campos. These faithfully reproduce the clocks originally made in the early eighteenth century.

The PILLAR and SCROLL CLOCK

At about the same time Simon Willard was developing the banjo movement and case, another innovative New England clock maker, Eli Terry, designed a weight driven wood movement with a much shorter weight drop than that required for the movements then being used in tall case clocks. He obtained a patent for this movement in 1816 and used it in his experimental box clock.

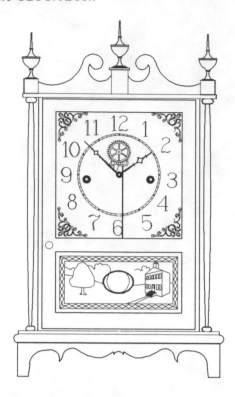

Figure 24 Eli Terry Pillar & Scroll Clock (ca. 1810)

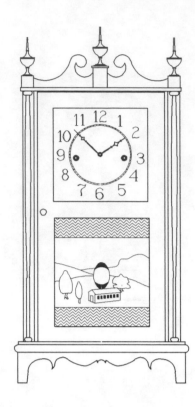

Figure 25   Ethel North Pillar & Scroll Clock (ca. 1825)

Unlike the brass Willard banjo movement that had no strike train, but ran for eight days, the Terry movement had a strike train but its running time was only 30 hours.

The short weight drop and the location of the weights on either side of the movement made it possible to house the movement in a case small enough to be placed on a shelf or mantel.

After several pilot models, Terry is generally credited with developing the Pillar and Scroll case, considered by many to be among the most beautiful clocks in the world. With a large square hand painted wood dial featuring Arabic numerals, time track and corner decorations, the case was nicely made and faced with exotic veneer.

The broken arch scroll at the top and the inverted scroll at the bottom were sawn from thin solid hard wood, such as native black walnut. This scroll inevitably warped, so that the ends of the scroll moved toward the back. The elegant urn shaped finials were of polished brass.

A very slender fully turned hard wood column extends the full length of the door on each side. The rectangular lower glass in the door was decorated with reverse painting. Subject matter ranged from scenic or elaborate geometric designs to public buildings and mythical allegory.

This painting, was done by local artisans, many of them young women, in their homes. Their work varied in quality from fine to crude. Some of the best are elegant works of art.

The cabinetry of nearly all Pillar and Scroll clock cases produced by Eli Terry, Seth Thomas and a few others was, in general, very good. They were nicely sanded and varnished with shellac.

Other contemporary clock makers were quick to mimic this popular case style. Their modifications resulted in a product often inferior to the original..

In the nearly 200 years since its introduction, the Pillar & Scroll design, with modifications has been produced repeatedly. This is a testament to its design integrity and basic appeal.

The Beginning of Production of
INTERCHANGEABLE PARTS

In 1807, to the astonishment of many of his contemporaries, Eli Terry negotiated an order to produce 4,000 traditional tall clock wood movements. This was an astronomical number at the time.

According to Terry's son, Henry:

"Three years elapsed while these clocks were being made. A great part of the first year was spent fitting up the machinery, the next in the manufacture of one thousand clocks (movements) and the third in completing the remaining three thousand."

At its peak rate, during the last year, Terry's shop produced 3,000 movements. Based on the usual six day work week of the time, this was some 58 clocks per week, or almost 10 per 10 hour work day.

While much more productive than traditional hand crafting of each part, this was hardly mass production. It was, however, the foundation on which the Industrial Revolution was built.

Terry's genius lay in his concept of interchangeability of parts of a mechanism and the methodical development of tools, water powered machines, jigs and fixtures to produce significant quantities of essentially identical parts. Unskilled workers were then able to assemble the various parts to produce completed movements. Later, he used similar methods to produce clock cases.

Since all units of each mechanism were alike, the previously necessary fitting of each part to the next, by tedious and time consuming hand methods was eliminated.

The first production movements were essentially the same as those made by traditional methods. No major changes were made in the design. . The loose tolerances of the movements made it possible for them to run satisfactorily, even with minor irregularities of individual parts. The genius of this development was the making of identical parts.

The FIRST WIDELY AFFORDABLE CLOCK

While in the process of completing this order, Terry conceived the idea of a smaller clock that could be placed on a mantel and would be much less expensive than the tall clocks and banjos then dominating the clock market.

The Pillar and Scroll case design discussed earlier was practical only because Terry developed a unique movement designed to take advantage of the methods of production he had pioneered. With its short weight drop, this clock took up little space and was suited to much more modest homes than those displaying tall clocks.

From the beginning, Pillar and Scroll clocks found a ready market and were produced in significant quantities by Terry and by Seth Thomas, who was licensed by Terry to produce his patented design.

Many more people could now afford to own a timepiece. For the first time, ordinary citizens could afford to have a nicely cased clock in their homes. The Pillar and Scroll clock became the decorative centerpiece in many households, but, more importantly, it provided reasonably accurate timekeeping. This meant that people began to organize their daily activities on a time-oriented basis. No longer did they have to rely solely on the town tower clock for the time of day.

From this period on, the lives of everyone in the civilized world began to become very time oriented. Hours of work and daily schedules were increasingly ruled by the relentless marking of time.

Most clocks made during this period were not

capable of keeping very accurate time. Customarily, they were reset on a daily, or more likely nightly, basis, using the chimes of tower clocks marking the most accurate time indication available. This was usually done at bedtime when winding the clock.

WOOD MOVEMENT MANUFACTURING

At the same time Eli Terry was developing and producing his Pillar and Scroll clocks, other makers also modified traditional wood movement design to make free-standing or mantel cases practical. Initially, they continued to use traditional methods of production, only later emulating Terry's more efficient techniques. These were all one-day or thirty-hour movements.

While interchangeable wood parts were then produced in lots by water powered machines, many time consuming turning and sawing operations were involved. Small factories for the manufacture of wood clock movements sprung up all over New England, but were most numerous in Connecticut.

As compared with later stamping of intricate clock movement parts from sheet brass, the making of wood movements was very slow. Even though the new methods were a great improvement over individual crafting of movements, they were inefficient by comparison with true mass production that was to follow.

For this reason, we have arbitrarily called this period of clock manufacture *limited* production.

TRANSITION CLOCK CASE DESIGNS

Seeing the success of the Terry Pillar and Scroll case, other manufacturers of the new short drop movements developed similar cases. Undoubtedly, the fact that Terry held a patent on his design deterred most clock manufacturers from copying it.

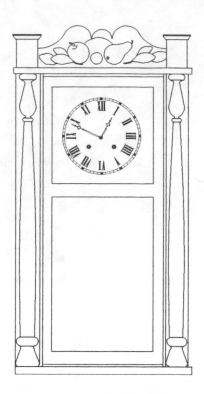

Figure 26　Boardman & Wells Mirror Clock (ca. 1825)

They did, however, retain certain elements of that successful style, notably a large square painted wood dial plate, side columns, scroll sawed top splats and a full length door with two glasses.

There were countless variations of these designs.

Spanning the years between the exclusive use of hand methods of making clocks to the beginning of true high volume mass production, clocks made generally between 1820 and 1840 are arbitrarily termed *Transition clocks*.

MIRROR CLOCKS

One of the most popular case designs to utilize these movements replaced the reverse painted lower glass tablet of the Pillar and Scroll with a simple glass mirror. These bubble glass sheets were silvered using mercury. The wavy, irregular surface of this type of glass produced a distorted reflection. This, however, was the only glass

Figure 27   Joseph Ives Mirror Clock (ca. 1820)

Figure 28   Typical Triple Deck Clock (ca. 1830)

available at the time. Half columns were attached by cut nails to the case, on either side of the door.

Half columns were made by lightly gluing two pieces of wood together, then turning the assembly on a lathe to produce a single column. Splitting this piece at the glue line produced two identical half columns.

Most half columns were made of pine painted black with gold leaf applied to their caps and bases. Some had designs made by stenciling clear shellac and then dusting it with bronze powder. Others were made of solid hard wood, notably cherry, finished with varnish (*shellac*). Some hard wood columns were decorated, after turning, with carved capitols, bases and, sometimes, carved main bodies.

Splats, the thin pieces mounted on top of the case, above the door, were almost always cut to form a curved or scroll shape. They were decoratively treated with various designs, either stenciled bronze, or carved. Common motifs were

groups of fruits and/or vegetables, or eagles.

In an effort to eliminate the cost of hand carving some splats were made by molding a mixture of sawdust, powdered clay or plaster and glue in a mold to form a piece resembling hand carving. The molds for this process were made by casting plaster of Paris over an original hand carving or clay model.. Such molding were usually painted to simulate wood. Some then had details painted in bright colors. Deemed not authentic by uninformed collectors, many have been destroyed.

TRIPLE DECK CLOCKS

Consisting of a basic box, of similar proportions to mirror clocks, the fronts of triple deck clocks have three sections. The top is a hinged door with a clear glass over the dial. The center section is a smaller, reverse painted or otherwise decorated

Figure 29   Sawin & Dyer Lyre Clock (ca. 1825)

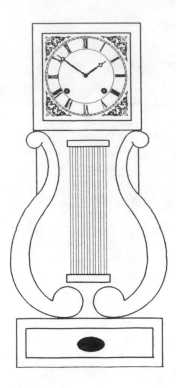

Figure 30   Joseph Ives Lyre Clock (ca. 1830)

glass, fixed into slots in the case, without a door or frame. The bottom section is a hinged door with reverse painted, stenciled or applied printed transfer decoration on its glass.

Three sets of half columns are mounted at the sides of each section. These were nearly always painted black, sometimes stippled, with gold leaf capitols and bases.

Top splats are similar to those of Mirror clock cases and turned feet are common.

While most of these clocks had 30-hour movements, a few ran 8 days.

Each manufacturer introduced minor variations of this basic case design. Literally hundreds of designs were developed for reverse painted tablets, and top splats.

Even though many thousands of these clocks were sold over a period of perhaps ten to twenty years, compared to other designs, they were relatively unpopular. Still, a significant number have survived.

LYRE CLOCKS

Of essentially the same size and overall proportions as Willard banjo clocks and using a similar 8-day individually made brass movement, Lyre Clocks replaced the brass sidearms and straight sided waist of that design with a hand carved solid hardwood shield in the shape of a lyre.

Sometimes the inside of the shield was cut out and a reverse painted glass inserted. More commonly the entire shield was of solid wood, naturally finished.

The bottom box, in which the pendulum swings, was a rectangular hinged door with a picture frame molding.

The top was usually decorated with a carved finial. Pineapple and Fleur de Lis motifs are common. In addition to fruit motifs, birds, particularly eagles, were often seen.

Dials are painted on metal and bezels are normally of turned hard wood in contrast to the

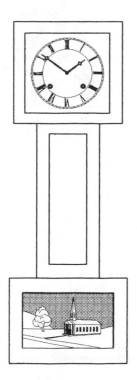

Figure 31 Connecticut Banjo Clock (ca. 1830)

Figure 32 Carved Case Clock (ca. 1832)

cast, turned and polished brass bezels of Willard style banjo clocks.

Joseph Ives was a most innovative clock maker. His essentially rectangular case made up of two box like elements reflected the lyre design, but was altogether different from most lyre cases. A simple lyre outline with only rounded edges, requiring no carving, but with dowels representing strings, was attached to the front of the box. Some examples of this style were simply varnished to show the wood grain, while others were painted and gold leafed.

The Ives lyre was unique in that it could be hung on a wall, like a conventional lyre or banjo clock, or could rest on a shelf or mantel.

CONNECTICUT BANJO CLOCKS

Another variation became known as the *Connecticut* banjo clock. Much less expensive to produce than other styles, it was made up of three rectangular boxes, all with glazed panels. The top was a glazed door with clear glass over the square dial. The middle, or throat, section was a narrow rectangle with plain or reverse painted glass.

The bottom panel was a rectangular door, usually with a reverse painted scene or geometric design. While they had flat bottoms and might conceivably be free standing, they were top-heavy and were nearly always hung on a wall.

CARVED CASE DECORATION

During the transition period of case design, there was an interesting development in the decoration of rectangular clock cases. As mentioned earlier, carving was used extensively for lyre clock cases and to a more limited degree on half column and splats. The example shown in Figure 31 is representative of a much more lavish use of carving for a clock case.

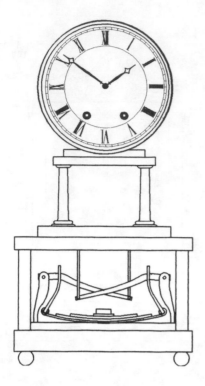

Figure 33   Joseph Ives Wagon Spring Clock
Door Removed   (ca. 1825)

Figure 34   Hollow Column Weight Clock
(ca. 1832)

With proportions obviously based on the Terry pillar and scroll, this case style replaced the delicate columns of that design with heavy, deeply carved half columns. For the delicate scroll, a carved large eagle was substituted.

The base scroll was eliminated and heavy carved claw feet were added.

MECHANICAL INNOVATIONS

During the transition period of case design, there was great activity among clock makers to design better and cheaper clock movements. Many visualized the significance of evolving machine manufacture, concurrent with the birth of an infant brass industry.

A significant limitation was imposed by the still relatively long drop required by weight driven movements. This meant that cases had to be comparatively tall. Reliable coil springs, like those then in use in England and other European countries for very high quality clocks were not available at prices and in quantities necessary for use in inexpensive clocks.

Observing the flat springs then common for carriages, Joseph Ives developed a movement powered by a smaller version to power clocks. Using hardened and tempered flat steel leaves, he anchored them through a hole in their centers to the bottom of the clock case.

Each end of the compound spring is attached to a strap that is hooked over a steel lever. At the end of each lever a rod is attached. The rod is then connected to a cord that wraps around the winding drum.

Winding the clock turns the drums, wrapping the cord around them and pulling up on the ends of the levers. This action raises the ends of the spring, storing increasing amounts of energy, sufficient to run the clock for eight days.

Others tried similar approaches, but leaf springs were never widely accepted for powering clocks.

Hollow Column Clock Cases

Another example of the innovations created by clock makers of this period was an interesting variation of the conventional weight driven clock. It was unique in that it had hollow sheet metal tubes, simulating the columns of other designs. The cord attached to the weights powering the movement was directed over two pulleys so that it rose and fell inside the column.

The example shown in Figure 34 has a carved top splat and carved claw feet. The center panel is a mirror and the bottom door contains a reverse painted or stenciled glass.

SIGNIFICANCE of the TRANSITION PERIOD in AMERICAN CLOCK MAKING

During this period, there were hundreds of clock makers, most of whom recognized that they were suddenly thrust into a battle for survival in a revolutionary industrial transition.

By 1820 clock making in the United States was on the threshold of becoming a major manufacturing industry, but its future makeup was only dimly visible. Many clock makers who failed to keep up with technological advances would not survive. Others would prosper.

rapidly changing environment. For the first time in history, clocks were being made in comparatively large quantities and sold at prices impossible to match, using time consuming traditional methods, making individual parts one at a time..

Many credit the mass production methods developed by the New England clock industry with starting the Industrial Revolution. The introduction and refinement of methods and machinery for producing fully interchangeable parts in quantity was certainly basic to all mass production.

It is interesting to consider that clocks made almost 200 years ago by these methods are still operating today.

CHAPTER THREE

Clock Case Materials and Construction

THE MATERIALS USED IN CLOCK cases range from wood to coal and an infinite variety of other substances, some mundane and some precious. Broad classes include *metals, woods, minerals* and *animal,* such as *ivory, bone* and *shell.*

As we have seen, the earliest clocks were made of iron and were not enclosed with cases of any kind. Even before enclosures were developed, there were efforts by the blacksmiths who made them to embellish their work. Small decorative touches were added to the shapes of wrought iron elements, especially the hands.

The stone of which early clock towers were made formed a case for the clock, even if a very large one.

The earliest full movable enclosures for clock movements were probably sheets of hammered wrought iron, followed closely by brass sheets. Both of these materials were extensively used for this purpose until well into the Twentieth Century. Even then, some clocks, notably those made in the *Frenche Comte* area of France, had movements encased in sheet iron with front shields of embossed sheets of thin brass, called *repousse'.* The art of making them was highly developed here.

CASES MADE PRIMARILY of METAL

Early English, German and French Clock Materials

While the earliest clocks were probably made in the latter part of the thirteenth century, they were strictly utilitarian and were not enclosed. It was not until the 16th century that European clock makers began to enclose their movements in sheet iron or brass.

The earliest English domestic clocks were open framed with a single hand and were weight driven. For protection against soot and household grease, the sides and back began to be covered with sheets of wrought iron, sometimes hinged to give access to the movement. The front was a sheet of wrought iron fastened to the posts of the movement, with the dial attached to it.

In Europe, as early as 1450, crude coil springs were developed. They were extremely inconsistent and incapable of providing the predictable power needed for even roughly accurate timekeeping. These springs did make it possible to power small mechanical devices that often included a clock of sorts.

In France and Germany, where the nobility was fascinated by automated devices which were part of clocks, clock makers were lavishly endowed and used materials that were very expensive at the time, notably brass.   Their cases were sometimes extremely complex and ornately decorated with cast and chased elements, quite frequently fire-gilt with pure gold, adding exceptional richness.

Many of these clocks were mounted on wheels that were powered by the clockwork. They were intended as a sort of centerpiece on the banquet table and would be set in motion during the meal, passing in front of each guest. Sometimes they transported items of food. The more intricate and amusing the antics of the automated elements, the greater the esteem in which the lord of the manor was held by his guests.

While they often had the hands and faces of clocks, these devices were not expected to keep good time. They were, literally, the toys of royalty.

It would appear that there was an ongoing contest among members of the nobility to see who possessed the cleverest and most intriguing animated toy.

The time keeping function of many of these so-called clocks commissioned by royalty was so subordinated that, in many, the dial or other time display was hardly visible.

Some of these elaborate clocks have survived to this day and may be seen in a few museums.

Clocks in continental Europe at this time seem to have been the exclusive preserve of the highest members of the court. In England clocks were becoming available to the affluent gentry. Many artisans were engaged in making clocks in all parts of the country, developing new skills and bringing devices for telling time in the home closer to the common people.

In a rural area of France, known as the *Franche Comte* that was blessed with iron ore and plentiful timber for charcoal, a crude clock making industry became established. The clocks produced here, commonly referred to in the United States as *Comtoise* or *Morbiere*, changed little over the course of some 300 years. Compared to Parisian clocks, they were crude, yet they functioned well..

As we will see later, in the nineteenth century, many clocks from this area were exported to the United States.

Techniques for making detailed castings in bronze and precious metals like gold and silver had existed for many centuries and were successfully adapted to brass. Iron castings could not accurately reproduce fine detail, so their use in clock cases was very limited for a long time.

In the late nineteenth century new alloys of iron were developed and casting techniques refined so that it was used for many American clock cases. Unacceptable imperfections still existed, but these were filled with mineral materials and the whole case painted.

A few foundries were able to produce extremely high quality iron castings that required little or no special finishing and, rarely, no painting.

Alarm clocks, manufactured in the millions for the past hundred years commonly had cases made of sheet steel, nickel or chrome plated, or painted. These cases are round or of rectangular shape with bases to make placing on a night stand or dresser convenient.

Some small clocks had cases made of die-cast zinc alloys, usually painted, but sometimes plated metal. From time to time, entire clock cases were made of cast bronze, brass or pot metal.

Metal and Other Materials Combined for Cases

During the nineteenth century, French clock makers produced thousands of clocks with cases artistically decorated in ormolu brass which was frequently fire gilt. These cases featured sculptured figures and other three-dimensional decor. Many of them were fine examples of the highest artistry of the period.

Some figures were modeled by highly acclaimed sculptors and many bore the signature of the artist in the casting..

A very popular type of clock, designed to be carried while traveling by horse drawn coach, evolved during the late eighteenth century in France. These clocks were small spring-driven and carried in plush lined leather cases. A sliding panel could be pulled up to reveal the clock face. The case of the clock was a framework of brass columns with glass panels between them and a brass top and base.

The Crystal Palace, a larger version of this design, emerged late in the nineteen hundreds and was designed as a shelf or mantle clock.

Metal decorative pieces have been attached to cases made of many other materials. Metal dial bezels are very common.

METAL CLOCK CASE DECORATION

Metals of many kinds have long been used to form decorative elements of clock cases. As we have seen, dial bezels of brass are one of the most common applications. Supplementing this is the application of formed sheet brass rings and other decorative elements to the face of the dial.

Another widespread use of metals is in pendulum bobs. When the pendulum bob is exposed to view, it becomes part of the visual aspect of a clock. Metals with a high coefficient of expansion, such as brass, lead and pot metal alloys, are used primarily because they provide temperature compensation, as pointed out earlier. Their malleability makes it possible to form them into attractive decorative shapes. Some very elaborate pendulum bobs can be found. Even simple discs are frequently embossed or incised with interesting designs.

The weights used to power the earliest clocks were crude, ranging from ordinary stones to cast iron in rough form. Later, weights were made of iron or lead and were encased in a thin brass shell.

In the late nineteenth and early twentieth century, these shells were frequently decorated with embossed or engraved designs.

French Comtoise clock makers evolved very large thin bas relief (*repousse'*) sheet brass covers for their long pendulums, complementing the shields around their dials. These clocks retained a large brass covered lead disc as the functioning bob.

Because they were so striking in appearance, many of these clocks found their way into some more affluent American homes.

Especially in shelf and kitchen clocks of American manufacture produced in the late nineteenth and early twentieth century, elaborate pendulums were common. There were many designs produced in both sheet brass and molded lead or pot metal, usually brass plated.

In the earliest efforts to make ordinary clock cases attractive, brass decorative elements were occasionally attached to the wrought iron dials and fronts of lantern clocks. This practice of embellishing cases has been common for almost 400 years.

When pewter was developed, its properties invited its application to clock cases, usually as inlays in wood.

Silver and gold have found limited use for decoration of clock cases. Gold plating of brass decorative elements, especially by French and Swiss clock makers was common during the late nineteenth and early twentieth centuries.

As a surface finish for parts of wooden cases, gold leaf and gold paint were often used. Even on cases produced in great quantities, such as the American half-column style, gold leaf was applied to the tops and bottoms of the turned columns. Gold leaf also found limited application as the finish for the front, or the entire case, as with some early banjos and some Ingraham *Ionic* wall clocks.

Gold leaf was used extensively by the artists who executed the reverse paintings for the tablets of American clocks made in the early 1800s. Some stenciled decoration on the glasses of a few later clock case designs also were of gold leaf.

Rarely, but at least in a few instances, entire cases have been formed of precious metals. This application has been limited to one-of-a-kind small clocks made for wealthy patrons of outstanding jewelers.

Metal hands made of iron, brass or pewter have, from the very beginning, been a vital decorative element of clock cases. Even the earliest wrought iron hands show efforts by the blacksmith to make them attractive. We have shown that the design of hands developed into a fine art form.

WOOD and WOOD PRODUCTS for CASES

No one can say when the first clock movement was enclosed in a wood case. It may have been simply a crude box made by a carpenter or cabinet maker. In England, as we saw in Chapter Two, wood was used to enclose the movement of clocks on shelves, followed by full length Tall Cases. From that time forward, for several centuries, wood became the preferred material.

Most early cases were custom made by skilled craftsmen whose major activity was the making of furniture or cabinetry. The styles of clock cases reflected those currently popular for these other products of the cabinet maker.

The materials used were those found in nearby forests and orchards, commonly pine, oak and cherry. Cabinet makers were familiar with the drying and aging of wood, necessary to limit warping and shrinkage.

Most old clock cases remain essentially sound and true, although a few were made of inadequately dried wood and may show severe shrinkage or warping of some elements, resulting in damage to the case. Prior to the introduction of thermostatically controlled heating and cooling of homes, severe changes in temperature caused elements of wood cases to expand and contract, placing severe stress on joints

Wood Veneer

As is the case for fine furniture and top of the line clocks today, unusual woods with interesting grain patterns have long been the preferred materials. Their relative scarcity led to the development of thin veneers that greatly multiplied the surface area that could be covered with a given volume of choice lumber.

Initially, veneer was created by sawing one thin layer after another from a log to make sheets. With sawing, the thinnest sheets practical were almost 1/8" thick. Much of the wood was wasted as sawdust and the sheets required fine planing and sanding to make them smooth.

Much later, machines with large extremely sharp knives were developed to *shave* slices from the log. This process permitted much thinner sheets, eliminated the loss of wood as sawdust and produced a very smooth surface, comparable to planing.

If two successive sheets of veneer are placed side by side, with the faces on either side of a cut facing up, the grain pattern of each appears to be a mirror image of the other. This is called book-matching. Careful selection by an expert of sheets of veneer for their grain pattern results in a most pleasing effect in the final product.

Woods with characteristically interesting grain which were not available locally were imported and converted to veneer sheets. Among the most popular such woods were mahogany and rosewood. These were frequently used in combination with veneers of local wood, such as oak and walnut.

Veneers of various colors and grain patterns were used to create interesting designs and accents on the surface of clock cases and other furniture. Intricate pictorial representations made of many varieties of wood were cut and fitted together and glued to the case to form a picture. This is called *inlaying*.

Less intricate, but more frequently used was a technique called *banding or cross-banding*. Strips of veneer contrasting in color and grain with adjacent surfaces was used to highlight and add interest. Frequently such bands were edged with narrow strips of veneer of a sharply contrasting color or shade, creating a miniature frame.

Exotic veneers, especially those with intricate grain patterns like rosewood and most cross grain and crotch veneers, are very brittle and it is difficult to make them conform to moldings or other curved surfaces.

Nineteenth century American clock manufacturers became adept at producing veneered cases in great numbers. They developed fast production methods of forming and gluing veneers of various kinds to flat lumber and moldings. Probably a majority of clocks made in America since before 1800 used veneer. Many thousands of these clock cases are found in American homes today.

Basic Clock Cases

Pine is the most common wood used for the basic case of both American and European clocks. On larger clocks, because the front and sides were usually covered with veneer, it was not usually of the highest grade. Knots, when present, were usually small and tight. Lumber was selected so that knots did not occur on or near the edges of individual pieces. Fortunately, such case lumber appears to have undergone effective curing, before being incorporated into clock cases.

The cases of smaller clocks are usually comparatively thin and made of a better grade of pine, since knots could not be accommodated. Back boards, the largest single element, were usually about a half inch thick and nearly always free of knots.

The quality of the cabinet work in non-production clock cases varies. Some demonstrate the finest techniques of cabinet making, while others are quite crude. With tall cases, especially, it frequently develops that one that is extremely attractive on its surface has a crudely constructed basic case. The interior wood surfaces of some cases may be quite rough, sometimes showing obvious saw marks.

Joints in manufactured cases are utilitarian. They are designed to be easy to produce, using machine methods, but in general are quite strong. There are a few mantle clocks with very intricate and precise joinery of many small elements such as the Seth Thomas *Arch Top*.

Glue was used extensively in old cases. Commonly, until about 1940, this was a hot glue made from animal matter like hide, hooves and bones. For added joint strength, dowels were sometimes employed. Hot glue has now been completely replaced by synthetic resin adhesives and dowels have been replaced with thin wood wafers, glued into slots in mating pieces.

Cut nails are found in early nineteenth century cases and manufactured nails in later ones. Screws were rarely used in older clocks. They became common in the late 1800s, especially to secure the movement to the case and are used extensively today. A comparatively recent development, found especially in lower quality cases, is the use of mechanically driven nails or staples.

Tall clock cases have evolved over the years into designs that are easiest to manufacture or assemble. This is especially true of cases made from kits and those provided in the lower price ranges.

Cases made by cabinet makers usually had a removable bonnet or hood. This is the top part of the case that surrounds the movement and carries a glazed door to cover the dial. This hood is positioned and held in place by mortise and tenon joints that make it possible to slide it forward and remove it from the case. This gives full access to the movement for maintenance, adjustment and repair.

The cases of better quality tall clocks manufactured in recent years have removable side panels in the hood that provide limited access to the movement. Clock cases of lesser quality provide no access to the movement, or at best have a removable panel at the back. This makes it necessary to move the clock away from the wall to remove the panel. Little adjustment can be accomplished from the back of the movement and, more often than not, chime rods are mounted behind the movement.

Most tall clock cases made in the last fifty years have adjustable feet to facilitate leveling. This feature is of little value however, when the clock stands on a thick carpet, as is usually the case today. Cups with nail-like projections that penetrate the carpet provide a much more solid support for clock feet and enable the adjustment to be effective.

Early tall clock cases had glass only in the door over the dial. The waist door was of solid wood. In recent years, the trend has been to install glass on the sides and front of the trunk in which the pendulum hangs. Very elaborate brass pendulums and weights are then highly visible.

Reconstituted Wood

Many attempts have been made to produce a moldable material made of sawdust or powdered wood with a binder of some plastic substance to create a sort of dough. This dough was then pressed into molds and allowed to harden to form a case. The earliest commercial application of this idea was probably as a substitute for hand carving in the splats of half column and triple decker American clocks.

Such materials were of some use for relatively small decorative pieces. When applied to entire cases, even small ones, problems of shrinkage,

warping and cracking developed and their use was limited.

Papier Mache'

With paper, often made of wood, as its main constituent, this material was used to a very limited extent for clock cases.

Papier Mache' is produced by soaking strips or scraps of paper in a glue solution, then packing the resulting mixture into molds, where it is allowed to dry and cure. The resulting molding, when properly cured and finished, is remarkably durable.

Its use in clock cases was essentially limited to the front panel, with the movement encased in a box attached to it. Commonly, decorative materials, such as mother of pearl, brass or pewter were embedded into the wet mixture.

MARBLE, ALABASTER, SLATE and Other STONES as CLOCK CASE MATERIALS

Sometime in the mid nineteenth century, French clock makers experimented with slabs of polished marble and alabaster to make mantle clock cases. By the end of that century, cases made of various types of stone were produced in large quantities.

For a substantial period, clocks made of stone appealed to American tastes and thousands of them were imported into this country.

In an effort to meet this competition, American clock makers began importing stone cases made in Europe and installing their own movements and decorative hardware, including bezels, feet and surface embellishments.

Stone cases were heavy and brittle, so they were easily damaged in transit. In addition their weight made for high shipping costs. Unable to develop competitive sources in the United States, American manufacturers set about developing cases in the same boxy style as most of the French clocks of this period, but made of other materials.

Wood, a material with which they were familiar, could be used easily since it was capable of being worked in much the same way as stone. Because some stone case clocks were made of slate or other solid black minerals, wood finished with black paint offered a possible solution.

With the development of special paints which were heated to a fluid state before application and produced a thick shiny black coating, this style was launched.

Later, when the burgeoning chemical industry produced *celluloid* (nitro-cellulose) a finish called *Adamantine* was developed and applied to clock cases. This was a thin film of celluloid of various colors, swirled to simulate marble. Adamantine finishes were also referred to as *marbleized*.

As indicated earlier, iron foundries by the late nineteenth century were able to produce fine castings only about 1/8" thick which were used to duplicate the appearance of stone cases. The finishes used were the much like those for wood cases.

Most of these wood and iron cases were finished in plain black, so clocks in this boxy style in all its variations have come to be known simply as *"Blacks."* Millions were produced and we will have more to say about them in a later chapter.

Solid Cases of Mineral Materials

In a few instances, clock cases have been made of a single piece of stone by carving or machining it from a solid block. French sculptors excelled at producing elaborate carved stone cases.

Especially for small *boudoir* or dressing table clocks, molded glass cases have been produced. Some such cases have also been made of cut glass. While most glass cases are clear, some are tinted with pastel colors. The movements in these cases are usually of near watch quality.

Semi-precious stones, such as jade and coral have been used for clock cases.

ANIMAL MATERIALS, IVORY, BONE Etc.

Clock movements have been encased in ivory, sometimes elaborately carved ivory from elephant, walrus and other mammals, and in tortoise shell mounted on wood. Even the preserved feet or other parts of trophy animals have served as mounts for clocks.

PLASTIC MATERIALS for CLOCK CASES

Celluloid (Nitro-cellulose)

Made from pyroxylin and camphor, this is a highly flammable material. Even old examples, when rubbed with a finger will often emit a characteristic camphor odor. This was the material originally used for photographic film, but its flammability resulted in the loss of many priceless original films and tremendous fire losses.

Probably the earliest use of plastics in clock cases was for the simulated marble columns that decorated the fronts of the black mantel clocks just discussed. This was followed by its use as a surface finish for marbleized clocks.

Celluloid was moldable, so columns could be formed with flutes. It was also capable of being colored, using suitable pigments. A unique property was the ability to simulate marble by floating liquid celluloid of various colors on water then gently swirling to create a marble-like pattern. This created a film which was applied to clock cases as mentioned earlier.

Celluloid was used for many items, notably rattles and floating bathtub toys like ducks and fish for babies. These items were very thin, made in halves and cemented together. They were easily dented and cracked.

Small clock movements which became available in the early 1900 period were housed in cases made of celluloid, usually in an ivory color. These cases were produced in a remarkable variety of styles and in great numbers. Because celluloid shrinks and becomes extremely brittle with age, these cases were easily damaged and relatively few have survived. Those that have are in great demand by certain collectors.

Celluloid is a highly flammable substance and is very easily ignited.

Bakelite (Phenolic Resin)

Developed early in the twentieth century by L. H. Baekeland, this was probably the first commercially successful synthetic resin plastic. Its first applications were in the field of electricity, because of its outstanding insulating properties. For this use, it was produced in sheets and blocks, usually reinforced with fabric. It was readily sawed and could be machined to any shape. It is characteristically a warm brown in color, although rarely it may be found in black.

Bakelite had a distinctive odor, resulting from the formaldehyde and phenol of which it was made.

The first application of Bakelite to clock cases has not been determined accurately. The author has in his collection a case identical in shape and wall thickness to many cast iron black clocks, but cast in natural brown Bakelite. This case was probably made around 1910.

Other styles of cases with mechanical movements were made of Bakelite on a limited scale until around 1930.

With the introduction of synchronous electric motors to power clocks in the late 20's, clock making was revolutionized. The combination of this new technology and the use of durable molded plastic for clock cases was a natural combination. Many small cases for electric clocks were made of bakelite, both in natural brown and black.

While most mechanical and electrical applications using bakelite were reinforced with one or more layers of fabric, clock cases were not.

Because of Bakelite's inherent brittleness, many of these cases were damaged or destroyed when they fell off a table or other supporting surface.

Of the millions of these clocks produced, only a few have survived.

Thermo Plastics

Since World War II, there has been phenomenal development and application of an endless variety of plastic materials. Many have been and are currently being used to form very inexpensive clock cases. The variety of styles is almost infinite.

CHINA and PORCELAIN CLOCK CASES

Capable of being molded into almost any shape, ceramic materials have long been employed as cases for clocks. Fired clock cases of all kinds are loosely referred to as *China*. Some of the finest manufacturers of fine china and porcelain have applied their skills and facilities to this activity. Many china clock cases bear the trademark signature of famous makers.

Typically, china cases have gracefully curved shapes with various color glazed bases and applied decoration. They are usually five sided, with the bottom open and a circular hole in the back.

Movements in China clocks are usually round and are attached to the dial plate with posts and taper pins. A decorative bezel with glass is secured to the dial plate. Two straps are attached to the back of the bezel and their opposite ends are bent and threaded. A round brass plate designed to fit over the hole in the back of the case has two holes through which long screws are threaded into the ends of the bezel straps. When tightened, these screws create tension between the bezel and back plate, securing the assembly firmly in place.

A wood platform may be mounted inside the case near the bottom to support a circular gong.

Alternatively, the hours are struck on a small bell attached to the movement itself.

CASE MANUFACTURE

Throughout the history of clock making, the operating mechanism or movement and the case in which it was housed have frequently been made by different craftsmen. In the early days of English brass movements, the back plates were often elaborately engraved and bore the name of the maker and the date. Cases, on the other hand, were seldom identified. When case and movement were assembled to form what we know as a clock, it was identified by the maker of the movement.

There is some justification for this, since it was common practice for the movement maker to order the case for each clock from one or more cabinet makers or makers of cases of other materials.

Today, many clocks sold in the United States have German movements in American cases, assembled by a company whose name they bear.

Until about 1820, all clock cases, whatever the material from which they were constructed, were essentially individually made by hand. In many instances, the entire case was crafted and finished by one man. In others, artisans with special skills, notably dial painting and metal casting, made elements that were incorporated into the finished product.

With the beginning of production of interchangeable parts for wooden clock movements, through the use of jigs and fixtures, similar ideas were applied to case making.

CHAPTER FOUR

CASE and MOVEMENT DECORATION

THE EARLY DECORATION of clocks, before the evolution of cases, was limited to the dial and the movement. Later, the appearance of the case seemed to become more important than the time-telling function of the dial and hands.

Even when the entire movement was made of wrought iron, numerals were sometimes formed in dials by indenting in the hot metal, using flat faced punches. Decoration of the hand or hands was sometimes achieved in the same manner.

In the earliest stages, the posts which spaced and secured the front and back plates of the movement were shaped by the blacksmith to make them as attractive as possible.

ENGRAVING of BRASS ELEMENTS

Very early in the development of clock movements, it was found that brass combined a number of characteristics that were desirable for this application. Brass is much easier to cut than iron or steel. It could more readily be fashioned into relatively thin plates or sheets by casting a small ingot, then hammering it on an anvil. It would not rust and could be polished to a high luster.

Brass was used for gears (*wheels*) mounted on steel shafts (*arbors*) with steel pinions. The pivots on the end of the shaft run in holes in brass plates, minimizing wear due to friction.

Brass was comparatively soft, and easily worked by steel tools. *Engraving*, the removal of brass by sharp steel tools in a decorative manner, began to appear on clock movements and dials. It was included as one of the skills learned and mastered during a clock maker's apprenticeship.

At the zenith of the art clock making in England, beginning around 1650, it was customary to decoratively engrave the back plates of movements. The entire surface of the plate was usually covered with intricately intertwined designs, including the maker's name and often the year the movement was made. These plates are excellent examples of the best of the engraver's art. The dials of clocks were made of brass with the time track, numerals and

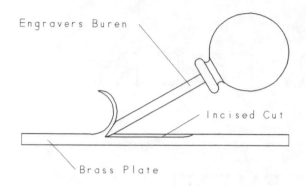

Figure 35 Engraving Brass

other decorative elements engraved and often filled with black sealing wax. The face of the dial was usually silvered.

When clocks ceased to be individually crafted by skilled artisans, but were made by mass production methods, engraving fell by the wayside. It continued to be practiced, but was limited to the inscription of silver ware, trophies, commemorative plates, or jewelry. Even these applications are now accomplished almost exclusively by machines.

CABINET MAKER'S DECORATION

As we mentioned earlier, clock cases have reflected the aesthetic tastes of the period in which they were made. In fact, cases for clocks have been made by some of the most renowned cabinet makers to house movements by journeyman clock makers.

Some of the most complex forms of cabinetry are to be found in early tall case (*grandfather*) clocks, especially those made in England and New England, France and Holland. They were individually crafted by journeyman cabinet makers, to the highest possible standards. English and American tall case clocks featured broken arch tops, beautifully proportioned turned finials and spandrels, tastefully done veneer and inlay.

The selection of solid woods and veneers and their combination on the case surface, along with careful choices of woods used for finials and moldings were expressions of the cabinet maker's artistry.

Wood Selection

When the wood, whether solid or veneer, of which a clock case is made will form the finished surface, the color and grain pattern of each piece must be carefully chosen by the cabinet maker. This is especially critical when using woods which have wide variations in either color or grain. Coarse grained woods like oak, or those with deep color like black walnut, unless carefully matched, can create less than pleasing results.

One reason for the use of veneers for clock cases is the ability to obtain many sheets from the same log, making it possible to match grain and color patterns in adjacent or facing areas.

Veneering is very time consuming and labor intensive. With modern automatic wood working tools, clock cases produced in recent years nearly always are made of solid wood, oak walnut, or cherry. The lumber from which they are made is commercially produced and only very broad grade and color specifications prevail.. While manufacturers may make an attempt at color and grain matching, the result is never equal to veneered surfaces.

In classic clock cases, solid wood boards more than twelve inches wide were common. Today, such boards are not available. To reduce costs, large flat pieces are often made up of several narrow boards, glued together.

Modern furniture factories making cases of solid woods use sprayed stains and toners to disguise or blend varying grain patterns and colors. This results in a degree of uniformity, but eliminates the uniqueness of a case with artistic selection of distinctive matching veneer wood grains and colors.

Figure 36 Representative Finials

Tastes have changed and bland atonal grain patterns now seem to be as acceptable as the atonal music currently in vogue. As has traditionally been true, this is a reflection of the tastes of our time. Panels of laminated wood, made up of several pieces glued together, have become so common that they are generally accepted as a suitable material for decorative uses of all kinds.

Finials

The design and execution of finials, columns and other turnings that decorate clocks can be almost a signature of the maker. Some are delicate, gracefully proportioned and are beautifully produced and finished. Others are poorly designed and may be crudely executed. Among the finest are those found on the cases of Vienna Regulator Clocks.

In general, it may be said that finials that have long, thin tops are more pleasing than those that are bulkier. Perhaps a reason for the somewhat

limited use of these attractive types is the susceptibility to breakage during manufacture and in use.

It has long been customary to make finials so that they may be easily removed and replaced. This is usually accomplished by having a short round stub on the bottom of the finial that fits into a matching hole in the case. Especially when finials are on the bottom of the case, the fit is usually tight enough so that some force is necessary to insert or remove them.

Many finials have been glued in place by an owner and cannot be removed without the likelihood of serious damage.

Columns

Columns and half columns have been used extensively to decorate clock cases. They are found on many tall clock cases, pillar and scroll, half column, mirror, triple decker, column and cornice and black mantel cases of American clocks.

Proportions of columns vary widely from long and slender, to short and stubby. They may be fully formed round, half round or have rectangular sections. Clock columns nearly always have capitals at the top and some sort of pediment or base. These may be ornate or quite simple.

Some columns are twisted, in the Queen Anne style and some are decorated with incised carved patterns. A few are fully formed carvings, including human and animal figures, in imitation of columns on classic Greek or Roman buildings.

Most American half columns have bulbous capitals and bases which are covered with gold leaf. The body of these columns was nearly always painted black, but some were of pine with artificial painted wood grain. A few were of solid cherry with natural shellac finish.

Many Vienna Regulator wall clocks have smooth turned column bodies with separate turned capitols and finials which have been beautifully carved with

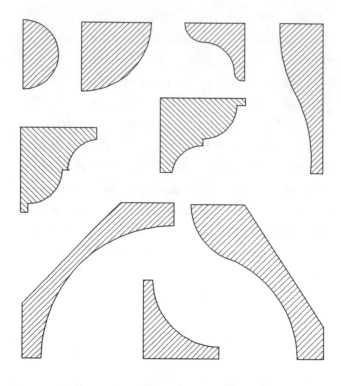

Figure 37 Representative Clock Moldings

incised designs. These elements, when glued to the door front of the case appear to be a single entity. Vienna clock columns are nearly always nicely proportioned.

Molding

Molding is the process of shaping a board into a decorative cross section. Originally, moldings were made by craftsmen using planes with blades curved to the desired shape. With the beginning of mass production, machines called *shapers* produced them in a fraction of the time required by hand methods.

Wood molding is found on nearly all cases made of wood. Molding shapes in clock cases vary from simple half-round and quarter-round to elaborate curved cross sections. Molding is always applied to flat elements of the case, often using nails and glue to hold it in place, but sometimes only glue.

Molding may be straight, as when used to accent rectangular cases, or curved as in circular dial bezels. Parts of circles, or compound curved

moldings are also common on clock cases. These types are known as *full* moldings.

When the edges of flat pieces are shaped, it is called *edge molding*. Edge molding is widely found on clock cases to soften otherwise sharp edges.

Geometric Wood Decorative Elements

Circular thin medallions with molded patterns are found on some clock cases, notably Ingraham *Ionic* and Vienna Regulator wall clocks. Some are turned and some are formed by pressing with a die.

Thin rectangular pieces of wood, with their sides tapered upward to form a ridge, are used as decorative elements on some Vienna Regulator clocks. They are frequently painted black before being glued to the wood of the case.

Carving

Additional three-dimensional decoration of wood cases is provided by carving and embossing. Designs which are carved *into* a flat surface are known as *Intaglio* carvings. Those which are fully formed and raised *above* the surface are *Relief* carvings.

The distinguishing feature of German Cuckoo clocks is the carving that covers the shield, or front of the clock, the pendulum and often the front of the roof-like top. While smaller clocks usually have relatively simple carving, larger ones, up to several feet high, may have very fine and intricate modeling of animal and bird figures and foliage of trees or vines..

While never mass-produced, many large carved pieces made in the Black Forest of Germany and incorporating cuckoo clock movements have been made by the skilled wood carvers of that area.

Usually made from a single large log or stump of a tree, these pieces usually depict a complex rural scene, usually hilly and heavily wooded. They commonly incorporate a number of trees, foliage, animals and birds, notably deer, goats, rabbits, cuckoos and hawks. Sometimes a single large animal or bird is featured. When a clock is inserted, its dial is usually insignificantly small.

Some of these Black Forest wood carvings are as much as three feet in diameter and five feet or more in height. The artistry of some is so fine as to be truly sculptural. They are treasured by owners and collectors of Black Forest clocks.

Metallic Decorative Elements

Brass or other metallic embellishment details have been added. to clock cases for hundreds of years. As we have seen, bezels of brass, either as doors carrying glass to protect the dial, or as a decorative surround for the dial itself, are found on a great many cases.

Other metals, notably pot metal and bronze, have been used to a lesser extent.

SURFACE FINISHES as DECORATION

Regardless of the material from which they are constructed, clock cases usually have a surface finished with some other substance. This is true, even when the final appearance shows the characteristics of the base material.

Clear Finishes on Natural Bases

On wood cases, especially when the grain is attractive, a clear finish was commonly employed. For hundreds of years such finishes were waxes, resins or oils derived from natural sources. Probably the most common was long known as *Varnish*. This was a solution of resinous substances dissolved in vegetable oils to make *oil varnish*, or in more rapidly evaporating alcohol to make *spirit varnish*. Essentially, both are what is more commonly known today as *Shellac*.

Several coats of such varnish, or shellac, filled the pores of the wood and created a relatively thick transparent high luster film that emphasized the richness and color of the grain. It provided a relatively durable finish, but is easily damaged by heat, alcohol and other fluids.

When such finishes are to be used, the wood must be carefully selected to display attractive color and grain patterns.

In addition to creating an attractive surface, these finishes provided a degree of protection to the wood. Accumulated dust and dirt will not penetrate the pores of the wood and can be removed from the surface with a damp cloth.

Pigmented Paint Finishes

Pigmented finishes completely cover the grain and color of the materials on which they are applied. The most common such finish is paint. Paint not only has pigments to give it color, there is nearly always a mineral filler to provide body and thus a thicker coat, with better hiding properties.

Black is the color most often used on clock cases. Most old black paints derived their color and body from tar.

A few mantel clock styles had cases painted in pastel shades.

A technique called *artificial wood graining* employed a combination of paints to simulate the appearance of exotic wood grains on cases made of cheap pine. In this process, a coat of light colored paint is applied, then a darker coat is spread over it and streaked with a dry brush to create the appearance of wood graining.

Nitro Cellulose Film Finishes

We have touched on the use of nitro cellulose films to simulate marble on the cases of rectangular mantel clocks. This was by far its greatest application.

Cellulose film was also produced in artificial wood grain patterns, almost indistinguishable from the real thing. It was used on several styles of clocks, notably the Seth Thomas *Sonora Chime* series made early in the twentieth century.

Japanese clock makers used this finish extensively, especially on miniature drop octagon or *Schoolhouse* regulator wall clocks. Made for their own domestic use and sold in large quantities in Japan, many thousands of these clocks have lately been brought into this country and sold as collector items.

PAINTED DECORATION

Beginning in the late 1700s, painted dials began to be made for tall clocks in England and the United States. In England the dial plates were made of iron, while in the United States they were commonly of wood. The face of the dial was white, the time track, numerals and the name of the maker black.

Especially for English tall clocks, the semi-circular space above the dial that often contained a moon phase indicator, was sometimes decorated with a scenic painting of a feature found on the estate of the owner of the clock.

Painted dials were commonly used for American clocks of all types, from around 1700 until well past 1750. Most of these, in addition to the numerals and time train, had hand painted corner decorations, often including highlights of gold leaf.

While the earliest American dial plates were wood and were hand painted. When mass production of clocks got into full swing, nearly all dial plates were made of thin rolled zinc sheet. The details were either printed or stenciled.

A significant difference in the rate of expansion of the zinc and the paint applied to it, with changes in temperature, caused the paint to check and separate from the zinc. It is rare to find zinc dials today with the original paint in even passably good condition.

Clocks with colored painted cases, especially those made of *Papier Mache'* often had hand painted floral decorations on their fronts. In addition, inlays of mother of pearl and other materials are often found. This form of embellishment may have been in imitation of more expensive china cases.

Reverse Painting and Stenciling on Glass

Developed as a novelty art form, the technique of painting on glass to be viewed from the unpainted side became popular late in the seventeenth century. Initially it was used only to create pictures for framing and display like conventional paintings.

Aaron Willard was taken with this technique and persuaded artist friends to apply it to the glasses of his banjo clocks. In clocks, these glass panels are referred to as *tablets*. They were used on all banjo clocks made by Willard and his many imitators.

When Eli Terry developed the Pillar and Scroll case, his first experimental models had dials reverse painted on the back of the top glass of the door. When the design was finalized and put into production, the lower tablet was a reverse painted scene.

All reverse painting was done by hand by artists, usually working in their homes. Some were talented children. The quality of the art varies widely, reflecting the skill level of the artist.

Reverse painting was used for early half-column and ogee clocks, but was later replaced by much less expensive stenciling and transfers.

For the nearly 100 years during which they were manufactured, Ogee cases carried some form of colorful decoration in their lower tablets. The variety of designs used may well exceed 1000. The same design might have been used by a number of clock makers.

Chinoiserie Decoration

In Europe, during the eighteenth century, there was a wave of interest in all things oriental. A style of decoration in imitation of the Chinese became extremely popular. Clock cases reflected this trend. Many tall clock cases, while retaining traditional styling, were painted black and their trunks illuminated with Chinese landscapes. There was a great deal of gold in these hand painted illustrations, many of which were true works of art.

A few of these clocks were imported into the United States and some American makers affected the style. Few examples are known to exist today.

Fabric Case Covering

Fine fabrics have been used, to a very limited extent, to cover the cases of clocks. Limited mostly to very small clocks, fabric proved to be impractical because of its vulnerability to damage and the tendency of its colors to fade when continuously exposed to light. The doors over the opening in the back of the case of many French clocks were made of thin brass with a cut out filigree pattern so the chime could be heard. A small square of silk was glued to the inside over the openings in the door.

Fabrics were used more successfully, but also to a limited extent, as accents on the insides of some cases.

Tortoise Shell, Snake and Lizard Skin

In France, during the regency period of the early eighteenth century, an elaborate shelf clock case style was developed which had a gracefully curved wood case covered in tortoise shell and with fire-gilt brass garnitures. These were beautiful examples of the French clock makers' art and the style has been produced sporadically even to the present day.

While tortoise shell is no longer used, for environmental reasons, it has been replaced by simulated finishes on clocks purchase in Europe and brought home as prized souvenirs by present day travelers.

Tortoise shell was used extensively in other styles of clock cases as trim or incidental inlay decoration.

Reptile skin has found its way into clock cases, especially smaller ones, like those used by travelers. It is occasionally found as incidental decoration on other styles of cases.

OTHER CASE MATERIALS

There is almost no limit to the kinds of materials that can and probably have been used to a very limited extent for clock cases.

Clock movements, over the years have been installed in all sorts of interesting artifacts, including animal parts, as noted earlier.

CHAPTER FIVE

CLOCK MOVEMENTS

WHILE THE MOVEMENT of a clock is usually concealed inside the case, its design and size may dictate the basic appearance of the case. Here we will not bore the reader with intricate details of movement design, only enough to help in basic understanding of clock characteristics and identification of broad categories.

In sketching the history of clock development, we have highlighted the importance of the pendulum in achieving more accurate timekeeping and the resulting development of long floor standing cases. Later refinements in movement design permitted the use of shorter pendulums and even the replacement of the pendulum with lever or floating balance escapements. Their size no longer controlled by pendulum length, movements became smaller, making smaller cases possible.

The QUEST for ACCURATE TIME KEEPING

Over the centuries, the most enterprising of clock makers constantly sought ways of improving the accuracy of their movements. The pendulum, as a device for dividing increments of time was discovered by Christian Huygens and patented in Amsterdam in 1657 by Solomon Coster, a master clock maker in the Hague. The first Huygens pendulums were 9 3/4 inches long and oscillated at half second intervals. He determined that a 39 inch pendulum, swinging at one second intervals, was more accurate.

The first pendulum clocks made for sale were made in England in 1658 by a Dutch immigrant, John Fromanteel, who trained under Coster and was granted rights to use the Huygens patent.

Another most significant advance in the art of timekeeping was the invention, around 1660, of the balance spring by an English scientist, Robert Hooke. While initially applied to clocks, this invention, was soon employed in large watches and eventually made practical very tiny watch movements which kept good time.

Probably because the making and treating of the steel necessary to produce consistently accurate hair springs was an imprecise art at the time of their invention, clocks incorporating them were far from accurate timekeepers. Because the time intervals marked by the swinging of a pendulum were constant and predictable, pendulum clocks continued to be most popular.

By 1675, English clock makers, notably Thomas Tompion and Joseph Knibb, were making wood cased short pendulum clocks designed to be placed on wall brackets or tables. They are known as *bracket* clocks today and their case designs have been widely imitated.

Hairspring balance wheel escapements made the pocket watch possible and were used from the time of their invention until the present, going through many technical refinements of metallurgy, design and manufacture.

For hundreds of years clock movements continued to use pendulums as the means of dividing time. Some smaller clocks, such as carriage and later alarm and boudoir clocks had movements with hairspring balance wheel lever escapements.

AMERICAN CLOCK MOVEMENTS

English clock makers were among the earliest immigrants to America. The traditions of English craftsmanship were continued until mass production of clock movements revolutionized clock making.

Colonial Clock Making

It is probable that, until the early eighteenth century, there was little clock making in the English colonies of the New World. Some of the more affluent settlers possessed fine clocks made in England.

Brooks Palmer, in his *"The Book of American Clocks,"* provides an apt description of clock making in colonial America:

"The craftsman, working alone, or aided by an apprentice or two, used only the simplest of hand tools-hammer, drill and file -with sand for casting. It was tedious, painstaking, wearing labor. Brass plates and blanks for the wheels were cast, using molds of sand. The brass was an alloy of copper and zinc and, on occasion, tin, for which each craftsman had his own formula. After the casting had cooled, it was still too soft and had to be beaten for a long period with light blows of the hammer until hard. This "planishing" could go on for days. Early manuals gave exact instructions, and one of them advised that, if a crack developed in the plate, the brass should be put under water and the planishing continued. This must have furnished a fine shower bath on a cold winter's day at a time long before central heating.

After the brass was of suitable hardness, it was filed smooth and polished to the necessary thickness. A later process for casting brass between two polished marble slabs gave it a more uniform thickness and reduced the amount of tedious filing. Later still, the clock maker was able to buy brass castings and blanks ready for filing, cutting and finishing; some of them came from Europe, some were made here.

Gears had to be cast in blank, cut, and filed; some of the old clocks still bear the marks of the lines used for cutting the teeth; all this was hand work. Despite the scarcity of metals and the amount of time involved, some few clocks were made in this country in the eighteenth century; but they were made only at the order of a purchaser. In those days there were no trains to catch and split second accuracy was not necessary."

With the outbreak of the Revolutionary War, clock makers were among the few artisans equipped with tools and training to make articles of armament, especially guns. This they turned to with a will.

Clock Making in the Early United States

Following the war, metal, particularly brass, was very scarce and the price of traditional clocks escalated.

This posed a challenge to the Yankee ingenuity of a few clock makers. As noted earlier, the Willard family of Grafton, Massachusetts set about developing and producing small weight driven wall clock movements.

Simon Willard, starting with hand methods, then progressing to the use of machines and with the help of apprentices, produced around four thousand clocks in forty years, beginning in 1802. While an average of some 100 units a year could not be considered mass production, it was an achievement in its time.

Both the movements, which were quite simple, and the cases of these clocks, some of which were very elaborate, were of the highest quality.

Their selling price was around $35.00. At a time when a skilled craftsman earned only about $1.00 a week, this was a considerable sum.

Wood Movements

In colonial and early post-revolutionary America, there was an abundance of wood, but little metal of any kind. There were immigrants from the black forest area of Germany, where wood was also plentiful and a cottage industry, including the making of wood clock movements had developed. Around 1790, Gideon Roberts began making clock movements of wood in Bristol, Connecticut and if not the first, was one of the earliest to do so in America.

In 1806, Eli Terry of Plymouth, Connecticut accepted an order for 4,000 wood movement clocks, which he proceeded to fill In doing so, he employed water power and developed the idea of using jigs and fixtures to make several parts at one time. This system produced interchangeable parts, laying the groundwork for true mass production. This was the true beginning of the Industrial Revolution. Other clock makers were quick to adopt similar approaches and before long, clocks were being produced in the hundreds of thousands each year, at prices affordable by a large segment of the population.

The big depression of 1837 halted clock production and marked the end of the manufacture of wood movements, except for a few smaller producers.

Sheet Brass Weight Driven Movements

Paul Revere had devised a means of rolling copper into sheets used to cover the hull of the famous ship *Constitution*. Not until 1838, did rolled *brass* sheets become available. Noble Jerome used brass strips and stampings to make 30-hour weight driven movements. These movements could be sold at a very low price and other clock makers were quick to follow Jerome's lead. The Connecticut clock industry was revitalized and took over the world clock market.

Coiled Springs in American Clocks

About 1845, coiled steel main springs became available in America, making much smaller clock movements and cases practical. Millions of small thirty hour clocks, called *Cottage Clocks*, were manufactured over the next half century.

Movements with eight day running time soon became common. To achieve the longer duration, a somewhat longer pendulum than that used in cottage clocks was necessary. A great many case designs for these movements evolved. The most popular were probably those generally referred to as *Kitchen* clocks, *Black Mantel*, and *Tambour* or *Humpback*.. These styles were all manufactured over a period of many years and many millions were sold.

Weight driven clocks, especially the Ogee case style, continued to be made in some quantity until late in the nineteenth century. Those driven by springs became far more popular.

Limited numbers of high quality tall and wall clocks have been produced continuously in America, even to the present day. The movements currently used, however, are made in foreign countries. At this writing, nearly all such movements are produced in Germany.

Balance Wheel Escapements

About 1850, movements employing an oscillating balance wheel instead of a pendulum to control the release of energy and referred to as *Marine* movements were introduced by several manufacturers. This is something of a misnomer, since these movements were much inferior to marine *chronometers* developed in England.

The small size of movements with balance wheel escapements made it possible to house them in smaller cases than movements with pendulums. They were less accurate , however.

The major advantage of this type of movement was that it could be moved without stopping it. This made it especially suitable to small clocks that were subject to accidental bumping.

For obvious reasons, it was the movement of choice for inexpensive alarm clocks, of which millions were made each year for many decades.

ELECTRIC CLOCK MOVEMENTS

Direct Current Battery Powered

Many attempts were made to use electricity as the motive power for clocks. One approach was to drive the pendulum by passing it through an electro-magnetic field that not only regulated the escape interval, but imparted power. Dry cell 6-volt batteries were the source of electricity. Some usable devices were developed, but never achieved great popularity.

Since these attempts merely introduced a different source of power with the only benefit being the elimination of winding a spring, they contributed little to the art of timekeeping. The batteries and wiring were bulky, cumbersome and unsightly.

They are an interesting novelty and are sought by many collectors.

Synchronous Electric Clock Movements

In the United States, almost all companies generating electrical power standardized on 110 volt 60 cycle alternating current for domestic use. This system sends pulses of alternating positive and negative electricity over the wires. The rate of oscillation was nominally 60 cycles per second, but this rate varied significantly.

Synchronous motors took advantage of this alternating pattern to develop motion and turn their rotors. In 1914 Henry Warren of Ashland, Massachusetts, developed a very small synchronous motor-powered clock movement. Its speed was controlled by the number of oscillations sent out by the generator at the local power plant. Thus it was *synchronized* with the generator.

The relative uncertainty of the speed of a generator made such a clock somewhat less than accurate. Before long, however power companies adopted a means of correcting for any discrepancy every hour by sending out compensating impulses. Synchronous electric clocks became a very desirable form of timekeeping.

Because they were very inexpensive to manufacture, were simply plugged into available electric outlets and kept such good time, synchronous clocks almost completely displaced mechanical clocks.

By the 1930's, electric clocks so dominated the market that many manufacturers of mechanical movements succumbed to the generally adverse conditions brought about by the Great Depression and closed their doors.

Battery Powered Electric Movements

Partly as an offshoot of the technical developments fostered by the space program and the surge in electronic development, a number of elements came together to make possible very small, inexpensive clock movements.

Powered by a single small flashlight battery, these movements had a tiny solenoid that periodically wound a small spring to power a balance wheel movement with plastic gears.

A later, similar movement incorporated a minuscule electric motor to operate strike hammers to sound the hours. Each time the motor is activated to move the hammers, it also powers a gear to wind the spring that powers the movement.

Batteries for these clocks may provide power for a year. or more of operation.

Quartz Regulated Battery Movements

The electronic miniaturization technology that spawned the computer industry included the quartz chip. This is a device that oscillates at a very high, very precise rate of speed when a current is passed through it. By electronically dividing this rate of oscillation, very accurate time keeping is possible.

Electronic miniaturization technology also resulted in the light emitting diode (LED) used to show time in digital watches.

Quartz chips are now used in very inexpensive clock movements and in watches of all grades.

FOREIGN CLOCK MOVEMENTS

Over the centuries that cover the history of clock making, several nations have dominated the market, as did England from about 1600 to 1840 and the United States from 1840 through about 1940. Large clock making industries have fallen by the wayside as other countries have gained ascendancy. In some cases, a small residual manufacturing base has survived.

French Clocks

Two centers of clock making existed in France. In and around Paris, originally as an adjunct to the royal court, a highly skilled and sophisticated clock industry developed. With the introduction of mass production, it retained very high quality standards and the movements it produced are among the finest anywhere.

These *Parisian* movements were small by comparison with most American clocks, the plates much heavier, arbors of fine steel with their pivots hardened and polished. Striking was usually on a small nickel-silver bell attached to the back plate of the movement, producing a most pleasing, delicate ring. Parisian French movements are nearly always round with solid front and back plates.

The dial plate and bezel are usually attached to the front plate of the movement. Riveted to the bezel are two steel straps, a little shorter than the depth of the clock case. Round holes only slightly larger than the diameter of the movement are cut in both the front and the back of the case.

The movement is installed from the front of the case, with the back of the bezel in contact with the front of the case. A simple bezel with a pierced brass door attached fits in the hole at the back of the case. Two long machine screws pass through holes on either side of this bezel and are threaded into holes at the ends of the straps attached to the front bezel. When tightened, they securely hold the movement in place. The door allows access for installation or removal of the pendulum.

The cases in which these fine movements were housed were of the same high quality. In many instances they were elegant and were sold in the United States through fine jewelry houses, such as Tiffany, and exclusive department stores. The name of the *seller* often appears on the dial. The maker's name and trademark are stamped on the back plate of the movement.

The second area of French clock making was in the province of *Franche Comte* in Southeastern France. The movements produced here were comparatively large and crude, but solidly built and very durable. They were made of iron, steel and brass.

Designed for sale to the middle class, these clocks lacked the fine finishes and attention to detail of Parisian clocks and were much larger.

Even during the domination of the international clock market by England and America, the French clock industry managed to survive, largely because its very high quality appealed the sophisticated tastes of the elite. There is little if any clock making in France today.

German and Austrian Clock Movements

A clock making industry has existed in Germany for centuries and continues active today supplying movements to the United States where they are housed in domestically made cases.

Especially during the 1930's, German *Box Clocks*, a simple rectangular case style of wall clock was very popular in this country. Tall clocks of similar style also found favor. Usually made of oak with beveled and sometimes leaded glass in the door and side panels, these cases housed rugged and well built movements. German tall clocks, complete with cases clocks were imported into the United States in substantial numbers, mostly between the two world wars, 1920 to 1939.

The German clock industry also developed a unique clock movement with a rotary pendulum. Using highly polished brass, decorated porcelain dial and displaying the movement and pendulum under a glass dome. The result is a fascinating decorative object with spell binding motion.

Using very little power, this design was capable of running well over a year on a single winding of the heavy spring. A very popular anniversary gift, because it needed to be wound only once a year on an anniversary date, it is commonly known as an *Anniversary* Clock and alternately, a *400 Day* clock.

German Black Forest Cuckoo Clocks

In the *Schwartzwald* or Black Forest of Germany, a clock making industry has existed for some two hundred years. Its primary output has been the unique cuckoo clock and its cousin, the trumpeter clock. Unlike most clocks, the hours and sometimes quarter hours are announced by sequential whistles, as well as by coil gongs.

The cases are designed to look like a house with the front decorated with carving. A small opening in the gable is covered by a door that opens to allow a carved cuckoo to pop out and bob up and down as the hours are sounded. Since about 1945, the bird has been made of plastic, not wood.

Very old cuckoo clock movements had wooden wheels or gears, old ones had brass wheels and steel arbors with wood front and back plates. Later movements had front and back plates of cast brass. For almost a hundred years, stamped sheet brass plates and wheels have been used. Following World War II, sheet steel and plastic have been used extensively for movement parts.

Cuckoo clocks have always been popular in the United States. Few American soldiers serving in the American Army of Occupation in Germany, after World War II returned home without bringing or sending at least one cuckoo clock.

Viennese Clock Movements

Beginning around 1800, a sophisticated clock making industry developed in Vienna. Both the movements and cases of Vienna weight driven wall clocks are among the finest examples of the clock maker's art.

The movements in these clocks are invariably well made, matching in quality and workmanship those of the best French clocks. As with the French, the Viennese converted to mass production systems while maintaining the high quality for which they had become known.

Most Vienna movements have two trains and two weights. They strike the hours and half hours on a fine coil gong, usually attached to the movement. A number have only one weight, indicating time, with no strike. A few have three trains, three weights and sound quarter hours in the *grande sonnerie* manner, in addition to striking the hours. All are collector's items, with the three weight style the rarest and most desirable.

A few early hand made Vienna movements will run for a year or more on a winding. Some are very complicated, providing all sorts of information in addition to the time of day.

Swiss Clock Movements

Many people, perhaps because the cases are suggestive of Swiss chalets, associate cuckoo clocks with Switzerland. True cuckoo clocks, are German. Very limited numbers of imitations have been made in Japan and in the United States..

The Swiss claim to horological fame lies mostly in the area of watches. The word *Swiss* has long been a synonym for high quality watches. The Swiss have also excelled in the production of small watch-like clocks, especially those commonly called *Travel Clocks*.

ATMOS Perpetual Clocks

These clocks, with movements that are of high watch quality, are unique and fascinating. Like Anniversary clocks, they employ a rotary pendulum, requiring very little power to operated. The uniqueness of *Atmos* lies in the means of winding.

The *Atmos* movement is powered by a small spring. It is housed in a barrel mounted on an arbor with a ratchet sprocket and has a chain connecting it to a large metal bellows diaphragm, much like that of an aneroid barometer.

The diaphragm is filled with a gas that expands and contracts very significantly with only small changes in temperature.

As the temperature decreases, the gas in the diaphragm contracts, pulling the chain and winding the clock spring. When the temperature increases, the gas expands and the bellows moves out. A small return spring turns the barrel ratchet to pull the chain back, ready for the next rise in temperature and a winding movement of the chain.

Changes in temperature of only a degree or two will wind the spring sufficiently to power the movement for twenty four hours. In effect, the owner need never wind the clock. In this sense the clock movement runs *perpetually*, without human winding.

Atmos movements are of very high quality, usually gold plated and encased in glass with gold plated brass corner posts, tops and bases. They are relatively expensive, usually sold in fine jewelry stores and often given as anniversary or retirement gifts.

Under average conditions in a home, they will keep quite good time over a long life.

Tourist Clocks

Today, American tourists frequently purchase very high quality clocks in Switzerland, notably replicas of the French Regency style of shelf or bracket clock.. Such clocks are usually of high quality and are relatively expensive.

Japanese Clock Movements

Long before World War II, there was a clock industry in Japan. Among the earliest Japanese clock cases were elongated vertical rectangles with a slot in the center of the front, known in the United States as *stick clocks*. A pointer, driven by clockwork, moved up and down in this slot. Hour markers beside the slot indicated the time as the pointer moved past them.

When these clocks were in use, Japan had its own unique system of telling time. It divided the periods of daylight and dark into equal divisions, regardless of the length of each period in real time.

In the summer, when daylight lasted perhaps sixteen hours, as measured in true time, the hours in Japanese time were very long and the divisions on a clock had to be far apart. Conversely, the period of darkness lasted only about eight hours, so the divisions had to be short or closer together.

To accommodate this unusual system, it was necessary to move what we would think of as the hour indicators, as the seasons progressed. Stick clocks were made so the position of the numeral indicators could be easily changed. Clock makers regularly visited the homes of their clients to perform this adjustment.

In the early twentieth century, as Japan began to adopt elements of western culture, the European system of timekeeping was gradually introduced. This, of course, required clocks with circular dials and hands.

Initially, American clocks were imported, but soon Japanese manufacturers began making Western style clocks. The movements produced in Japan for these clocks were almost exact copies of American movements. Initially, the case styles were copies of those made in the United States, but with Japanese characters. Later, Roman numerals and inscriptions, including trade names, were used. The most common case style was the miniature drop octagon or school clock.

Japan was not able to successfully compete with manufacturers of mechanical clocks in the American market, but it did develop a significant market for its clocks in the Orient.

There was a tremendous surge of progress in American electronic technology, miniaturization and robotic manufacturing techniques associated with the conquest of space.

Japanese manufacturers quickly capitalized on this technology and soon became preeminent in the field of electronics, especially in radio, television and clock movements. In recent times, Japanese manufacturers have set up factories in other Asian countries. For at least twenty- five years they have dominated the worldwide clock and watch market.

With high labor costs and lagging manufacturing techniques, Americans were unable to compete. Most electronic clock movements sold in the United States today are made in the Orient.

Korean Clock Movements

Before about 1975, Korea had no clock industry. Like other Eastern countries who had been economically dominated by Japan, prior to World War II, all manufacturing was discouraged in Korea and what clocks there were came from Japan.

Several factors in the United States were operating in the 1970's. There was rampant inflation that caused prices in the antique market to soar. For this and other reasons, there developed what was referred to as a *Nostalgia Boom*. Old clocks became highly desirable collectibles, prices began rising dramatically and Antique shops were stripped of their stock of clocks. A brisk trade in old clocks developed and attics, barns and abandoned chicken houses were scoured for discarded treasures.

Enterprising importers in America became aware of this boom. One or more who were familiar with the capabilities of Korean craftsmen and their low labor costs, took several examples of old, scarce American clocks, with cases featuring fine turning and carving, to Korea and arranged to have both movement and cases duplicated there.

To their credit, the earliest of these replicas to be made in Korea, were remarkably good. They were imported into the United States and other countries and offered to dealers and clock collectors at prices sometimes only a quarter of those prevailing for the originals. A brisk market soon developed.

In addition to complete clocks, a market was found in the United States for movements to install in original American cases when the original movement had been damaged or discarded.

The success of this original foray led many other importers to follow suit and before long there were a number of clock factories in Korea, turning out movements and cases by the thousands.

Recognizing that a much larger market might be reached by more current styles sold through mass marketers, some importers began selling Korean clocks at extremely low prices to large chain stores. Unfortunately, importers pressured for lower and lower prices and the inexperienced Korean manufacturers succumbed. Quality suffered and, as a result, in the public's eye, all Korean clocks were looked down upon as inferior.

During this period, Korea began a concerted effort to upgrade its economy, including its manufacturing base. It was remarkably successful and has become a major factor in the manufacture of computers and has developed a successful automobile industry.

As with other economically emerging nations, these developments resulted in rising labor costs.

Even before American inflation was brought under control and the nostalgia boom faded, the entire clock industry in Korea, which had produced millions of clocks, disappeared. By 1990 there were no clock factories in that country.

Indian Clock Movements

When the Korean clock industry began to dissolve, American importers sought other sources for clock movements. India was one of the potential source countries where labor costs were low and there were technicians capable of setting up clock manufacturing.

A limited number of movements were manufactured in India and imported into the United States and other countries. No complete clocks are known to have been made in India for export.

Chinese Clock Manufacture

In recent years, both clock and watchmaking for export have blossomed in the Peoples Republic of China. More and more items of Chinese manufacture are being offered for sale in the United States.

CHAPTER SIX

BASICS of CLOCK IDENTIFICATION And VALUATION

THE FIRST STEP in identifying a clock is determining its case style. Definition of broad clock case styles is generally based on where they are normally located, in the home, office, place of business, or institution.

PUBLIC CLOCKS

When a clock is intended to be seen by many people in a gathering place of any kind, it is considered a *Public* clock. Clocks mounted in or on buildings that can be seen from outdoor locations are most often located in towers and are commonly referred to as *Tower* clocks.

Clocks mounted in or on commercial buildings, or outside the building and designed to be viewed by the public are also termed public clocks. When located on pillars on the sidewalk in front of a place of business, they are called *sidewalk clocks*

Public clock faces may be very large, as in the case of the clock known as Big Ben in the tower of the Houses of Parliament in London, or quite small like those found in store windows. Commercial public clocks varied widely in size. Advertising clock dials on buildings might be several stories high.

GALLERY CLOCKS

A form of wall mounted Public Clock found in large meeting places, such as churches, legislative assembly chambers, courtrooms, banks and similar large areas where many people gather, are referred to as *Gallery* clocks. They usually consist of a large round case with a dial measuring about two feet in diameter.

Gallery clocks are often permanently attached to a balcony or *gallery* wall and are wound through an access hole from the opposite side of the wall. Cases may be decorated with carved elements and may be made of wood, marble or metal. Because Gallery clocks are so large, they are almost never found in homes.

STATION CLOCKS

As railroads perfected the art of running passenger trains so they departed and arrived at scheduled times, railroad time became synonymous with accuracy. To inform passengers of railroad time, large clocks began to appear in station waiting rooms. They were periodically adjusted to reflect true railroad time by periodic signals sent over the company telegraph. In early

EARLY AMERICAN
REGULAR TALL CLOCK
ca. 1700

EARLY AMERICAN
MINIATURE TALL CLOCK
ca. 1700

CONTEMPORARY AMERICAN
GRANDMOTHER CLOCK
ca. 1990

GERMAN TALL CLOCK
ca. 1910

CONTEMPORARY AMERICAN
TALL CLOCK
ca. 1990

Figure 38 TALL CLOCK TYPES - Size Comparison

times, this was done by manually resetting the hands. Later, adjustment was accomplished by automatic electric signal impulses.

In the United States, various clock case styles were used for Station clocks. In Europe, especially in Great Britain, Railroad Station clocks were very plain, consisting of a large round dial with a simple wood bezel. The movements were of very high quality, commonly incorporating a fusee system to provide good timekeeping for eight days.

Large round clocks were a prominent feature in Western Union and Postal Telegraph offices that proliferated across America in the early twentieth century. These companies prided themselves on the accuracy of their clocks. Like railroad clocks, they were periodically reset, by a telegraphed signal.

Western Union time was the standard used by communities large and small.

In the late 1920's and early 1930's, fledgling airlines established *stations* at primitive landing fields around the country. They were among the first to make commercial use of synchronous electric clocks. Small round clocks showing 24 hour time became common in their waiting rooms.

While not commonly found in homes, Station Clocks are prized by many clock collectors today. In general, they are of high quality.

DOMESTIC CLOCKS

With the exception of public clocks, almost any clock, whether originally intended for use in offices, commercial establishments or other specific locations, may be found in American homes today. For purpose of this evaluation, we will include any clock style that was designed for use inside a building. This class is subdivided into three basic types; floor standing, wall, or shelf.

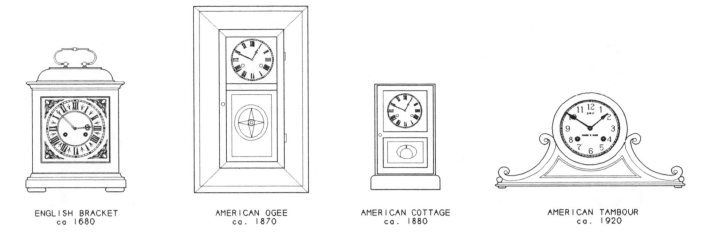

Figure 39 SHELF CLOCKS - Comparative Sizes

FLOOR STANDING, or Tall Case Clocks

In the United States, tall case clocks are usually referred to as *Grandfather or Grandmother* clocks. This nomenclature came about following the publication of the famous poem describing the death of a grandfather who owned a tall case clock that stopped at the time of his passing.

While there is no sharp visual line of demarcation between these two styles, the *Grandfather* has a longer pendulum that swings once a second (*seconds beat*), while the pendulum of the *Grandmother* style is several inches shorter.

Grandfather clock cases are usually a bit over six feet tall, while Grandmother cases are under six feet. There is wide variety in tall clock case styles.

WALL Clocks

Suspended Types

Many clock styles are intended to be displayed on a wall. To support them, some are provided with a metal ring attached to the back of the case.

Others have a hole in the back of the case itself. A few have a slot in the back board with a steel bar attached horizontally across its top, designed to hang on a nail.

All of these clocks are meant to be suspended from a large nail or hook firmly attached to the wall, preferably into a stud.. For security some are further fastened to the wall by a screw through the back of the clock.

Shelf Supported Types

The earliest domestic weight driven clocks were supported on a *bracket* or small shelf, that was securely fastened to the wall. Later, weight driven wood movement clocks made in America were often mounted on such brackets until a floor standing case could be made for them locally

When springs were introduced to replace weights as a source of power in early English hand made clocks, they no longer had to accommodate the long drop required by weights.

Because people were used to seeing clock faces at or above eye level, these clocks were frequently supported on shelves or brackets. They became known as *Bracket Clocks*.

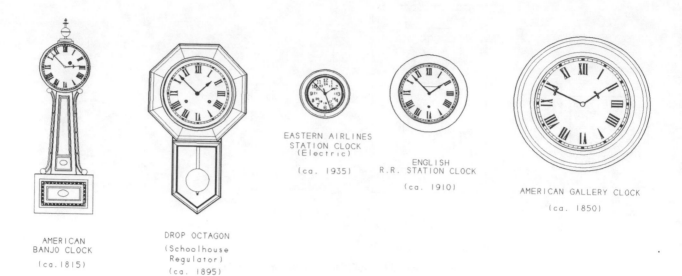

EASTERN AIRLINES
STATION CLOCK
(Electric)
(ca. 1935)

ENGLISH
R.R. STATION CLOCK
(ca. 1910)

AMERICAN GALLERY CLOCK
(ca. 1850)

AMERICAN
BANJO CLOCK
(ca. 1815)

DROP OCTAGON
(Schoolhouse
Regulator)
(ca. 1895)

Figure 40 WALL CLOCKS - Size Comparison

It was not long before they were most commonly placed on tables or mantles, rather than shelves or mantels. The name, however, continued.

SHELF or MANTEL Clocks

In America, clocks designed to rest on their bottoms and intended to be placed on existing shelves or mantels were the most popular type. The terms *Shelf Clock* and *Mantel Clock* are essentially synonymous, but among collectors, there are some distinctions. In essence, the names derive from the location in which a particular style of clock was usually found at the time of its original sale.

SUPERFICIAL IDENTIFICATION

After determining the basic type of a particular specimen, the proportions of the case, the character of the dial, hands, glass and other characteristics will help to more closely categorize it. The name of a maker may appear on the dial and/or a glass, but this may not be definitive. Dials and glasses are easily changed or altered.

Each of the major classes of clock we have defined here constitutes a very broad category. With hundreds of makers producing clocks, there is almost infinite variety within each group. In some instances, designs are unique to a particular maker. In others, copies and mutations of original designs have multiplied and it is impossible to ascribe any clock case of that type to a particular manufacturer simply by looking at it.

Most, but not all, case styles have been produced by many makers. Some have been copied in almost exact detail. Some are simply based on a particular design, but obviously vary from it to a greater or lesser degree.

While these clocks may be *copies*, they nearly always bear the name of the *actual* maker, not the one from whom the design was copied. In some early American clocks, the copies are licensed by the originator and that fact may be noted on a label in the case.

When there is reproduction with intent to mislead or defraud, including the marking of case, tablets, dial and/or movement with the name of a famous maker, it is *counterfeiting*. Careful examination is required to detect counterfeiting.

DETAIL IDENTIFICATION

In most cases, especially with mass produced clocks, the movement back or front plate is marked with a die-impressed trademark of the manufacturer. If the movement bears this mark, and it agrees with the name on the dial, it is likely that the clock is made by that maker. Other information, such as pendulum length, model number or date code may be stamped as well.

Not infrequently, movements, dials and other elements of a clock have been removed from damaged cases and installed in ones of the same or different style that are in better condition. The resulting clock is called a *marriage*.

When a movement or dial is installed in a case other than the one of which it was originally a part, the mounting holes usually do not match. Careful inspection will reveal extra screw holes in the case. The mutation may appear to be authentic, but it is not .

Early manufactured clock cases usually had a paper label pasted to the inside of the back board, or the top of the base board. These labels included the name of the maker and instructions for operating the clock.

Unfortunately, makers of some of the most desirable clocks did not always mark either the dial or the movement. This invites counterfeiting. Only someone very knowledgeable about the details of the case and movements produced by the presumed maker can be reasonably sure of the authenticity of a particular specimen.

CLOCK MAKERS

The determination of which clock maker produced a particular clock is an important aspect of accurately identifying it. As we have indicated, names engraved or stamped on movement plates are more likely to be authentic, but even they are subject to counterfeiting. It is reasonable to assume that, in most cases, names with trademarks on movements are likely to be authentic.

Before the mass production manufacture of clocks, when they were individually crafted by master clock makers, each maker frequently left his name or a unique mark on his work. As with works of art, experts are sometimes required to authenticate the maker of a particular early clock.

By far the majority of the clocks found in American homes today were mass produced in factories. Most are of American manufacture, but many were produced in Europe, notably Germany, France and England, and the Orient. Today nearly all movements in clocks sold in the United States are of foreign origin, most of them are made in Germany.

American and European clock movements are usually marked with the maker's name and/or trade mark and the country in which they were made. Other markings may indicate the pendulum length, model or style type and sometimes a serial number and a code for the date of manufacture.

Movements of Oriental manufacture are often unmarked, except sometimes with the name of the country in which they were made. In recent years, a simple easily removable self-adhesive label has been used to show the country of origin.

Rather than incur the sometimes large expense of repairing a movement, some owners have replaced original movements with these comparatively inexpensive reproduction movements, or with even less expensive battery operated quartz movements.

These practices may severely reduce, or even completely destroy the value of an otherwise collectible clock.

Makers' Names as Related to Quality

In the days before mass production, clocks were hand crafted and were nearly always of essentially high quality. These clocks were almost invariably made to order. The livelihood of clock makers depended on the reliability and overall integrity of their product. Quality was essential.

European manufacturers, especially before World War II, produced generally high quality movements with their own identification, or that of an American importer, with the name of the country of origin, i.e., *Made in Germany*, added.

Some American mass production manufacturers turned out a limited number of very high quality clocks, along with untold hundreds of thousands of lesser quality. There was a great difference in the selling price of the two types.

The higher quality clocks were usually floor standing or wall mounted and weight driven. They were used in professional offices, churches, fraternal meeting halls and other public places. Occasionally, they found their way into the homes of the more affluent, where they frequently became prized heirlooms. Many are still in the families of the original owners.

The movements of these higher quality American clocks had heavier plates, machine cut wheels *(gears)*, high strength steel arbors *(shafts)* and hardened and polished pivots. All of this resulted in better timekeeping and much longer life of the clock movement.

Manufacturers who made both types of clocks include, *Seth Thomas, New Haven, Ingraham, Sessions*, and *Waterbury*. A few manufacturers produced *only* high quality clocks in comparatively limited numbers. Among these are the *E. Howard* and *Chelsea* clock companies, both of Boston and the *Herschede Hall Clock Company* of Cincinnati.

The output of the hundreds of factories that made the millions of low priced clocks during the latter half of the nineteenth and the first quarter of the twentieth centuries was of remarkably uniform quality. The movements were made as cheaply as possible, with little regard to their serviceable life. Their accuracy was marginal, but acceptable to a population who could reset their clocks daily by local factory whistles. Cases were also made as cheaply as possible while still appealing to the buyers' taste and were also of uniform quality.

In fact, for the vast majority of ordinary clocks made during this period, there is little to differentiate one manufacturer from another.

Because the *Seth Thomas* clock company was in business in one form or another for more than a hundred years and had a very successful marketing program, this is a familiar name to most people. To many it is synonymous with quality. In fact, many other companies made millions of clocks of equal quality.

DATE of MANUFACTURE

To most owners, the age of their prized clock is important. In many cases, family lore dates such artifacts as belonging to a particular ancestor, often given as a wedding gift..

Most manufactured clocks are undated. Some of the earlier weight driven ones had large labels pasted on the front of the backboard. Clock manufacturers changed printers frequently. Labels usually bear the name of the printer who made them and, rarely, the year they were printed.

Horological historians have pieced together information showing dates when a manufacturer used labels by a particular printer. Labels in early American clocks can usually be dated within a few years.

From the middle of the nineteenth century onward, American clock manufacturers introduced several new case styles each year. In addition, they copied, imitated, or adapted earlier designs and those of competitor's more recent output. This makes for confusion, but diligent research of company catalogs and other documentation make dating the introduction of a case style by a particular manufacturer possible. However, a style may have been manufactured for many years, so precise dating of a particular clock may be difficult if not impossible.

It is important to bear in mind that some case styles, notably the weight driven *Ogee*, were made by many manufacturers over a period of almost a hundred years. Many millions were produced with little identifiable difference between the first and the last produced. Fortunately, nearly all of them have a large label pasted on the front of the case back, which may assist in dating.

As we have previously noted, many artful mass produced reproductions of older American clocks were imported from Korea during the 1970s. The movements were hardly ever marked, except, rarely, with a self-adhesive label imprinted *KOREA*. With the passing years, such labels have separated and these clocks may become more and more difficult to distinguish from the originals.

VALUE

The price of a clock, when new, nearly always reflects its cost, plus a reasonable profit for the manufacturer and others necessary to the chain of distribution. Essentially, selling price was dictated by the very stiff competition that existed in the clock industry from its inception.

When clocks were all hand made, they were usually sold by the maker directly to the buyer at a negotiated price. Barter for goods of various kinds in lieu of cash was common. There were no middle men, but the clock maker and his apprentices were required to expend many hours in the making of each clock. By today's standards, labor costs were very high, so clocks were expensive.

As the manufacturing methods introduced by Eli Terry were further developed, much less labor was required and the bulk of the work force was made up of unskilled or semi-skilled workers operating machines. Not only was the cost per clock drastically reduced, but it became possible to produce huge quantities.

For the first time, the clock maker, now an enterprising manufacturer, sought to sell his product outside the immediate geographical area of his shop. Salesmen were employed to establish sales outlets and in some cases, sales offices were set up in metropolitan areas. American clock manufacturers' sales forces invaded European markets and eventually dominated them.

Clocks were now found on the shelves of a variety of retail outlets, even on the Western Frontier, ready for immediate sale.

Clocks had to be transported from the factory to stores all over the country, salesmen had to be paid and retailers had to make a profit. The retail selling price of a clock reflected not only the manufacturer's price, but the added costs of distribution. In spite of all this, the cost to the consumer was still much lower than it would have been under the old craft system. In addition, clocks were available 'off the shelf'.

In the mid-nineteenth century, clock manufacturers began publishing catalogs with woodcut illustrations of clocks they manufactured, along with list prices. These catalogs indicate the relative value of different styles and types when they were produced. Usually a reflection of the cost of manufacture at the time, these list prices provide a basic starting point for assessing current values.

The value of any clock today is dependent on its worth to a particular prospective buyer. The selling price of old clocks put up for sale at auction is one indicator of value.

Clock price guides provide another indicator. The prices shown in these books are based on a subjective assessment by the author of sales in various arenas just preceding the date of publication. It must be remembered that Price Guides are just that - *Guides*. The prices shown assume the clock is in mint condition and fully authentic. In point of fact, clocks often are sold for prices well below those shown in these guides.

Economic conditions have a profound effect on the prices of old clocks. When inflation runs wild, clocks and other antiques experience a disproportionate increase in price. In downturns, prices may plummet.

In the United States and some other countries, large displays of clocks for sale are found at Regional meetings of the *American Association of Watch and Clock Collectors* which are held in various parts of the country. Admission is limited to members of that association, but such membership is open to anyone interested in clocks or watches.

This Association publishes the finest horological magazine in the world, the bi-monthly NAWCC BULLETIN and, on alternate months, the NAWCC MART, in which members may advertise horological items wanted or for sale.

Further information may be obtained by contacting the Association at:

NAWCC
514 Poplar Street
Columbia   PA   17512

Factors Affecting Current Value of Old Clocks

While price guides purport to list current prices of old clocks, the values shown are educated guesses based on asking prices of sellers at large clock marts and auctions. It is important to remember that the rarer and/or more valuable a clock may be in relation to other clocks, the fewer potential buyers there are. Actual selling prices of high end clocks can vary tremendously.

There are few qualified appraisers of clocks. Most people who do appraisals are auctioneers and those rare ones who specialize in clocks are probably the most knowledgeable. Appraisals given for insurance valuation purposes are commonly higher than prices realized at auction.

It is axiomatic that any sale requires a seller willing to sell an item at a price and a potential buyer who wants to obtain that item and is willing to pay for it. Ultimately, the decision is completely up to the buyer. If he considers the final offering price to be reasonable, a sale is made. It must be remembered that the value of a clock to one buyer establishes worth for only that transaction.

In general, asking prices for old clocks reflect the owner's perception of what collectors are likely to pay at a particular time and place. Formal appraisals for insurance coverage are based on this same principle. Unlike the prices listed in the manufacturers' catalogs, there can be wide swings in such determinations.

Inflation has a tremendous effect on the selling prices of old clocks. In times of runaway inflation, investors have bought clocks and other antique artifacts as hedges expected to escalate in value. Under these conditions, the demand results in increased prices. When inflation is controlled, clock prices tend to remain more or less constant, or, more probably, to decline.

An interesting phenomenon is the broad perception of value of a style or manufacturer. Large groups of collectors sometimes become enchanted with a particular type of clock and it suddenly is in great demand. Competition to obtain these clocks reduces the available supply and prices shoot up. As often happens, when the enthusiasm wanes, prices fall, sometimes below those just before the boom.

Availability is sometimes a key factor in value. As with any commodity, clocks in short supply often command higher prices.

Quality or the lack thereof can have a profound effect on value.

Intrinsic Value

While certain clocks have become extremely collectible based on emotional appeal or perceived rapid increase in value, unless they are of basically good quality, their monetary value frequently deteriorates over time.

Clocks with finely made movements and very well crafted cases are almost invariably excellent time keepers and objects of beauty. These qualities make up the *intrinsic* value of a clock. An owner can take pride it such a timekeeper, regardless of the price paid for it. For most collectors, *intrinsic* value is the overriding consideration.

New Clocks Currently on the Market

In recent years there has been a steady increase in interest in high quality mechanical clocks of all kinds. While some of the shelf and mantel styles are fitted with inexpensive quartz movements, their cases show excellent workmanship and many people acquire them, even though prices are comparatively high.

Tall Clocks - Grandfather and Grandmother

The Herschede Hall Clock Company of Cincinnati was noted for its extremely high quality tall clocks. This company made excellent chiming movements with tubular chimes. They also used less expensive bar chimes. Other major clock manufacturers also made elaborate chiming tall clocks, notably Seth Thomas, New Haven, E. Howard, Waterbury and E.N. Welch.

These American manufacturers have been out of business for many years. The growing public demand for similar clocks is being met by companies who buy or make cases in the United States and purchase movements made in Germany, assembling them to form a complete clock.

There are essentially two classes of the latter type of clock. The higher quality makers include *Howard Miller, Baldwin, Sligh, Ridgeway* and others. These companies sell through retail outlets often located in shopping malls and through quality furniture stores.

Prices of these clocks in 1994 generally ran from around $1,500 to $5,000.

Available by mail order are clocks with simpler case designs and workmanship of lesser quality. Movements are of lesser quality. Cases are available in kit form. Kits are assembled by amateur handymen who then may sell them from their homes or small shops in rural areas advertised by highway billboards..

Smaller Grandmother clocks are common, although some full size grandfather cases have been available.

The Empire Clock Co. pioneered this type of clock and is still actively in business. Other companies have since entered the market. A number have failed

Current Value of Recently Purchased Clocks

In considering the current value of Grandfather or Grandmother clocks purchased in the past twenty or thirty years, there is a parallel with automobiles.

When the clock is delivered to your home by the retailer, it is like a car being driven off the showroom floor. The value drops. That is, you would not be able to sell it and recover the money you paid for it.

Over time, your clock may appreciate in value, but don't expect this for many years. If you have purchased a new Grandfather clock because you are impressed with its appearance, the deep resonance of its chime and its contribution to gracious living in your home, you will be rewarded every time you see it or listen to it chime. This should be more than enough to justify your investment.

BUYING CLOCKS at AUCTION

Clocks continue to appear at auctions of various kinds. There are several kinds of auctions, from those in rural areas, or small towns, to specialty or fine art auctions.

Rural Auctions

Rural auctions are typically *Estate Sales* where essentially all the possessions of an owner are offered for sale to the highest bidder. Such auctions nearly always include many items of little value. These are generally offered at the beginning of a sale and their disposal can be very time consuming. Occasionally, real treasures, true family heirlooms, including rare clocks, are included. Depending on the auctioneer, such items may be offered for sale at any time during the auction. If you are interested in a particular object, it is important to closely observe the ongoing proceedings, so that you are ready to bid when it is offered.

City Estate Auctions

Many auctions in larger cities are for owners of modest means whose possessions are likely to be unremarkable. Ordinary clocks are often found. Occasionally, however, as with country auctions, a rare heirloom piece will appear. Larger estates are more likely to include high quality clocks.

Clock Auctions

A few auctions are limited to clocks only. These may include clocks of many owners, or may involve the liquidation of a clock collection. They usually include many types of clocks.

Suggestions for Buying at Auction

Carefully study the published listing of items offered at a particular auction. If you find something that interests you, arrive early and carefully inspect your selections. Request permission from the auctioneer to remove hands and dial to inspect the movement. Make sure all of the necessary parts of the clock are there.

Carefully examine the condition of all elements, especially the finish of the case. Remember that it is *your responsibility* to assess the condition of objects you may buy. Sales are on an *as is* basis and often there is no recourse if unnoticed defects are discovered after the sale

Most importantly, *determine the maximum amount you are willing to pay.*

STOP BIDDING when you reach the value you have set.

CHAPTER SEVEN

Early Manufactured American Clocks

(Manufacturing as used here, is the production of interchangeable parts capable of random assembly to create a finished product. *Mass Production*, the making of such parts in large numbers at very high speed, followed at a later date.)

T HE MANUFACTURE of clocks in America began in 1806 when Eli Terry accepted an order for the production of 4000 wooden movements. This was an audacious act on his part, since up to that time all clock movements had been made one at a time by individual craftsmen with the assistance of one or two apprentices.

The genius behind Terry's seemingly foolhardy commitment was that he conceived the idea that he could devise equipment and methods to make many essentially identical replications of each part. He developed tools, jigs and fixtures to position and hold the parts. Water power was used to run lathes and saws to shape and cut the wood parts that made up the movement.

A number of wheel (gear) blanks were stacked together and saw cuts for the teeth made through all the blanks in the same pass. The stack of blanks was indexed from one cut to the next. Since only one setup was required, hundreds of parts were turned out in a fraction of the time formerly required, when teeth on each blank were cut one at a time.

The development of these methods resulted in fully interchangeable parts and the fact that the design of the movement did not require close tolerances eliminated the traditional time consuming need to make each part to fit those mating with it. Once a machine was set up, it could be operated by unskilled workmen. Now, every part of a particular type was essentially identical to all others. Human error was greatly reduced. People with limited skills were quickly trained to operate the machines and to assemble the various parts into finished movements. From this point on, tools, fixtures and production machinery were constantly improved. In a few years, true mass production would be achieved.

At the peak of production, Terry turned out about 60 movements a day. While a tremendous accomplishment at the time and a real milestone in manufacturing history, this was a very modest number when compared to the rate of thousands per day achieved by many manufacturers, when true mass production methods were developed.

The new concept of making a number of parts at the same time was adopted by other clock makers, who then produced hundreds of clocks a year, several times their former output. They, too, employed unskilled workers.

The combined total annual production of all American clock makers then was at best only a few thousand clocks. Specimens made during this stage of development that have survived are highly prized by collectors.

REPRODUCTIONS and COPIES

With the possible exception of the Pillar and Scroll case and that of the Willard Banjo, most clock case styles of this period were adaptations of contemporary furniture designs. Some were innovative enough to be considered original conceptions and were produced in fairly large quantities for the time.

Along with the revolutionary changes in the making of clock movements, there was a surge of creativity in clock case design. This phenomenon became rampant later, with the introduction of true mass production.

It is significant that, while a design may have originated at a certain date, other styles were produced by most of the originators over a period of many years. Original case designs were widely copied or adapted, so the appearance of a case, even when the name of the manufacturer is known, does not necessarily indicate that the clock was made early in the history of the production of that style.

In the discussion of particular designs that follows, we will give the name of the originator, the approximate earliest known date of manufacture and comments on subsequent production.

MANUFACTURING INNOVATIONS

During this early period, Yankee ingenuity was devising new manufacturing methods for the production of cases as well as movements. Water powered machinery, including circular saws was constantly improved. Tools, jigs and fixtures were designed so that increasing numbers of the same part could be made by unskilled workers using powered and automated machinery.

Labor costs were slashed and the finished product could profitably be sold at a much lower price than was the case when each part was individually hand made.

Suitable coil springs were not commercially available, so almost all of the clock movements made in the early 1800's were weight driven.

Prior to the American Revolution, sheet brass was available only from England. It was made by hand planishing or pounding chunks of cast brass to form plates, then hand filing them to eliminate hammer marks. Not only was this a time consuming, tedious and expensive process, but the end product was of inconsistent and frequently inferior quality.

There was no source of large quantities of brass plates, even in England, that would have been adequate to support manufacturing of movements on the scale now possible with the new manufacturing methods.

While the supply of brass plates made in England was embargoed after the Revolution, small quantities were made by American craftsmen. Brass continued to be used for traditional individually commissioned weight driven tall clock movements.   The Willards and a few other manufacturers with limited production capacity were among those who continued to make brass movements. These followed the traditional English style with heavy brass plates and wheels. Prices of clocks with

Figure 41 Seth Thomas Pillar & Scroll Clock

brass movements continued to be high and these clocks were affordable only by the more affluent.

During this period, in spite of the limited availability and very high cost, there was some experimentation and limited production of a few unusual *brass* spring driven movements and the cases to house them. Brass springs were never made in large quantities, since they were not a good substitute for steel.

PILLAR and SCROLL CLOCKS

Designed and patented by Eli Terry, and licensed to Seth Thomas, the Pillar and Scroll clock was the first *manufactured* clock. It dominated the clock market from its introduction in 1817 until about 1840. A weight driven wood movement designed by Terry required less drop for the weights, facilitated the shorter pendulum, and made possible the compact case.

The cases of original pillar and scroll clocks are indeed outstanding examples of the cabinet makers' art.

The top and bottom scrolls are not only gracefully designed, but are scroll-sawed and nicely finished. They are made of thin solid wood, usually mahogany, with the grain running horizontally. The corners are neatly mitered. Almost invariably, the wood has warped so that the scrolls of the top splat are curved toward the back of the case. Attempts to flatten them by applying pressure are likely to result in splitting the scroll..

The door, which constitutes the front of the case, and the sides, are all made of pine faced with veneer. The quality of the veneer is usually excellent. Grain normally runs at a 45 degree angle and is tastefully matched.

The bottom glass tablet of Pillar and Scroll clocks was decorated with reverse painted scenic or allegorical subjects. Each of these was individually painted and there was great variety in both quality and subject matter. Gold leaf was often used as a highlight in borders, and sometimes in the main illustration.

The comparatively small size, extremely attractive case and low price of the Pillar and Scroll clock made it possible for upper middle class families to have a time keeper in their homes for the first time..

These clocks were among the most prized possessions of their owners and were usually accorded a place of honor in the main room of the house.

THIRTY HOUR RUNNING TIME

Prior to this time, hand made clocks with running times up to one year had been designed and built by a few outstanding clock makers. They required extraordinary craftsmanship, took an

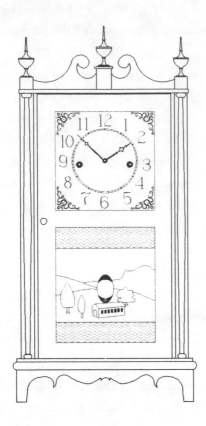

Figure 42 Ethel North Pillar & Scroll Clock
(ca. 1825)

inordinate amount of time to build and were very expensive. Most tall clocks with brass movements had running times of eight days.

While Simon Willard's patented movements for Banjo clocks ran for more than a week and are commonly referred to as *Eight Day,* this was achieved only by using very expensive heavy hand hammered brass for the comparatively small movement and a large, very heavy lead weight to provide necessary additional power. These were single train movements and had no strike train. Sometimes a *passing strike,* activated by the time train, producing only one note at every hour, was added.

Most clocks of this period and all of those manufactured in quantity ran for about thirty hours. This necessitated winding each day. They were powered by cast iron weights and had a strike train for striking the hours, usually on a cast iron bell.

Commonly, only the head of the household was permitted to wind and set these clocks. Early American homes usually had a cat to control the mouse population. These cats spent the day in the house as pets, but were relegated to the outdoors at night. Fathers' usual ritual, before retiring, was to *wind the clock and throw out the cat.* This phrase was in common use for almost a hundred years.

Winding a clock, or even a watch, every day used to be the accepted thing. With the advent of eight day clocks, this nightly exercise began to lose favor.

Unfortunately, when longer running clocks became available, a great many thirty hour clocks including those of Pillar and Scroll design, were considered obsolete and were summarily discarded. Comparatively few were stored away in the attic or abandoned hen house and have survived. A few were retained as family heirlooms.

MANY MANUFACTURERS

Other clock makers who were trained in and used traditional methods, notably those also located in Connecticut, were acutely aware of the development of manufacturing methods by Terry and Thomas. Some tried to emulate these innovations with varying degrees of success. Most simply altered proportions while some made versions that retained only a vague resemblance to the original.

Recognizing the success of the new methods, there was a scramble by entrepreneurs to establish clock factories. They sensed the significance of these revolutionary methods and the opportunity for profit.

This was the beginning of true mass production and laid the foundation for what was later to be known as the Industrial Revolution. It made it possible for the young United States to become the

  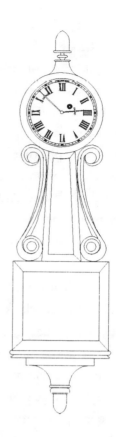

Figure 43 Banjo Clock Case Styles (ca. 1825-1830)

world leader in the production of manufactured goods.

enabled the young United States to become the world leader in the production of manufactured goods.

Over succeeding years, an efficient and highly competitive American clock industry came to dominate world markets. In Connecticut, clock manufacturing led all others industries.

EARLY EIGHT DAY BRASS MOVEMENTS

Around 1820, Heman Clark, who had served as an apprentice to Eli Terry, made eight day movements using cast brass elements which he then machined and assembled. These movements were usually housed in modified pillar and scroll cases. Such clocks were necessarily expensive and it is not sur-

prising that this venture, like others of a similar nature, had a short life.

Other clock makers pursued similar courses, but were not able to compete with the much less expensive wood movement clocks then being produced by Seth Thomas and other clock factories.

This activity established Seth Thomas as a leading manufacturer of clocks. In the years to follow, the company grew and produced millions of clocks. The name is found on clocks marketed today, but the movements are made in Europe or Asia, not in America.

SMALL EIGHT DAY BRASS MOVEMENTS

Probably the most successful maker of brass movements was Simon Willard, who developed a small weight driven brass 8-day movement and housed it in a case style to become known as the *Banjo Clock*. The Willard design movement was small and did not have a strike train. It only told time and did not strike the hours. It had a comparatively large and heavy weight for power. The pendulum was suspended from a flat spring with a transverse pin that rested in grooves on top of a slotted bracket on the front plate of the movement. A cord, with one end anchored to a pillar of the movement and the other to the winding drum ran over a brass pulley on which the weight was suspended.

The Willard movement was made small as compared to tall clock movements to use less brass. Parts were made in groups of several pieces machined at one time, so they were interchangeable, but were still relatively expensive. Sales of Willard Clocks were essentially limited to the more affluent members of society.

This movement achieved sufficient popularity that other clock makers copied or adapted it, in spite of the patent protection Willard had obtained. While total production over the years, by Simon and his sons, probably reached the thousands, very few original Willard type movements have survived. They are highly prized by collectors .

BANJO CLOCKS

The Willard Banjo Clock case was designed to take advantage of Willard's Eight Day PATENT MOVEMENT. It was a relatively small wall clock with a uniquely American style. It is classic in its proportions and derives its name from its vague resemblance to the stringed musical instrument called a banjo.

Many variations of this basic type were produced by a number of makers, mostly during the ten year period between about 1825 and 1835. Typically, they had painted sheet zinc dials, very delicate

blued steel hands with arrow points, double side arms of polished brass, a narrow throat, just large enough to accommodate the weight and pendulum and a rectangular base.

The round bezel was usually made of cast brass, turned on a lathe, then polished to a high luster. A convex glass was mounted in the bezel. The bezel assembly was supported on a single hinge, with a button latch on the opposite side.

Brass finials usually decorated the top of the case. These were of various shapes, usually balls or urns, but sometimes a cast brass eagle with wings outspread.

Banjo cases were generally made of locally grown, not very high quality, pine. They were veneered with mahogany or other imported exotic woods. The throat and bottom door frames usually were covered with carefully selected and applied cross-banded veneer. Some were gilded with beading. Glasses in the throat and bottom door were decorated with sometimes very colorful and intricate reverse painted designs, commonly using bright colors and gold leaf.

The comparatively limited individually crafted making of these clocks was such that the Willards could accommodate orders for special cases with details meeting the customer's requirements. These were known as *Presentation* banjos.

Presentation banjo clocks were more elaborate variations of the basic design. They were used as gifts for special occasions, such as weddings. The most common was the substitution of wood beading or roping applied to the front of the case, a bracket added to the bottom and the entire case gilded. Custom reverse paintings in both throat and bottom glasses were not unusual, sometimes including a legend commemorating a special event.

A very ornate version, having a round bottom box with a convex reverse painted glass, was decorated with wooden balls and the entire case was

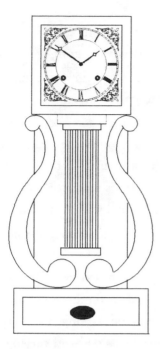

Figure 44 Lyre Clock Variation - Joseph Ives
(ca. 1830)

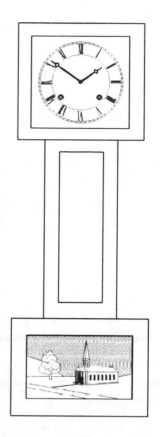

Figure 45 Connecticut Banjo Clock

beautifully gold leafed. These are among the most highly prized of all American clocks.

The variation by Sawin and Dyer shown at the right of Figure 42 has a wooden bezel and wood side arms with the bottom curved inward. This resulted in a shape that may have been the precursor of the soon to follow Lyre clock style.

Simon Willard was granted a patent for his moment and labels placed in his banjo clocks and even some of the reverse-painted glasses, proclaimed that this was a *WILLARD PATENT CLOCK*. Other makers obtained from Willard the right to use his patents and their clocks frequently bore the same legend.

The Willard banjo type movements in these clocks were very durable and some have run for almost two hundred years.   Unfortunately, relatively few have survived, not because they wore out, but because they went out of style and were relegated to the dump.

In later years, however, the case design was repeatedly revived, but with few exceptions, the quality of both the movement and the case was not duplicated.

Later versions, except for a relative few hand made by dedicated craftsmen and sold at high prices, almost never employed the very costly reverse painting technique for decoration.

Since its introduction, reproductions or adaptations of the banjo style have made in a wide variety of sizes. Great liberties have sometimes been taken with the overall design, yet they   still maintain the essentials of the banjo design.

Only early examples and carefully crafted reproductions are weight driven and have a single winding hole at the two o'clock position on the dial.

LYRE CLOCKS

Using banjo or similar movements, lyre clocks are about the same size as banjos. The essential difference is that, because they used no brass for the case and minimized or eliminated the glass with reverse painting that added cost to the banjo, they were less expensive.

This was true, even though they substituted hand carved wood as the decorative motif. Skilled carvers produced the central shields or throat pieces and finials in very short order. It is evident from surviving examples that the custom was to use big very sharp gouges that removed large pieces of wood with each carefully controlled stroke. The carving of some specimens is far from perfect and might even be considered crude. Most, however, were of high quality.

Deriving its name from the lyre shape of the center portion, or throat, this style of case nearly always had an acanthus leaf motif. Bezels were of turned wood. Carved wood finials decorated the top, rather than brass, as was the case with banjo clocks. The bottom doors were usually solid wood, with a frame and panel. Some were wood framed with a reverse painted glass.

While the cases of these clocks, like the banjo style, were made of native pine, the bezels and fronts were of solid hard wood. with only the sides of the basic case veneered. Native wild cherry and imported mahogany were commonly used woods. Native wild cherry and imported mahogany were commonly used hard woods.

Many clock makers adapted the lyre style and there was wide variation in the quality and depth of the carving. Although usually there was an opening in the center of the shield, with a reverse painted glass, often the shield was entirely of solid wood.

While the banjo style of case was later copied or adapted to mass-produced clocks, the lyre style was not, to any significant extent. This was probably because mass production methods of satisfactorily duplicating the hand carving had not been developed. The cost of using hand carving would have made them uncompetitive.

Bearing little resemblance to the Willard style banjo, a simpler design with square top and bottom boxes was developed around 1830. It has been called the *Connecticut Banjo*. The case of this clock was much simpler and less expensive to make than the original.

The rectangular box and dial of the top and the wide, straight neck lacked esthetic appeal and this style found little favor with the public. Its manufacture soon ceased.

Most lyre clocks were unsigned and it is often difficult or impossible to identify their makers with certainty.

CHAPTER EIGHT

Mass Produced American Clocks

The importance of the American Clock Making Industry
in the Industrial Revolution

MASS PRODUCTION OF HARD GOODS
-An American Innovation

The English often claim to be the instigators of the Industrial Revolution, with some justification. Significant innovations in the textile industry began with the invention of the flying shuttle in 1733 that made it possible for one person to operate a wide loom instead of requiring two people. They also developed mechanized spinning of cotton thread. In 1770 a patent was issued for a spinning jenny that enabled a worker to run eight spindles at a time rather than only one.

The first power loom was patented in England in 1785, but was not in general use until 1813. Flowing water was the primary source of power at this time. Steam engines were then in operation to pump water from coal and to turn blowers to create the draft in iron mine smelting furnaces.

All of the major inventions related to manufacturing developed in England up to this time affected only the textile and mining industries and had little application to the making of other goods.

The clock making industry in the United States, on the other hand developed basic mass production manufacturing concepts, equipment and tooling techniques that were applicable to a wide range of hard goods other than clocks. It also developed the concept of dividing the work into sub-assemblies, such as wheels and arbors, ready for final assembly on a production line.

The BEGINNING of TRUE MASS PRODUCTION

In the United States, enterprising clock makers in Connecticut set out to make a profit by producing timepieces in a price range affordable by a large segment of the population.

While certain materials such as brass, steel springs and other high grade steels made in England had been embargoed and were not available in America, the new nation was rich in natural resources and what later came to be known as *Yankee Ingenuity*.

In 1837 a serious depression struck the young United States. The burgeoning American clock manufacturing industry, still producing mostly wood movements, was seriously affected and many makers were bankrupted.

One who was determined to find ways to survive was named Chauncey Jerome. He and his brother, Noble, developed a small, 30-hour weight driven movement with a count wheel strike system.

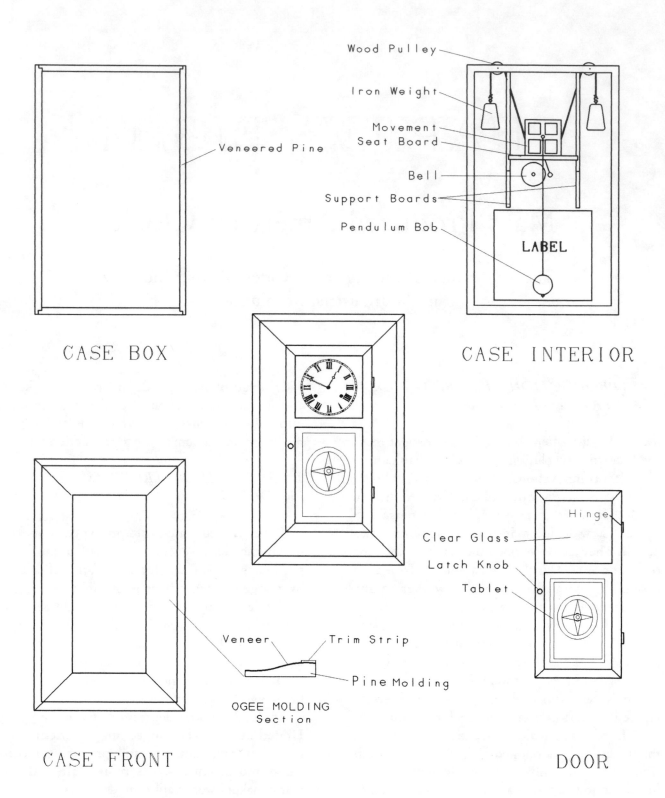

CASE BOX

Wood Pulley

Iron Weight

Movement
Seat Board

Bell

Support Boards

Pendulum Bob

LABEL

CASE INTERIOR

Veneered Pine

Hinge

Clear Glass

Latch Knob

Tablet

DOOR

Veneer

Trim Strip

Pine Molding

OGEE MOLDING
Section

CASE FRONT

Figure 45 OGEE CLOCK CASE - Construction Details

To produce this movement, the Jeromes used newly available, domestically produced machine rolled sheet brass for the plates and wheels. Water or steam powered stamping presses equipped with steel dies were developed. These powerful machines formed and punched out movement plates and wheels complete with teeth, in one quick motion. This innovation drastically reduced the amount of machining required. Thousands of parts and movements could be produced in a fraction of the time required to cut out or turn wood elements for the then standard wood movements.

Jerome was probably the first to recognize that a great deal of brass could be salvaged by punching out unnecessary areas of the movement plates. The resulting scrap was sold to the brass mill for remelting., significantly reducing the cost of materials. Was this the first instance of recycling?

The Jerome movements were so much less expensive than those they had been making that other manufacturers quickly copied their manufacturing methods. Almost overnight, wood movements became obsolete.

Power from a water wheel was used to turn a system of shafts, pulleys and leather belts that transmitted motion to individual machines. These included lathes, drills, and presses. As time went on these machines were increasingly automated.

Assembly and testing of movements was conducted on an assembly line.

There were a number of essential supporting industries that made possible the revolutionary manufacturing methods developed in the clock industry. Among these was brass manufacturing which came of age and provided sheet brass of consistent quality and in sufficient quantity to keep up with the demands of the exploding clock manufacturing industry.

Equally important was the development and availability of high strength steels for the making of punches, dies and other tools and fixtures. Steel rod mills also produced quality steel for arbors, verges and other steel parts of the movement.

Along with all this came the birth of the highly skilled craft of tool and die making. It is difficult to imagine how die makers of that era made the intricately shaped punches and perfectly matching dies necessary to produce the plates and fine toothed wheels essential to clock movements. There was also constant improvement in the design of production jigs and fixtures.

Mass Production of CLOCK CASES

While the manufacture of mechanical devices such as clock movements received more attention, producing clock cases of high quality at the lowest possible price was essential to the ultimate success of the manufacturing venture.

Early wood clock cases employed conventional cabinet making methods. Planks were sawed from trees using two-man pit saws. They were smoothed with hand planes and cut with vertical reciprocating saws, often foot powered. Scroll work was done by hand with a scroll saw, or with a treadle operated vertical saw.

After gluing, clamping was accomplished with wood furniture clamps. Hot animal glue set rapidly, so clamping time was short. Joints were often nailed, using cut iron nails.

Veneer was sawed by hand and was quite thick as compared to that available today. Before sawing, the surface to be finished was planed smooth, the other side, to be glued to the case, retained saw marks. The board had to be planed again before the next saw cut was made.

A great deal of tedious hand work was involved in jointing and finishing. Cabinet or case making was, like movement making, a labor intensive and therefore expensive activity.

When movements were produced by the thousands, it was essential that the making of cases for them keep pace. This meant that manufacturing methods and wood processing machinery had to be developed that would speed up case production and significantly reduce costs.

Again, designs, machines, tools, fixtures and processes were developed to meet the need.

Introduction of the OGEE CASE (Figure 45)

Having successfully developed an inexpensive movement, the Jeromes had to come up with a comparably inexpensive case in which to house it. They started with a simple rectangular box made of native pine, with four sides and a back. The top, bottom and side pieces were rabeted. The corners were simply rabeted, glued and nailed. A thin pine back board was inserted in a rabbet at the back and nailed in place, without glue. The outer surface of the side boards was veneered, usually with mahogany, but sometimes rosewood.

A pair of narrow pine boards, about 3/8" thick, each with a mortise to support a seat board for the movement and a slot at the top, were then nailed to the back. The top board of the case had a slot near each end into which a wooden pulley with its supporting steel shaft were inserted.

The movement was attached to the seat board with J-bolts and the board then inserted into the slots of the uprights. Cords attached to the winding arbors were threaded through openings at the top of the support boards, over the pulleys and down to be attached by hooks to the driving weights.

An iron bell was attached to the back board just below the seat board. A hammer on an arm projecting from the bottom of the movement struck the bell to toll the hours. A steel wire pendulum rod was flattened at its top to form a suspension spring and hung from a slotted post on the front of the movement. A small brass faced lead filled round bob with a threaded wire insert and brass nut was hooked to the bottom of the rod. The dial was a thin sheet of pine, later zinc, painted white with time track, numerals and decorations painted by hand. Hands were typically of the design originated by Terry for the Pillar and Scroll clock.

The case was designed to rest flat on its bottom board. There were no feet. It is not uncommon to find a hole in the backboard near the top, used to suspend the clock on a nail in the wall.

The front of the Ogee case is made of an ogive, or S-shaped pine molding, veneered with mahogany or rosewood. This molding was commonly used in building and was cheap and readily available. To form the case front, four pieces were simply mitered and nailed to the case box. A finishing touch was added by placing a narrow strip around the outer edges of the frame.

Standard ogee cases have flat strips around the inner and outer edges. When these strips are rounded, the case is referred to as a *Double* Ogee.

A simple door made of veneered pine with two glass panels is attached to the right side of the ogee molding with inexpensive sheet metal hinges. The upper panel over the dial is clear, while the lower one, the *tablet*, is decorated with a stenciled or transfer design.

Certainly hundreds and perhaps thousands of different designs were used for the tablets, some by several different manufacturers.

With his inexpensive movement and the Ogee case, Jerome revolutionized clock making. He proudly called his clocks "Cheap" and the market for them expanded at an incredible rate.

Millions of Ogee Clocks were made by many manufacturers from the date of their origin around 1840 until the last was produced about 1914. Some early ones had wood movements by clock makers who had not yet converted to the less expensive brass movements.

While some Ogee clocks were made with 8 Day movements, the less expensive 30 Hour weight driven movements in the original 26" high cases remained by far the most popular. Many of these have survived.

The first 8 Day weight driven Ogee clocks were about 30"-34" tall. Later spring driven versions were made in both 30 Hour and 8 Day styles and were housed in cases 16"-18" high.

Ogee clocks commonly have a paper label pasted to the inside bottom of the backboard, prominently displaying the name of the manufacturer and frequently the statement *Warranted if Well Used*. Simple instructions for the care and operation of the clock are also commonly included. The labels often carried the name of the firm that printed them. Many manufacturers changed printers at frequent intervals and, where records have been found, this provides a comparatively accurate means of dating a clock.

A great many Ogee clocks have survived, many in excellent condition. The earliest ones, even after the passage of a century and a half, are still attractive and capable of keeping good time. Most of them are well over 100 years old, true Antiques. Readily available at modest prices, Ogee clocks are great for beginning clock collectors, antique buffs, decorators and the average home maker who simply wants a ticking and

Figure 46   Seth Thomas Arch Top Clock

striking clock with a touch of history attached..

Both movement and case manufacture underwent constant improvement over the years. Cases became more elaborate and ornate and the jointing and finishing more complex. Veneering on a production basis, begun with the ogee molding with its sweeping curves, was extended to much smaller and more intricate molding.

Perhaps the most complex and complicated small wooden clock case ever produced was the Seth Thomas *Arch Top*. (Figure 46) This case had well over a hundred pieces, each covered with thin rosewood or oak veneer.

LOW COST and EFFECTIVE MARKETING LEAD to DOMINATION of the WORLD CLOCK MARKET

Yankee traders in the clock industry matched the progressive ingenuity of their manufacturing brethren. England was soon displaced as the dominant clock making nation. Other European clock makers found themselves hard pressed to compete with the Americans.

When Connecticut manufacturers began to make clocks in numbers exceeding the local market, they started the first broad marketing of a manufactured product. Initially, peddlers packed several clock movements with their dials, hands and weights on their backs and walked to outlying areas to sell them to individual householders. As the trading area was enlarged, pack animals were used to carry larger numbers.

Expanding still farther away from the factory, enterprising peddlers began selling several clocks at a time to owners of general stores for resale to their customers. It was not long before clocks were available, even on the western frontier. With the coming of the railroads the shipping of clocks in large quantities was a reality.

American clock manufacturers even sent salesmen to foreign countries, where the low prices and acceptable quality of their clocks found a ready market. Even in England, which had dominated the international clock market, American clocks were sold by the millions, seriously affecting the British clock industry.

Connecticut clock manufacturers opened their own stores in large cities, notably New York. Some manufacturers set up shop outside Connecticut, but that state remained the largest producer for almost a century.

Manufacturers of clocks aggressively marketed their product, mounting elaborate exhibits at World's Fairs, State and Local Fairs and special exhibitions.

Soon after the introduction of the Ogee style, the annual production of American clocks climbed to more than a million clocks a year.

By 1850, there were more than thirty major clock factories in production. There was a deluge of case styles by every maker.

Catalogs illustrating their case styles with very fine woodcut engravings along with prices and a description were issued annually by each maker. In addition, wholesalers began to spring up and they issued their own catalogs. Top of the line marketers imported clocks from abroad and illustrated them in their catalogs. Notable among these were elaborate French clock cases of marble, bronze and brass, as well as Vienna Wall Regulators.

In the latter half of the nineteenth century, the German cuckoo clock, because of its unique animation and sound became very popular in the

United States. A few American manufacturers attempted to produce competing products, with little success. Some imported German clocks with their own names attached to them.

While new designs were introduced on an almost annual basis, some remained popular for years and repeatedly appeared in catalogs. There was a constant contest between manufacturers to hit on a clock case design that would be popular with the public and would result in increased sales and earnings.

As with automobiles in later times, a design that caught the public's fancy was seized on by competitors and either pirated outright or copied with minor changes.

While manufacturing innovations have justly earned acclaim, the marketing efforts of the American clock making industry set a new standard for all kinds of manufactured goods.

THE RISE AND FALL OF
THE AMERICAN CLOCK INDUSTRY

Hundreds of entrepreneurs, observing the phenomenal success of clock manufacturers like Seth Thomas and the Jeromes, entered into the market with varying degrees of success.

Successful makers often saw opportunities in the acquisition of factories started by others. There was a rash of mergers, combinations and outright purchases of competitors. There was a scramble to lure talented employees to their companies.

In 1850, ten years after the beginning of mass production clock manufacture, there were just under a thousand clock manufacturers in the United States.

Marketing strategies were copied, not always successfully, and improvements in manufacturing methods and equipment were shamelessly imitated

In 1850, there were more than seven thousand clock peddlers in the country. In addition to individual peddlers, this included wholesalers and large retailers, as well as smaller sales organizations. For almost a hundred years, American clock making factories prospered.

When synchronous electric clock movements became practical, they were much simpler and less expensive than mechanical clocks and required no winding. They quickly caught on with the public. In an effort to compete, some traditional clock makers added electric motors to replace springs as the power source in their clocks, retaining most of the traditional movement. This arrangement was not competitive and was soon dropped.

Other clock makers purchased synchronous movements and installed them in cases, the dial of which often bore the clock company name.

After 1900, only a very few of the major clock making companies remained in existence. The oldest was the *Seth Thomas Clock Company.* Others were; *Ansonia Clock Company, William L. Gilbert Clock Company, Ingraham Company, New Haven Clock Company, Waterbury Clock Company* and *E. N. Welch Manufacturing Company.*

Following World War II, the American clock industry entered a sharp decline as foreign manufacturers entered the market. The introduction of the very inexpensive quartz battery movement and other digital electric movements sounded the death knell. Today, there are no world class manufacturers of clocks in the United States.

Capitalizing on the Nostalgia Boom of the 1970's, a few enterprising individuals from the United States sought to have reproductions of old American clocks made abroad, where labor costs were much lower. The Orient appeared to offer the most likely opportunity. Korea, with an economy ravaged by years of war and determined to make a giant step into the world market, had a tradition of fine wood craftsmanship. There was no clock movement manufacturing industry in Korea at that time. Under Japanese domination for a very long time, manufacturing industries had been suppressed. Undaunted, American entrepreneurs prevailed on the government to support the creation of a clock manufacturing industry.

In a remarkably short time, factories for the production of movements and cases were set up and in the early 1970's quantities of Korean clocks began to appear in the United States and other countries. Many people were impressed by the fine carving of many of the cases and a market soon developed. Ultimately, millions of Korean clocks, designed for the current American market, were sold through discount stores and other retail outlets. Before 1990, the Korean clock industry completely collapsed.

CHAPTER NINE

The CLOCK INDUSTRY MATURES
1840 - 1850

WHEN TRUE MASS production got into full swing, during the decade from about 1840 to 1850, 30-hour weight driven hour striking clocks were still the standard type. They were produced in the hundreds of thousands by hundreds of clock manufacturers.

As machinery became more complex and expensive, a trend toward bigness resulted. Steam engines provided power which was transmitted to heavy stamping presses and small lathes, drill presses and other increasingly automated machines by *line shafts*. Very substantial investments were necessary to fund the building and equipping of a clock factory.

Line shafts transmitting power to many machines were the key to mass production manufacturing.

The steam engine had very large pistons driving a fly wheel six feet or more in diameter at low speed. A wide and heavy leather belt transmitted power from the fly wheel to a smaller pulley at the end of one or more line shafts. This turned the line shaft at a faster speed.

By varying the sizes of pulleys on the line shaft and on the machines, a wide range of operating speeds was obtained.

One or more line shafts running t the length of the building were supported by brackets attached to ceiling joists. Many pulleys were mounted on each line shaft to transmit power by belts to individual machines. Clutches activated by the machine operator engaged or disengaged the belt from the line shaft at each machine, as needed. Line shaft bearings were lined with babbitt. a soft low friction metal, ware rapidly and required frequent lubrication and replacement.

Stamping presses had a large, very heavy cast iron fly wheel, with a wide outer rim, turned, at relatively slow speed, by the line shaft .The inertia of this rotating wheel supplied energy for the stamping stroke and minimized surges in power demand.

Other machines powered by the line shaft had smaller pulleys to obtain higher speeds.

For efficiency, most large clock factories were quite long and narrow, with several line shafts.

Smaller machines, such as lathes, were placed in front of large, closely spaced windows that provided good working light for operators. Other machines used for less precision production, like stamping presses, were usually located in the center of the building.

Manufacturing buildings, often of two or three stories, were constructed of brick, with line shaft systems on each manufacturing floor.

Even when, late in the 19th Century, steam power began to be replaced by large direct current electric motors, line shaft power transmission was essential from the motor to individual machines. For many years this system was used extensively in all types of manufacturing operations.

As time progressed and the most efficient clock factories became more and more complex and costly to build, a handful of companies began to grow at a rapid rate, frequently as a combination of smaller firms. Others, unable or unwilling to make the investment necessary to compete, dropped by the wayside. This trend was aggravated by the financial depression that struck in 1837.

In the decade between 1850 and 1860 there were more than thirty substantial clock factories. Most were located in Connecticut and each produced around 100,000 clocks a year.

During that period, some eighteen companies went out of business. The largest of the surviving companies was the New Haven Clock Company, producing more than 200,000 clocks annually. William L. Gilbert Clock Company, E. N. Welch Co., and Seth Thomas each turned out some 100,000 clocks per year.

The predominant case style during this period was the Ogee, which continued to be manufactured in quantity until around 1920. Because many millions were made, a significant number have survived. There is little difference in appearance, inside and out between clocks made in 1850 and those that were manufactured in 1920.

Sometimes resulting from mergers and acquisitions, a few companies emerged as dominant factors in the clock industry. While all manufacturing by these companies has ceased, the names of some are still found on new imported clocks being sold in the American market today.

SETH THOMAS CLOCK COMPANY

The *Seth Thomas* Clock Company, growing out of the firm started early in the century by Seth Thomas, continued in business well into the 20th century. It was located in Plymouth Hollow, Connecticut.

Around 1840, Seth Thomas stopped making wood movements and converted production lines to make brass movements. At mid-century, the company manufactured almost 25,000 clocks a year.

In an early demonstration of the principle of integration in business, Seth Thomas built a brass rolling mill factory for the production of the sheet brass used in its clock movements. Converting the company to a stock corporation in 1853, Thomas gradually transferred operating authority to his sons, Aaron and Seth Jr. He died a wealthy man in 1859.

In recognition of his importance to the town and its economy, the people of Plymouth Hollow in 1865 renamed the town *Thomaston*. The labels pasted on the backboards of clocks were changed to show Thomaston as the Company address, providing a clue as to the period of manufacture. Seth Thomas Clocks with the Plymouth Hollow label were made before 1865, while those showing the Thomaston location were produced later.

By 1880, The Seth Thomas Clock Company represented a capital investment of over a half million dollars. The most skilled employees at that time earned about three dollars for a ten hour work day. Less skilled workers received about a dollar a day. For its time, this was a very large company. It employed more than 800 people.

While its primary production was low cost clocks for homes, the company also made a more limited number of very high quality clocks from time to time throughout its history.

Following World War II, the Seth Thomas Clock Company stopped manufacturing clock movements. The Seth Thomas name, however, continued to be used on clocks with movements produced overseas. Bearing little resemblance to the original, a company using the Seth Thomas name still exists.

Many current inheritors of family clocks think the name Seth Thomas represents the highest quality. In point of fact, most clocks by other manufacturers are of equivalent quality.

ANSONIA CLOCK COMPANY

The Ansonia Clock Company was formed in 1850 by Anson G. Phelps who had built a copper and brass rolling mill at a site near Derby, Connecticut, which he named *Ansonia*, based on his given name

The company operated a manufacturing plant at this location until 1878, when operations were moved to Brooklyn, New York.

As enterprising in marketing as in production, the company eventually had offices in New York, Chicago and London. It had sales agents around the world.

In 1929, Ansonia found itself in dire financial distress and was forced into bankruptcy. It was placed under the control of a Creditors Committee which found it impossible to reorganize. The

company went out of business and its remaining assets were liquidated.

Ansonia, like Seth Thomas made a few very high quality clocks, but its mainstay was clocks for ordinary homes.

NEW HAVEN CLOCK COMPANY

The New Haven Clock Company was established in 1853 to produce inexpensive brass movements for the Jerome Manufacturing Company, which soon after went into bankruptcy.
given name. The company operated at this location until 1878, when it relocated to Brooklyn, New York.

Following this move, the company began to manufacture complete clocks.

In addition to its own products, New Haven marketed clocks made by other manufacturers, notably F. Kroeber of New York City, E. Howard Company of Boston, and E. Ingraham & Company of Bristol, Connecticut. Later it discontinued representing these lines and took on lines of imported clocks, notably French and Viennese. Around 1885, the success of its own clock production caused it to drop all other lines.

New Haven was possibly the most prolific of all clock manufacturers in its introduction of new models. Other clock manufacturers considered the wide variety of designs offered for sale by New Haven a drawback.

After World War II the company experienced serious financial problems and in 1956 production was stopped. Ultimately, the company went completely out of business.

WATERBURY CLOCK COMPANY

Benedict and Burnham, a brass manufacturing company, in a move to enter the industry using most of its product, in 1857 organized the Waterbury Clock Company in Waterbury, Connecticut. In its early years, the company produced a few case designs, but installed most of the movements it produced in cast iron or bronze cases made by others.

Waterbury developed good marketing capabilities and acted as a distributor for the Ithaca Calendar Clock Company located in Ithaca, New York. In 1891, the company developed its own line of perpetual calendar clocks, and ceased to represent Ithaca. By 1917, New Haven manufactured more than 23,000 clocks and watches *per day*.

By the time of the Great Depression in 1929, the Waterbury Clock Company was in financial distress. Its assets were sold at Auction and the company name was sold to United States Time corporation.

E. INGRAHAM CLOCK COMPANY

The firm of Brewster & Ingrahams was started in 1835 by Elias and Andrew Ingraham, with Elisha Brewster in Bristol, Connecticut.

A series of events resulted in changing the name of the company to E. Ingraham Company in 1884.

An original design, the *Sharp Gothic* or *Steeple* clock was produced by Brewster & Ingrahams in 1845. This became a very popular style and was produced in large quantities by the originator and adapted by other manufacturers

Another innovative design credit to Ingraham was the introduction of cases painted black with a finish known as *japanning*. Over the years, more than two hundred models of this type were produced by Ingraham.

The company introduced a number of new case designs, notably ripple molding-decorated ogee top and beehive cases, *Ionic* figure eight wall clock cases and *Grecian Mosaic* shelf clock cases. These case styles became very popular and they were manufactured for a number of years.

Around 1915, the company brought out an eight day lever escapement movement.

Production of pendulum clock movements was stopped in 1942.

In 1958 the name of the company was again changed to The Ingraham Company. In 1967 the company was sold and all mechanical movement manufacture ceased.

WILLIAM L. GILBERT CLOCK COMPANY

The firm of Jerome, Grant, Gilbert & Company was formed in 1839 in Bristol, Connecticut, to manufacture and sell inexpensive brass movements designed by Chauncey Jerome.

In 1851, having moved to Winsted, Connecticut, the company name was changed to W. L. Gilbert Clock Company.

Except for the development of *papier mache'* cases, the Gilbert company appears not to have been as innovative in case or movement design as some of its competitors. It adapted styles introduced by others and kept pace with improving manufacturing methods.

Gilbert became one of the major producers of clocks, manufacturing many millions over the course of its existence. It was one of the survivors, staying in business for some 100 years.

Severely affected by the Great Depression of 1929, the company went into receivership in 1932. Reorganized in 1934, the name was changed to William L. Gilbert Clock Corporation.

During World War II, Gilbert was one of the few clock manufacturers permitted to continue making clocks, because it made mechanical alarm clock cases of *papier mache'*, rather than scarce metal needed for the military. Alarm clocks were essential to wake the American work force.

In the late 1940s, Gilbert encountered serious financial problems. Following a long series of profitless years, the company was sold to the Spartus Corporation. Clock production ceased in 1957.

E. N. WELCH MANUFACTURING CO. and SESSIONS CLOCK COMPANY

In 1841, the *Forestville Manufacturing Company* was formed in Bristol, Connecticut, by E. N. Welch and J. C. Brown. Following a devastating fire in 1853 at his Forestville Hardware and Clock Company, J. C. Brown was bankrupt and Welch purchased his remaining assets. He also acquired the Frederick S. Otis case making shop and, in 1856 started manufacturing clocks labeled

E. N. Welch
Successors to the Old Establishment
of the Late J. C. Brown

In 1864 the E. N. Welch Manufacturing Company was incorporated. This firm became the largest clock manufacturer in Bristol.

In 1868, Welch joined with Solomon Spring and others to form Welch Spring and Company. This new company manufactured clocks of higher quality than was the norm for the trade. It appeared that the public was not eager to pay the higher prices attached to such luxury and the company failed to be profitable. It was taken over by the E. N. Welch Manufacturing Company in 1884.

In 1893 the company was forced into bankruptcy and clock production ceased. Following reorganization in 1897, manufacturing of clocks was resumed.

Fire destroyed both the movement and case factories in 1899. They were replaced in 1900 with a modern group of buildings. Continuing financial problems resulted in the directors of the company deciding the situation was hopeless and the business should be liquidated.

William E. Sessions, owner of the Sessions Foundry Company, had been buying Welch stock. In 1902, he was elected president of the company. Sessions injected large sums of money to rebuild the company and in 1903, the company name was changed to Sessions Clock Company. The new company continued to make clocks in the old Welch line. Many thousands of black mantel and oak kitchen clocks were labeled *Sessions*.

Following introduction of synchronous electric clocks in the early 1930s, the company discontinued the making of mechanical clocks in 1936 and turned to the making of electric clocks.

After passing through several changes of ownership, all production of clocks was terminated in 1968.

IMPROVING MANUFACTURING METHODS

The continuing development and refinement of machinery and tooling was the key to survival of clock factories. It made production of both movements and cases more efficient and made it possible to sell clocks at prices affordable by more and more people.

At the beginning of this period, by far the most usual case style was the Ogee shelf clock. In an effort to increase sales, a somewhat more elaborate case style came into being. This was a *Half Column* design, vaguely similar to earlier wood movement half column cases, but smaller.

The half columns were mounted between cornice-like moldings at the top and bottom. Dials were painted on thin zinc sheets. The body of the columns was usually painted black with the top and bottom elements in gold. They were attached to the case with cut nails and glue.

Like the Ogee, case elements were of native pine, veneered with rarer woods, such as mahogany and rosewood. A single door was divided by a cross piece and glazed. The top area was clear and protected the dial. The lower section was decorated with colorful transfer designs, usually with an opening so that the movement of the pendulum bob could be seen.

Utilizing basically the same weight driven movements employed in the Ogee design, the dimensions of these cases were almost identical to the Ogee. Dials and tablets were essentially the same. A large printed label identifying the manufacturer and giving instructions for operating the clock was pasted to the inside of the back board.

Weights were made of cast iron, as was the bell on which the hours were struck, that was mounted on the back board.

MOVEMENT MAKING

In England, about 1850, Henry Bessemer invented a new process for making steel that resulted in much higher quality and lower cost. As it related to the clock industry, this meant that arbors and other steel parts could be machined more rapidly, with higher quality and less cost.

Steel wire of uniform quality was now available and was used for not only arbors, but pendulum rods. In the beginning, one piece rod and suspension springs were made by hand hammering one end to make a thin flat area to act as a spring. A hook on the other end was formed by hand, using round nose pliers. Now, the spring was formed in one blow by a powered press and the hook was machine formed.

Perhaps of even greater importance was the fact that better steels made it possible to make better tools, dies and punches used to produce brass parts.

Concurrently, the young brass manufacturing industry was undergoing similar changes. Brass metallurgists developed formulae for several grades of their material, with different characteristics. Sheet brass which was of more uniform quality and easier to stamp out became available to clock manufacturers.

Stamping machines (*punch presses*) used to make movement plates and wheels from sheet brass were greatly improved.

Tool and die makers emerged as the elite of the work force. They were true craftsmen who were highly skilled and inventive in developing new concepts and methods. Very high production of plates and wheels of very good quality became the rule for the industry.

While there appears to be no record of it, there must have been great strides made in the generation and transmission of power to run the increasing number of machines in a clock factory. Much improved bearings with automatic oilers, for example, greatly extended their life and significantly reduced downtime for repairs.

GONGS REPLACE IRON BELLS

Nearly all wood movement clocks employed a bowl shaped, thin walled, cast iron bell to strike the hours. These bells were cast in sand molds and were attached to the wood back of the clock case by a screw through the middle of the bell. They produced a dead sounding ring.

Improvements in metallurgy and machinery to produce thick wire and other machines to form wire into coils, resulted in the *coil gong* used in later ogee and other clocks.

Not only were these gongs less expensive than the bells, they produced a deeper, more resonant tone that vibrated for seconds and was much more pleasing to the ear.

CASE MAKING

To make high production of ogee cases possible, it was necessary to develop a number of technological improvements.

Ogee cases were many times larger than the movements they housed. Their sheer bulk created a space problem for most clock factories. When more than 100,000 cases a year were required, this meant that over 2,000 were made each week. With six ten hour working days in the week, *thirty cases* were completed *every hour.*

Pine timber for the case wood was sawed into lumber planks, then aged and air dried, to minimize warping.

Even though veneer would be applied over the pine top and sides of the box case and the exposed door faces, planing was necessary to true and provide a smooth surface on which to glue the veneer. Veneer was glued to the lumber before other operations were performed on it. The use of hot hide glue made it necessary to position and clamp the veneered boards quickly, before the glue set. Jigs were used to facilitate this process.

Easily constructed and durable joints had to be formed at the end of each board, pulley slots cut in the top board and a rabbet cut in the back edge to receive the case back. Cut nails and hot hide glue were used to secure the joints.

Simple fixtures were used to assemble the box case and the door for gluing and nailing.

Case backs were made of thin pine, often made up of two or more pieces glued together. Two thin boards to support the movement were secured in slots in the top and nailed to the back board. They each had a rabeted slot into which the movement base board would be fitted and oval shaped holes to permit passage of the cords from the winding drums of the movement to the weights. Like other case elements, they had to be smoothed and cut to size. Jigs and powered saws performed the cutting.

Pulleys, over which the weight cords ran, continued to be turned from wood. Jigs and drill presses were used to drill holes for the pin shaft.

Case fronts were made from pine boards about three inches wide and an inch thick. One surface was milled to an ogive shape and carefully selected thin hardwood veneer attached with hot hide glue. The veneered lumber was clamped in a fixture matching the ogee shape until the glue had set.

Such operations were performed in batches. As each piece reached the set time for the glue, clamps and fixtures were removed and returned to the assembly point to be used again.

Flake shellac, dissolved in alcohol, was used to finish the case. This was applied with animal hair brushes. Shellac dries fairly quickly, so a brief time on a drying rack was sufficient to permit further handling for final assembly.

The inside of the case, its back, top and bottom were unfinished. A label, showing the maker's name and giving brief instructions for the operation of the clock, was pasted on the back board

TABLET DECORATION

In the beginning, glass tablets for the lower section of Ogee case doors were reverse painted by hand. This was a labor intensive and slow process. As production of cases and movements accelerated, other, faster methods had to be found. The first of these was the use of stencils to apply an outline of the design to the glass. Color was added by hand painting, but required little skill and was accomplished much more rapidly than free-hand painting.

A bit later, images printed on special paper which, when wetted and placed in contact with the glass, allowed the image to be transferred from the paper to the glass. This process was similar to the later *decalcomania (decal)* process, with which it is often confused, except that only the ink was transferred.

Decals employ a special paper coated with a water soluble separating coat and then with a comparatively heavy lacquer film on which the design is printed. A coat of paste is applied on top of the laquer.

When the decal paper with the image on it is wetted, the paste is activated and the paper is placed on the glass. The decal must then be gently wiped or squeegeed to force out air bubbles and excess water. The image adheres to the glass, then the paper is slid away from it and removed.

True Decals (*decalcomania*) were developed long after decorated clock tablets had gone out of style, so were little used in clocks.

Transfers, because they lacked the lacquer reinforcing layer, were much less durable than decals and were easily damaged. To minimize this problem, after they had been applied to the glass and allowed to dry, a coat of paint or thin shellac was applied over the transfer.

DIALS and HANDS

In the early days of the Ogee case, hand painted dials similar to those used in Pillar and Scroll clocks were used. The most significant change was the use of thin sheet zinc in place of wood for the dial plate. To keep up with demand and reduce cost, methods of printing them were developed.

Suitable sheet steel for hands became available and stamping presses equipped with precision punches and dies, turned them out by the thousands. They were heat treated in batches to harden them and to produce a blue color. The quality of the finished product was excellent.

Here, again, great credit is due to the metallurgists who developed the steels for hands, as well as the hard and tough steel essential for dies that would efficiently and precisely punch the hands from thin sheet steel.

CHAPTER TEN

Mass Produced
WEIGHT DRIVEN SHELF CLOCKS

BECAUSE THEY PROVIDE a reliable, consistent and inexpensive source of power, cast iron and lead weights were used to drive shelf clocks well into the twentieth century. While their use required rather large cases to accommodate the necessary fall of the weights over a thirty hour period, such clocks maintained their popularity and were made by nearly every clock manufacturer over a period of almost 75 years.

When rounded, rather than flat, moldings were used next to the ogee molding, the cases are commonly referred to as *Double Ogee* style.

As we have seen, the simple Ogee case style and the similar half column case, provided an attractive and economical means of enclosing movement and weights.

Various manufacturers introduced some modifications in movement design and very minor changes in dimension and the shape of moldings and other decorative elements, while retaining the basic character of both these styles.

Ogee and half column cases for clocks were produced by the millions. A relatively large number have survived and continue to operate reliably. They require winding on a daily basis.

While many of them are true antiques, over a hundred years old, so many of these clocks were made that many collectors shun them and their market price has remained almost constant in spite of inflation.

HALF-COLUMN WEIGHT CLOCKS

Using the same movement, weights and box case that had become common with the Ogee style, an innovative look for the front of the clock evolved with the addition of columns and cornices. The door, with its clear glass over the dial and a decorated glass tablet in the lower portion, remained almost identical to that of the Ogee.

To reduce costs and simplify case construction, half columns were made by gluing two pieces of wood together and turning a full column to the desired shape. After turning, the two halves were then separated and became two identical half columns.

Figure 47   Seth Thomas Half Column Clock
ca. 1845

The body of each column was most commonly painted black. Occasionally they were turned from hard wood such as cherry or walnut and finished naturally. With black columns, the capitols and bases were gold-leafed.

Veneered ogee moldings formed the center portion of the top cornice and the base of the case. The exterior dimensions of Half Column clocks were essentially identical to those of the standard Ogee case.

Like Ogee clocks, Half Column clocks nearly always had a label pasted to the inside of the backboard of the case. The name and address of the manufacturer were prominently displayed, along with brief instructions for winding, setting and regulating the clock.

Over the years, the paper on which these labels was printed has usually become brittle and the paste has lost its adhesion. Many labels are now in poor condition; some are missing completely.

It was common practice for the printers who produced clock labels to put their name and address in small type at the bottom of the label. Clock manufacturers appear to have changed printers fairly frequently. Some printers moved during the time they printed clock labels. These events are often a matter of record, so the name and address of the printer offer clues to the date the clock was made.

TABLETS IN DOORS

Glass was used for both the clear pane over the dial and the decorated one in the lower part of the door, called the tablet. The only available flat glass for many years during the early production of Ogee and Half Column clock cases was hand made.

Glass makers rotated a blob of molten glass on the end of a blowpipe, then blew large bubbles of glass. When the bubble reached maximum size and while the hot glass was still plastic, the bubble was slit with shears and the resulting sheet of glass dropped onto a flat surface to cool and harden.

Called *bubble glass* because of the way it was made, it also contained small bubbles of air. In addition, the surface was not perfectly flat, but had small irregular ridges.

Later, glass was machine made in continuous sheets and had fewer imperfections. This manufactured glass is called *window glass*, and is made in two thicknesses, single and double strength. When available, it was used in clocks.

Considering the fact that millions of these clocks were made over a period of about a hundred years, it is not surprising that literally thousands of tablet decorative designs were created. While early tablets were hand painted inreverse on the back of the glass, other less expensive decorative techniques developed.

Figure 48   8-Day Ogee Clock. 37" High
ca. 1840

Figure 49   Column & Cornice Clock
ca. 1845

Several manufacturers specialized in making tablets. It is not unusual to find the same design in the tablets used by various clock manufacturers.

Perhaps the earliest mass production method of making and applying tablet designs to glass was a transfer system in which paper was coated with a starchy paste that was allowed to dry. A colored image was then printed on the paste surface. When the paper was wetted, and the printed side placed in contact with the glass, the image separated from the paper and was transferred to the glass.

Another method involved printing directly on the glass, using soft plates that conformed to irregularities in the glass surface, without damaging the glass itself.

Toward the end of the production of ogee and half column clocks, true decalcomania, designs printed on a lacquer film on special paper were employed. Like transfers, wetting the backing paper allowed the film to be transferred to the glass.

Another method involved silk screen printing directly on the glass.

Decorated glass was used in many other case styles, sometimes as individual tablets and sometimes as the glass for the entire door, as in the case of Kitchen clocks.

8 DAY WEIGHT DRIVEN CLOCKS

OGEE

Not long after 30 Hour Ogee clocks began to be produced in quantity, manufacturers sought to expand their line with an Ogee that needed to be wound only once a week. This was achieved by

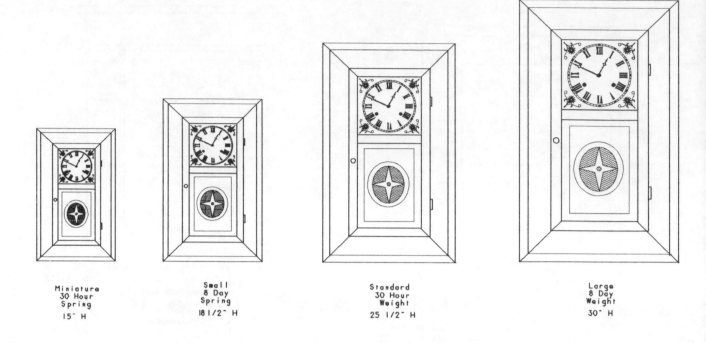

Miniature 30 Hour Spring 15" H

Small 8 Day Spring 18 1/2" H

Standard 30 Hour Weight 25 1/2" H

Large 8 Day Weight 30" H

Figure 50 Size Comparison, Ogee Cased Clocks

adding another wheel (*gear*) to the time train of the movement, increasing the height of the case by about four inches and almost doubling the size of the weights.

While priced significantly higher than the standard 30 hour Ogee clocks, the 8 Day version sold in reasonable quantities, though not nearly matching sales of the standard model. Probably because they only had to be wound once a week, a number have survived and are considered collector's items.

COLUMN AND CORNICE

Using the same basic box case of the Ogee and an eight day movement, the more ornate Column and Cornice style was a modest success.

This style had two doors. The top one was divided into two sections, much like the 30 Hour Half Column clocks, with a clear glass in the top and a decorated tablet in the bottom. Half columns with gold leafed capitols and bases and black bodies were attached to the case on either side of the top door by nails and glue.

Above the door and columns was a veneered ogee molding that projected from the front over each column.

The base of the case consisted of a smaller door with S-shaped veneered blocks on either side and with a decorated glass tablet. The entire case and doors were veneered with hard woods, such as rosewood, oak and mahogany.

SPRING DRIVEN OGEE CLOCKS

When 30 hour coiled springs became available and achieved popularity for movements used in small *cottage* clocks., Enterprising clock manufacturers soon used these movements in a scaled down version of the popular Ogee style.

The first of these measured 18 ½" high, seven inches shorter than the standard weight driven Ogee. This is designated a *Small Ogee*. Another, even smaller version, the *Miniature Ogee*, measured only 15" in height. In all respects these clocks were true scaled down versions of the original. The smaller sizes are very collectible.

While many Ogee clocks are true antiques and well over a hundred years old, partly because they must be wound every day, they have never been popular with most clock collectors.

VARIATIONS OF 8 DAY WEIGHT DRIVEN CLOCKS

As with other case designs, many clock manufacturers altered the basic column and cornice style to produce a different, but generically similar design. Movement designs were also modified, primarily to avoid patent infringement

In addition, a few enterprising clock producers used this basic case design to house unique mechanisms supplementing the basic clock functions.

One of the most interesting of these is the Kirk and Todd Whistle Pipe Organ Clock shown in Figure 51. A number of pipes, or whistles, play a tune at the hour, when activated by a pinned drum, like that of a music box, which directs air from a bellows to each whistle, as required by the tune being played.

CLASSIC CLOCK REPLICAS

In addition to mass produced adaptations of early hand made clocks, such as the Willard Banjo and Tall clocks, each generation for almost two hundred years has had a few craftsmen who

Figure 51 Kirk & Todd Organ Clock

faithfully hand crafted authentic replicas.

Several practice this art today and their very limited output is eagerly sought by collectors and interior decorators. One of the outstanding makers currently producing such pieces is Foster Campos of Massachusetts, a protégée of Elmer Stennes, a colorful character who made outstanding replicas of Willard clocks while serving a prison sentence for a serious felony.

While clocks made by both Stennes and Campos are identifiable by thier marks and signatures, the makers of many fine clocks made over the past nearly two hundred years cannot be determined.

Most early banjo clocks carried the name of the maker on the glass tablets oor throatpieces of the case. The movements of many original timepieces made by Simon Willard and his contemporary imitators are unmarked. When tablets of such clocks have been broken and replaced, only an parts that are easy to manufacture and assemble. They generally lack the niceties of cabinetry that characterized the originals. The movements in these kits are manufactered in the Orient or in Germany. Some are provided with inexpensive quartz battery movements.

While many such kits assembled by inexperienced people appear somewhat crude, some are nicely finished and reflect the care and patience of a true amateur craftsman. As gifts to relatives and friends of the assembler, they are highly prized by the recipients.

CHAPTER ELEVEN

SHELF CLOCKS

CLOCK MANUFACTURERS were quick to make use of the spring steel of good quality produced by the Bessemer process around 1850. Coil springs made of this material were used as main springs to power small shelf clocks, instead of the weights then commonly employed.

Springs of one sort or another had been used to power clock works for a long time prior to this, but the material of which they were made did not provide consistent force and they were generally unreliable.

As early as the fourteenth century, some artisans did develop alloys that were more satisfactory than most for clock and watch springs, but the materials and methods they used were very jealously guarded secrets.

The availability of suitable spring steel in quantity, at very reasonable cost, resulted in what amounted to a revolution in clock making.

Jerome was an early developer, but every clock manufacturer quickly came out with a line of comparatively small 30-hour spring-driven clocks. Because nearly all such clocks were initially made in that state, they became known as *Connecticut Shelf Clocks* or *Cottage Clocks*. They were signifi-

cantly smaller, from 12" to 14" in height, and lighter than traditional weight-driven clocks and were less expensive.

While weight driven clocks continued to be made for many years, spring-powered timepieces soon dominated the market. It was not long before spring-driven movements capable of running for eight days were in production. Unlike those powered by weights, these clocks were only slightly larger than their 30-hour cousins. The springs are thicker, wider and longer, but require little more space.

The movements of each manufacturer were very similar to those of its competitors. Cases were typically made of wood with a hinged door in which decorative glass was fitted to form the front. Dials were often printed on paper and glued to the face of a light steel round pan, attached to the case with screws.

Pendulum bobs were usually simple round brass covered lead, with a convex face and back. The bob had a hole through which the pendulum rod passed. The rod was threaded at the bottom, with a round nut. Turning the nut raised or lowered the bob to adjust the rate of swing to make the clock run faster or slower.

Because 30-hour springs were relatively thin and narrow, it took little effort to wind them and smaller winding keys were provided. Clocks with 8-day running time required larger keys.

While there were some without strike, most such clocks struck the hours on a brass bell attached to the inside back of the case. Many carried a label giving simple instructions for operating the clock and the manufacturer's name and address. Sometimes a warranty statement was included.

Case design of these small shelf clocks ranged from a simple rectangular box to those with tops of round, hexagonal, octagonal, ogive, or roof shape. Joints were simply nailed and glued.

Regardless of the style, cases were made of native New England pine, with sides, top and front veneered with hardwoods, notably rosewood, walnut and mahogany. The surface was finished with shellac, then known as *varnish*.

With reliable springs and highly efficient manufacturing methods, plus aggressive marketing, the American clock industry soon dominated the world market for clocks.

Weight-driven clocks were heavy, bulky and the weights had to be packaged separately for shipment. They were difficult and costly to ship. Distribution of the new smaller and lighter spring-driven type was significantly less expensive and helped make their cost to the consumer low.

Connecticut Shelf Clocks were sold by the millions, not only at home, but worldwide.

CHAUNCEY JEROME

An innovator, always in the forefront of development in the clock industry, Chauncey Jerome was again a leader in the move from weight driven to spring operated domestic clocks. Around 1850, his Jerome & Co. firm introduced 30-hour spring-driven clocks in a several designs.

The case for these clocks consisted of a simple box, the front of which was a door, divided by a single cross piece. Glass panes were mounted in the door, the top one clear and the lower one, the *tablet*, decorated with any of a very wide variety of decorative designs.

In a very short time, all major clock manufacturers followed suit and these thirty hour clocks were produced by the hundreds of thousands. Over the years, far more shelf clocks have been sold than any other kind.

SHELF CLOCK CHARACTERISTICS

Shelf clocks usually are from 12 to 14 inches in height, with a single front door. The door may be divided into two panels and, in some instances, there may be two doors. In all cases, the doors are frames for glass panes. The upper part of the glass that protects the dial is clear, while the lower portion is decorated with geometric or figural designs in several colors, or in plain gold or silver.

The earliest shelf clock movements were nearly always time only, that is, they did not strike the hours. For this reason, they were technically *timepieces* rather than clocks. Some did have what is known as a *passing strike*, providing a single strike of a bell at each hour.

It was not long until a second, or *strike train* was added to the movement to provide true hour striking. This required no increase in the size of the case, but upped the price somewhat.

Time Only clocks had a single train in the movement and only *one winding hole* appears on the dial. *Striking* clocks have an additional train to power the strike function and *two winding holes* in the dial.

Soon, in an effort to meet the public demand for clocks that did not require winding every day, spring driven movements that run for 8 days on a winding were developed.

Figure 52 Jerome & Co. Tablet Shelf Clock
ca. 1850

Figure 53 Jerome & Co. Mirror Shelf Clock
ca. 1855

To achieve the longer running time economically, it was necessary to make the pendulum rod a bit longer than that used with 30 hour movements. To accommodate this, case height was sometimes arbitrarily increased to about 18 to 20 inches tall.

These clocks were very popular and millions of them were made over almost a half century.

The movements developed for early cottage clocks, with minor adaptations, were used for many decades in millions of clocks, with an almost infinite variety of case styles. These movements, while relatively unsophisticated and inexpensive, were very durable. Many are still in working order today.

The PERSISTENCE of SHELF CLOCK STYLES

Case styles developed to utilize spring movements, with minor modifications, continued to be produced for more than fifty years.

As late as 1910, cottage clocks were being manufactured in both 30-hour and 8-day versions by several manufacturers.

The most obvious innovation of later models, as compared to the earliest versions, was elimination of painted tablets and the use of elaborate pendulum bobs to replace the simple brass disks originally employed.

Some were fitted with separate alarm movements mounted on the backboard and controlled by a small brass setting dial on the hour hand shaft, which could be rotated to the desired hour of alarm. The alarm rang the same bell as was used for striking.

Because they were manufactured over a period of many years with little apparent change in design, it is often difficult to accurately date individual examples. Experts rely on details of the movement, case, labels, etc. for clues.

REPRESENTATIVE SHELF CLOCK STYLES

Figure 52 shows a very early 30-hour shelf clock. This is an extremely simple design. It consists of a simple rectangular box made of thin

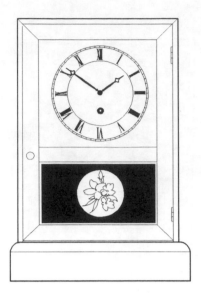

Figure 54 Jerome & Co. Cottage Shelf Clock
ca. 1852

Figure 55   Ansonia 8-Day Cottage Shelf Clock
ca. 1900

pine boards attached to a base made of pine molding. The door is a rectangle with a crosspiece just below the dial. Fitting within the case box, it is hinged on the right and has a rotating latch on the left.

Visible surfaces on the sides, top and front of the case are covered with hard wood veneer. The upper and lower glass tablets in the door are clear. The lower tablet of some examples is decorated with reverse painted or stenciled designs.

The pendulum bob is of the same type used on weight-driven 30-hour clocks.

The clock in figure 53 is nearly identical to that in Figure 52, except that mirror glass is used for the lower tablet and small gold leafed quarter-round molding around the inside edges of the door. Surprisingly, the use of gold leaf in small areas like this did not add appreciably to the cost

The clock in Figure 54 is of slightly different proportions than those shown in the previous illustrations. The design in the lower tablet is a simple reverse painting. The area surrounding the flower is black asphaltum paint. The case is

identical in construction to the previous examples.

This thirty hour timepiece (note the single winding hole), like other early examples, had a thin zinc plate on which the dial was painted. As with weight-driven clocks employing this type of dial, changes in temperature caused the white paint to separate from the zinc, resulting in flaking.

Demonstrating that clocks of this style persisted in production for many years is the one shown in Figure 55, made around 1900, nearly half a century after the first Connecticut shelf clocks were made.

This Ansonia Clock had a movement that ran 30 hours and also had an additional train in the movement for striking the hours. Note the two winding holes in the dial.

Other than the molding, all outside surfaces, except the back, were veneered.

Another innovation is the much simpler and less expensive spring latch to secure the door, in place of the earlier knob and rotating latch.

The tablet decoration is a multi-colored printed

Figure 56 Jerome & Co. Half Decagon Shelf Clock
ca. 1853

Figure 57 Jerome & Co. Gothic or *Beehive* Clock
ca. 1855

transfer, much cheaper and sometimes more intricate than earlier reverse painted designs.

This and many other examples of the cottage clock type became available in both 30-hour and 8-day options and time only, or striking. In 1900, this clock was listed for sale at $2.30 in the 30-hour time only version, $3.50 for 30-hour strike and $4.10 for the 8-day striking model.

While we may think it odd for anyone to choose a 30-hour version over an 8-day one, when the difference in price is only 70 cents, it should be remembered that the average worker in 1900 earned less than $1.00 a day. Probably primarily for this reason, 1-day clocks continued to be available as long as mechanical movements were produced in the United States.

By far the majority of mechanical alarm clocks made in this country during the first half of the 20th Century were of 30-hour or 1-day duration. These clocks were found in nearly every home, in America until well after 1940.

Mechanical alarm clocks are still readily available today.

Among the more intricate shelf clock case styles, from the standpoint of cabinetry, is the one shown in Figure 56. The tops of both the case and the door are constructed of four individual pieces which, with the sides, form half of a ten-sided geometric figure known as a decagon.

The front of the case is made up of half-round molding. The elements of the door are thicker at the outer edge than at the inner one and are rabeted to retain the door glass. A small quarter-round molding is attached to the inner edge. Two hinges support the door and it is secured by a rotating latch. The base is rectangular and is topped by an ogee molding. Hours are struck on a round brass bell attached to the back board. The pendulum is like those used on weight clocks.

The door glass of the clock shown is decorated with an intricate applied printed design in gold and does not have a solid background, so that the swinging pendulum bob may be observed.

As with all shelf clocks, this basic case style was made by many clock manufacturers, with infinite variations.

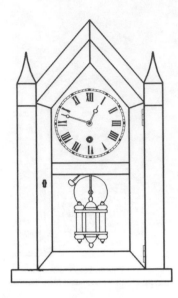

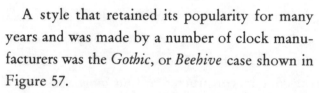

Figure 58 Jerome & Co. Sharp Gothic or *Steeple* Clock
ca.1855

Figure 59 German 30-Hour Shelf Clock
ca. 1890

A style that retained its popularity for many years and was made by a number of clock manufacturers was the *Gothic*, or *Beehive* case shown in Figure 57.

The rounded molding forming the top of the case front was veneered with exotic hard woods. Perhaps the most popular was distinctively colored *rosewood*. The veneer was applied so that its grain was perpendicular to the molding. How this was done on a production basis appears to have been lost in time. In some cases, this veneer has remained tightly adhered to its pine base for almost a hundred and fifty years.

The curved portion of the case top is part of the same pine board comprising the side. Bending was made possible by multiple saw cuts on the outside surface. Unlike other shelf clock cases, a separate hinged bezel, bearing a round glass, covers the dial. It is secured by a spring clip.

A lower rectangular door is framed in veneered rounded pine molding and carries a decorative glass tablet. In this case the glass is almost completely covered with the design and the

swinging pendulum bob may only be seen through a very small opening in the design.

Historians generally credit Chauncey Jerome with introducing a most popular case style that persisted for a great many years, the *Sharp Gothic* or *Steeple* in Figure 58. Its popularity prompted other clock makers to imitate the design. While retaining the basic characteristics of a steeply pitched top, or roof, a great many adaptations were made by nearly every clock manufacturer. Front and side case surfaces are veneered.

Characterized by rounded side columns, a sharply sloped top, and a dial plate with a pointed top to match that of the case, variations of this style of clocks were made by several manufacturers in both 30-hour and 8-day versions. The style has been popular for many years.

Principal variations were in the shape of the finials, or steeples, topping the side columns the treatment of the tablet, or glass in the door and the style of the pendulum. In addition, there were changes in the design of the base and, of course, in the veneers used.

Figure 60 Ansonia Round Top Shelf Clock
ca. 1878

Figure 61 New Haven Roof Top Shelf Clock
ca. 1870

The early version shown in Figure 58 has a 30-hour passing strike movement, producing a single strike at each hour. It has a fairly elaborate pendulum bob which is fully visible through the clear lower glass of the door.

Not to be outdone by their American counterparts, foreign clock manufacturers, especially those in Germany were quick to produce cases like those which the Yankee clock producers had so successfully marketed.

The example shown in Figure 59 is typical of German output. A small clock, it is 30-hour time only, having no striking capability. It has a half-octagon top and door. The glass in the door is clear and reveals a decorative pendulum made up of three rods and an embossed brass bob

The base has a rounded top and all front, side and top surfaces of the case are veneered with hardwood, In this case, walnut.

Unlike American clocks, a round metal dial with a brass bezel is mounted on a thin wooden board with a scalloped bottom. For a relatively short period of time, German shelf clocks in

various styles were imported to the American market.

Since few German shelf clocks have been found by collectors, it is likely that they were unable to successfully compete, at least in the American market.

The basic *round top* shelf clock case style, Figure 60, was popular for many years and was made by nearly all clock manufacturers. Its basic construction was similar to the *beehive* style discussed earlier. Exposed surfaces of the case were veneered with hard woods and the top portion of the basic pine case was serrated with closely spaced saw cuts so that it could be easily bent to the round shape, without cracking..

The door was always made of pine with hard wood veneer. Molding of various shapes was frequently added. It usually carried a single pane of glass, the lower portion of which was commonly decorated with intricate gold or silver printed transfers. The example shown in Figure 60 has been decorated with half-round solid hardwood turnings glued to the flat surface of the side

Figure 62 E. N. Welch *Patti No. 2* Shelf Clock
ca. 1875

Figure 63 New Haven Walnut Kitchen Clocks
ca. 1880

of the case front. A semi-circular rounded hardwood molding is attached to the top.

The door is flat pine with hardwood veneer and a small inside molding. Frequently, this molding was covered with gold leaf. In this and other styles where the pendulum bob was highly visible, manufacturers vied with each other to develop the most attractive and elaborate pendulum bobs .

Nickel plating was widely used on the cylinders of the bob and other pendulum parts.

The very simple *roof top* case style shown in Figure 61 was found in every clock maker's line. There were countless variations in details such as the angle of the top, design and decoration of the door and base and decoration of the door glass.

In some versions, the door glass was decorated with transfers similar to that shown in Figure 60 in order to expose the fancy pendulums that came into fashion.

The glass in Figure 61 is an example of a fully opaque decorative treatment. The entire glass is totally opaque, except for the dial area, which is clear.

The case front was sometimes simply flat, or might carry any of a wide variety of solid wood molding. The base might be plainly rectangular, or could be ornamented with molding of various contours on its upper surface.

As with nearly all shelf clock styles, the sides, top and front were covered with hard wood veneer. Solid wood decorative elements, including molding, were nearly always made of the same wood as the veneer.

Most clocks bore labels. Jerome and others attached the label on the inside bottom of the case. More usually, a label was pasted to the outside back of the case. These labels were adhered with library paste.

Complying with contemporary design trends in furniture and other decorative objects, clock designers developed more and more elaborate case styles. The *Patti* introduced by E. N. Welch was a comparatively expensive and very popular example.

While maintaining the essential characteristics of the first *Patti*, Welch introduced a number of

Figure 64 Kroeber *California* Statue Clock
1898

Figure 65 Ansonia *Symbol* Crystal Regulator Clock
ca. 1901

variations over the years. Included among these were wall models and miniatures.

Other manufacturers developed similar styles, but few if any very closely resembled the original.

The *Patti* cases are characterized by turned half-columns on either side, with square sections on which are mounted turned wood medallions, a rounded top and three turned finials. Flat surfaces are veneered with hard wood.

Door glasses are nearly always decorated with delicate, colorful transfers, with the center area fairly open to make it possible to observe the fancy pendulum.

As part of the trend toward more and more ornate clock case designs, pretentious additions were made to basic shelf clock cases. For reasons that are obscure, this genre became know as *Kitchen Clocks.*

They were so popular that millions were made over roughly a thirty year period. There was an almost infinite variety of designs over the years and bobs were often the major distinguishing

feature of different models of the same basic clocks.

An elaborate monogram bearing the E. N. Welch initials, *ENW* often appeared as decoration on a cut glass insert Welch pendulum bobs.

The clock shown in Figure 63 is an early example of a kitchen clock. The front of the basic *round top* shelf clock case has simply been added to. Thin sheets of walnut have been scroll-sawed in a rather bizarre shape and attached to the case. The base is much wider than that in the basic shelf clock style.

To these flat elements are added various decorative details. In this case a shallow, curved rounded molding is also applied near the top. Carved and incised designs are added to both the top and side pieces. The lower portion of the door glass is decorated with colorful transfers, with a clear area so the pendulum can be viewed.

As with other case designs produced during this period, there were many designs of elabo-

Figure 66 Waterbury *Willard* Mantel or Shelf Banjo
ca. 1913

Figure 67 Gilbert Porcelain *Case No.423*
ca. 1910

rate pendulum bobs. They were finished in bright or antiqued brass.

In the late 19th century, tastes in decoration became increasingly ornate. One of the manifestations in clock design was the addition of small statues. Usually made of pot metal, an alloy of lead and other metals, they were plated with brass or gold that was sometimes antiqued. They were not part of the clock case, but were added on a separate pedestal. Most statues were in the classic Greco-Roman style and were usually very well executed.

Statues for clocks often depicted classic mythical, historical or military figures. Animals of all kinds, alone, or as part of a figural group are sometimes found.

The clock itself is usually housed in a case of the same material as the statue. Case designs are often very intricate. Cast brass bezels with bevel inserts are attached to the case with a single hinge and have a snap catch to keep them closed. Bases are of cast metal or stone. Decorative feet of cast pot metal support the base.

While nearly all manufacturers produced statue clocks, Ansonia was the most prolific. Their catalogs show a great many designs offered as part of a clock, or separately. These were sometimes added to ordinary flat top clocks.

In the late 1890's, reflecting the tastes of the time, clock manufacturers produced an elegant style of case featuring beveled glass front and sides. The then famous *Crystal Palace* a huge glass structure erected in London, England, for a World's Fair was the inspiration for this. The case of the Crystal Regulator clock is constructed entirely of glass in a brass frame. The example shown in Figure 65 is one of the plainer versions. It features simple brass half columns on either side with rather plain finials and pediments. Dials are nearly always of porcelain, surrounded by elaborate cast brass bezels. The interesting exposed *Brocot* escapement shown in the illustration is often found, especially on those made by Ansonia and occasionally on clocks by other makers.

Figure 68 Howard Miller Quartz Bracket Clock
ca. 1993

Figure 69 Howard Miller Mechanical Bracket Clock
ca. 1993

The 8-Day movement has a strike train with the hours and half hours struck on a coil gong mounted on a steel post attached to the base plate by a nut. This support is usually decorated with brass trim. Crystal Regulator clocks, each with a variation of the basic design, were made by most manufacturers.

The clock shown in Figure 66 is an interesting example of reproduction of the early Willard banjo design modified so it could be used as a shelf clock. The proportions of the case have been changed by widening. Simple block feet have been added.

A cast brass eagle finial rests on a wood base atop the case. A cast brass bezel surrounds the dial. The throat and door glasses are executed in a manner similar to the original Willards. The movement is typical of those used at this time in other shelf clocks.

Figure 67 shows a porcelain cased clock which is representative of hundreds of styles sold by many clock manufacturers. The porcelain was molded in three dimensional relief, then colorfully

hand decorated before glazing.

The cases were made by china makers among whom are some of the prized names in that field. Like other china products, clock cases are often signed or trademarked by their makers, notably *Spode, Delft, R.S. Prussia, Royal Doulton, Royal Bonn* and others.

In 1901, Ansonia Clock Co. Showed 42 *different* Royal Bonn china cases in its catalog.

Movements are 8-Day with round front and back plates. A wood base inside the clock at the bottom supports a coil gong.

Following early English bracket clock designs, the Howard Miller *Bracket Clock* shown in Figure 68 is representative of some of the higher quality timepieces being offered for sale in the late 20th century. The case is of solid hard wood, usually walnut or cherry. The veneer of the originals is prohibitively costly in today's economy, even when compared to the cost of using solid woods.

The cabinet work of these cases is of a high order. Since there is considerable variation in the

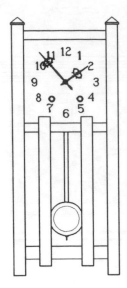

Figure 70 Tall Mission Style Shelf Clock
ca. 1920

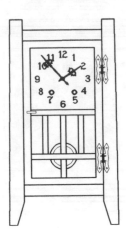

Figure 71 Enclosed Mission Style Shelf Clock
ca. 1920

color and grain of natural woods, the furniture manufacturers who produce such cases use a process called *toning* to subdue and blend the colors. After the case has been stained, a small spray gun is used to apply pigmented liquid toner to darken lighter areas to match darker ones. After this, the final finish lacquer or varnish coat is applied.

The battery powered quartz movement used in this model is made in Germany and has an electronic Westminster chime. The chime simulates, but does not approach the tonal quality of mechanical chimes.

The dial is embossed brass with corner escutcheons, the raised brass decorative elements in the corners of the dial..

Superficially alike, the case design of the clock in Figure 68 and the one in Figure 69 are somewhat different. Their bases vary significantly as do the handles at the top.

Made in Germany, the spring driven mechanical movement of the clock in figure 69 has three trains for the time, chime and strike functions.

Three winding holes appear on the dial. Howard Miller uses high quality movements, among the best available at the time.

Movements and cases in contract lots by the company whose name appears on the dial. It is not uncommon to find movements by different German makers in the same style of cases made by a particular clock company. The maker of the case is almost never identified.

Mechanical movements may have a pendulum, or more likely in current clocks, a balance wheel escapement.

Bar chime rods, usually five in number, are mounted on the bottom of the case. Hammers with molded nylon inserts at the striking face are activated by the movement to chime at the quarters hours.

On the hour, two or three of the hammers then simultaneously strike selected chime bars to produce a reverberating tone.

In the early 20th century, there was a general fascination with simple, even rustic, furniture styles.

Figure 72 Mission Style Shelf Clock
ca. 1920

styles.

An example of this trend was the severely plain *Mission* style, based on furniture associated with old Spanish missions in California.

Quickly adapted by clock manufacturers, the Mission style was very popular for clock cases for a short span of time. When applied to Mission style clocks, the word *case* is often a misnomer, since the movement is often housed in a small sheet metal enclosure attached to the back of the dial. The rest is an open slat work of wood, usually unsanded oak with dark stain and only a thin coat of varnish, to obtain a rustic appearance.

The clock illustrated in Figure 70 is typical of the basic Mission style. It is essentially a scaled down version of a Mission style tall clock, but is only 24" high. It is made up of oak slats with a thin oak board forming the face.

There is no time track, only brass numerals attached to the face. It is more a stand to support the movement than a case. The movement is mounted in a small wooden box on the back of the face board.

The clock example shown in Figure 71 is slightly less stark in its design than that in Figure 70. While retaining the simplicity characteristic of Mission furniture, this is a true clock *case* in which the movement and dial are completely enclosed in the case.

A hinged door with decorative hinges has a full pane of glass with a grill of wood slats in front of it. There is a rotating latch to secure the door.

While all other case elements are square, the two outside pieces are tapered on the outside and have a bevel on the inside edge at the bottom.

The face is a thin wood slab on which antiqued brass numerals are mounted. There is no time track. The oak of which the case is made is darkly stained and comparatively rough in texture.

While maintaining the basic austerity of the type, there was a surprising number of variations, using simple slats of oak.

The clock in Figure 72, while obviously of the Mission style, gets away from the stark slatted look of most such clocks. The case door has a single pane of glass with a slatted grill over the lower portion. Antiqued brass hinges support the door and it has a rotating latch.

The side pieces are sawed in a curved outline, as is the piece under the door. An unusual molding adorns the edges of the top board.

The 8-Day movement uses a short pendulum and strikes the hours on a coil gong mounted on the back board. The face is a thin slab of oak with antiqued brass numerals.

All wood parts are rough, darkly stained and finished with a thin varnish coat.

Typical of other clock case styles produced at this time, a standard pendulum time and strike movement was installed.

For many years, Mission style clocks were looked down upon by collectors and they were of little value. Recently, some collectors have specialized in this style and their value is on the rise. This is an example of how clock values can change.

Today's trash often becomes tomorrow's treasure. The reverse can also happen when a style loses favor, values can also go down.

SUMMARY

Because there have been so many different shelf clock case designs, it would be impossible to include all of them in a single volume. In this chapter we have tried to trace the development of those still commonly found in American homes.

In succeeding chapters we will amplify on the most popular types.

There are a surprising number of shelf clocks of all kinds, most of them well over fifty years old, sometimes in use, but more often stored away in attics and basements still in homes all over the country. Most can be very easily restored to useful running condition.

CHAPTER TWELVE

KITCHEN CLOCKS

WE TOUCHED BRIEFLY on the Kitchen Clock style in the last chapter. Because they were so popular and so many of them were produced over a period of many years, this chapter will explore the type in more detail.

Because of the hundreds, perhaps thousands of different designs made by many manufacturers, we can only scratch the surface here. We will try, however, to paint a broad picture and point out typical features.

It must be borne in mind that there were two basic types of Kitchen Clock cases, walnut and oak. In addition to the material of which they were made, there was a basic difference in the decoration or embellishment of the fronts. While walnut clocks had turned or scroll-sawed elements applied to the surface, those made of oak were decorated by pressing a hot die with a raised design into the moistened oak, under great force. There are a few collections of these dies still preserved.

The objective was to create a design that appeared to be carved in the wood and, at first glance, this goal may seem to have been attained. A closer inspection reveals that the fibers of the wood have been compressed and in some cases ruptured.

One thing all oak Kitchen Clocks appear to have in common is the ornateness of their designs. There seems to have been an ongoing contest among manufacturers to produce the most complex design. This applies not only to the impressed designs, but to the outer scroll-sawed shapes of the pieces attached to the basic case.

Walnut Kitchen Clocks followed this trend. Their incised carved designs were never quite as elaborate as the impressed ones of the oak clocks. Very elaborate clock cases, no longer called *Kitchen* clocks, evolved from the early comparatively simple walnut kitchen clock case style..

No doubt because their production was semi-automated, oak kitchen clocks were manufactured in much greater quantities than the walnut variety, over many more years. Oak Kitchen Clocks were manufactured for almost half a century, from about 1870 to 1920. During this period literally millions were produced.

Each manufacturer used his own designs and there were sometimes dozens in his line each year. In a very competitive market, it is probable that more than a thousand kitchen clock styles were produced.

There were almost infinite combinations of wood elements and door glass designs.

All kitchen clocks, although not precision time pieces, kept reasonably good time, when properly adjusted. Many have survived well over a hundred years in running condition.

BACK BOARD WITH
MOVEMENT & GONG

BASIC CASE WITH DOOR ATTACHED
Note Glue Blocks at Top and
Either Side of Base

DOOR GLASS

EMBOSSED TOP & SIDE PIECES

DIAL PLATE

HANDS

BASE

FULLY ASSEMBLED CLOCK

Figure 73   Kitchen Clock Case Construction

Figure 73 shows the elements of nearly all kitchen clocks. The case is made of 3/8" thick pine with the outer surface veneered in oak or walnut. The inside at the middle is serrated with saw cuts so that it can be easily bent to the half-round shape. Two pine blocks glued to either side near the top support the dial. The door is made of oak or walnut molding. Door hinges are set in mortises in the case and door and secured with screws. The back of the door is rabeted to receive the glass.

The dial plate is of tinned steel painted white with black numerals. It is attached to the case by wood screws into the blocks on either side.

Top and side decorative pieces are made of 1/4" thick oak which has been die-embossed with designs. They are attached to the case by means of

Figure 74 Terry Clock Co., Walnut Kitchen Clock
ca. 1890

Figure 75 New Haven Walnut Kitchen Clock
ca. 1890

small nails and hot hide glue. Further support may be provided by small blocks nailed and/or glued to the case. Movement and gong are fastened to the back board with wood screws.

Bases are made up of one or more oak or walnut moldings glued and nailed together and to the case bottom. The molding combinations are infinite in number. Some are very plain and some, like the one shown, more elaborate.

The walnut kitchen clock pictured in Figure 74 is a fairly early example of this type. It is almost severely simple in appearance, but utilizes the case construction that lasted for half a century. The basic case housing the movement has a round top. Decorative top and side pieces are of solid walnut.

Two pieces of walnut molding and a shield-like decorative element are glued to the top piece. The side pieces are scroll-sawed and decorated carved incised designs.

The base is scroll-sawed and set at an angle. Three decorative designs in the shape of a leaf are glued to the front. The door is made up of pieces of walnut molding, mitered and glued. The door glass is decorated with an applied design.

Showing the beginning of a trend to more elaborate designs in kitchen clocks is the example shown in Figure 75. The basic box is the same as that shown in Figure 73. The door, rather than having a half-decagon top, is a semicircle. This curve is repeated in the molding in the top piece. The top is further decorated with carved scrolls on either side of a keystone shaped block carrying a figural bust.

The solid walnut side pieces are not only scroll-sawed on the outer edges, but have a cutout design in the middle. They are also decorated with carved incising.

Made of walnut, the base consists of flat pieces nailed and glued together, with incised floral decoration. Trim molding adorns the top and bottom of the base.

A cast pendulum bob carries a three-dimensional design and is plainly visible.

While the door glass in this example is undecorated, one of many applied designs might be found on glasses in identical cases. Walnut kitchen clocks were made by almost every clock manufacturer. They were a bit more expensive than oak clocks.

Figure 76   New Haven Walnut Kitchen Clock
ca. 1900

Figure 77   Sessions Oak Kitchen Clock
ca. 1900

One of the more pleasing walnut kitchen clock cases is shown in Figure 76. The lines of the scroll-sawed top and side pieces are comparatively simple and form a pleasing outline. The contour of the side pieces flows into that of the moldings forming the base.

The top piece has three turned half finials, that is they are made up of two pieces of walnut, temporarily glued together and turned, then separated and glued to the top piece.

The rest of the design of the top and side pieces is incised with chisels, by hand. They are generally well executed. The side pieces extend only about halfway up the case.

The door is typical, with a half-decagon top. It is made up of shaped walnut molding.

The door glass carries one of many possible designs applied in gold. A pendulum bob with sculpted design is readily visible through the glass.

The dial pan is of tin plate and is painted white, with black Roman numerals. Thin brass forms an outer bezel and an inner decorative ring.

Spade hands are shown in this illustration, but other shapes were used as well.

Seeming almost top-heavy, the die-embossed oak case of the clock in Figure 77 is typical of the more pretentious versions of this type.

The top piece of this case is notable for its size. It was made from a single 3/8" board more than 12" wide, fine grained and free of knots. The embossing required a very large die mounted in a large and powerful press. The resulting embossed piece in this example was of very good quality, with the design deeply indented and little if any broken grain showing in the wood.

The side pieces are in back of and overlap the top piece, which provides additional support.

The base of this clock is two-dimensional and is of embossed oak. It is contoured to make it compatible with the top and side pieces of the case.

The door is conventional. The door glass in this case carries a more elaborate gold design. The pendulum bob is a simple convex brass disk, but more intricate designs were also used with this case.

The usual finish for oak kitchen clocks was called *dark oak*. The wood was stained, then finished with shellac which was then known as *varnish*. The objective was to simulate a very old oak finish.

Figure 78 Ansonia Oak Kitchen Shelf Clock
ca. 1900

Figure 79 Ansonia Oak Kitchen Wall Clock
ca. 1900

The Ansonia Oak Kitchen clock in Figure 78 is notable for its exceptionally deep and well formed impressed designs.

The base is made of several moldings, including one with a deep and well executed impressed design. In other respects the case is quite conventional, employing the usual round top, with the movement and gong mounted on the back board.

As was customary, many different designs were used on the door glass. The one shown is opaque with an elliptical opening to show the pendulum bob. The door has the usual half-decagon top and is made up of shaped oak molding.

While a simple round pendulum bob is shown in the illustration, other, more elaborate pendulum bobs were also used, especially when the glass decoration was more open and the pendulum more readily visible.

When this clock was made, clock shelves were quite popular. They were available in a wide variety of styles and were usually made of oak or walnut. Although many of these shelves were produced, few have survived and they are much sought after by collectors.

The clock in Figure 79 is an excellent example of the way case elements were used in different combinations to radically alter the appearance of a clock.

In this instance, the case is identical to that of the clock in Figure 78. The base of the shelf model has been removed and a flat, embossed bottom piece substituted. Adding a steel hangar to the back of the case to facilitate hanging makes this a wall clock.

It appears to be a conventional shelf clock resting on its own shelf. Changing the door glass, a simple matter to accomplish, would further transform the clock.

While nearly all manufactures used this method of expanding their line, wall mounted kitchen clocks were never as popular as the shelf variety, although they continued to be made over a period of many years..

Like other wall clocks, this type was subject to movement from side to side when being wound, or even when the door was opened, upsetting the beat.

Many owners drilled one or more holes in the lower part of the back, then inserted a screw to secure the clock to the wall. Sometimes a nail was driven through the back board into the wall.

Figure 80 Seth Thomas "Capitol" No.5 Oak Kitchen Clock
ca. 1925

Figure 81 Waterbury "Radnor" Oak Kitchen Clock
ca. 1891

The clock in Figure 80, made in 1925, is an example of the durability of this style. Made almost 50 years after introduction of the kitchen clock design, its appearance is little changed from the earliest examples.

The basic case is still the same, with rounded top and a back board to which the movement and gong are attached. The top and side pieces are scroll-sawed in a fairly intricate shape and are further decorated with impressed designs. Three pressed oak round medallions are glued to the top piece.

The top piece extends down the sides of the case almost to the bottom of the dial and there is a space between them and the side pieces at the bottom of the case.

The door molding is of picture frame contour.

A simple fluted base has attached feet at the corners.

The movement, dial and gong differ very little from those of the earliest kitchen clocks.

It is clear from this example why dating of kitchen clock manufacture is difficult. Only subtle differences in movement design and case construction provide clues as to the date of manufacture.

This is a rather unusual model of an oak kitchen clock.

While in most respects, it conforms to the basic kitchen clock design, with round top box, inserted back board on which the movement and gong are mounted and impressed designs in the top and side pieces, it also has applied molding and turned half-finials applied to the top piece.

This feature is common with walnut kitchen clocks. In the case of the "Radnor" model and others made by different manufacturers, the design was available in *both* oak and walnut. It is not surprising that some of the features of each basic style are incorporated in such a clock.

Making a particular design in both walnut and oak was an effort on the part of the manufacturer to provide additional choices to the buyer and, hopefully, to gain a competitive advantage.

This model had a fancy 3-dimensional cast pendulum bob, further decorated with a nickel plated sheet metal escutcheon at the top of the bob.

Decoration of the glass is in gold, with a very light, almost lacy pattern, so that the bob is readily visible.

CHAPTER THIRTEEN

WALL CLOCKS

WALL CLOCKS HAVE been around for hundreds of years, in many forms. Even today, few kitchens are without a clock, usually electric, on a wall. Wall clocks are frequently larger than shelf, mantel, or table clocks and they take up much less space than tall clocks.

As a rule, wall clocks become a major focus of attention in any room. It is not surprising that, except for the smaller versions, like those found in kitchens, they have always been relatively expensive.

We have already looked briefly at some wall clocks, notably the early banjo style developed by Aaron Willard. In this chapter, we will take a somewhat broader view. In later chapters, we will look at certain special groups of wall clocks.

As we have seen, the earliest forms of wall clocks were mounted there as an effective way of accommodating the long drop of weights necessary to achieve the desired running time. Later examples were more decorative in nature and often, because of the longer pendulum they contained, were adjustable to a higher degree of accuracy than smaller clocks.

Because of this latter feature, some enterprising manufacturer applied the word *REGULATOR* to his wall clocks. The public inferred a high degree of accuracy from this designation and other makers were quick to adopt it. Even some notoriously poor time keepers carried this appellation in bold gold leafed letters. The fact of the matter is that almost all clocks can be regulated to make them run faster or slower. With patience and making tiny adjustments, most clocks can be made to keep good time, gaining or losing only a few seconds a day.

Among the most accurate time keepers are those designated as *Jeweler's Regulators*. These clocks are equipped with precision movements and can be adjusted to keep very accurate time. Before precision time keeping became available through atomic clocks and time signals broadcast on the radio, a jeweler's livelihood depended on his ability to adjust watches to keep accurate time. This required that he have an accurate timepiece himself, to check the time keeping ability of watches he repaired.

True jeweler's regulator clocks are eagerly sought by many collectors.

Like jewelry shops, wall clocks were found in many public places, notably banks, department and other retail stores, offices, railroad stations, airline terminals and governmental buildings. Their dials were large enough to be easily read at a distance and, before the days when everyone had a watch, they performed an invaluable public service.

With a few exceptions, wall clocks were of the highest quality and workmanship. As a result, they were comparatively expensive.

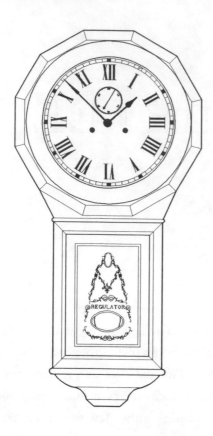

Figure 82   Seth Thomas Regulator No.1
ca. 1864

Figure 83   E. Howard Gallery Clock
ca. 1860

Many wall clocks, such as the one in Figure 82, were intended for use in offices, schools, public and commercial establishments of all kinds. With the introduction and eventual dominance of electric clocks, mechanical wall clocks were soon replaced with the newer and more accurate timepieces. They often found their way into homes, where they became prized posessions and ultimately, heirlooms. Many collectors specialize in such clocks.

While the banjo style of wall clock remained popular for almost two centuries, mostly in homes, clock manufacturers perceived a new market in commercial establishments. The Seth Thomas Regulator No.1 was among the earliest of this type.

A rather large clock, almost three feet high, it has a dial painted on metal. The top portion of the case has a turned rounded molding around the dial. Outside this are 12 pieces of half round molding.

The door glass is black with gold decoration and an oval opening through which the pendulum bob may be seen.

The case is of pine overlaid with veneer, usually walnut. All molding is of solid wood.

One of the unique features of this style is the seconds bit, a small dial and hand in the top part of the dial that shows seconds elapsed.

Some public places, notably churches and large meeting rooms, such as legislative houses and court rooms required a rather large, easy to read timepiece. The most common type was round and comparatively simple in design, such as the gallery clock by E. Howard shown in Figure 83.

Gallery clocks were often mounted on the wall at the back of a public room. In the case of churches and other buildings with balconies, the clock was mounted on the front of the low wall fronting the balcony, facing the preacher. Thus, he could easily see it, but the congregation would have to turn around to time his sermons. An opening in the wall permitted winding the posts at the back of the movement. Thus there are no holes in the dial.

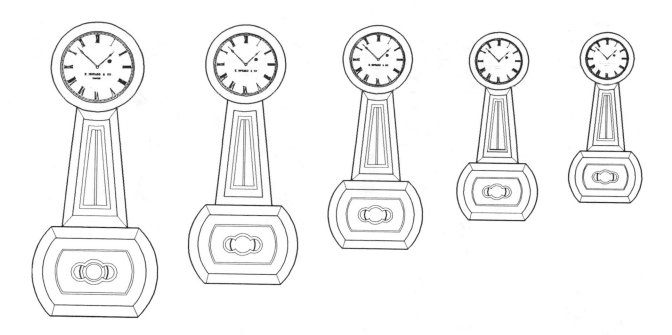

Figure 84 E. Howard & Co. Regulators Nos. 1 through 5
ca. 1874

Among the earliest manufacturers to capitalize on the new market for office clocks was the E. Howard Co. The first such clock was their *Regulator No.1* . It was a very impressive large timepiece, measuring 50" high. It was driven by a heavy lead weight suspended on a pulley and concealed behind a thin wood board in back of the pendulum, which was mounted on the front of the movement.

The movement was attached to the back of the case. It was of simple design, but was beautifully made, with heavy plates, finely cut wheels and polished pivots. These movements, even after more than 100 years, are remarkably free of wear.

Essentially all office clocks were time only, no strike. Apparently a striking clock would have been considered too distracting. Note that there is only one winding hole in the dial.

The case is of pine with all exterior flat surfaces veneered. The top bezel and bottom door are of solid walnut with a rounded cross-section.

The pendulum consists of a metal strap or rod and a round brass bob with circular grooves in its surface. This is a distinctive feature of clocks made by Howard.

The throat glass and bottom door glass have a solid black background with gold leaf designs. A clear place in the center of the throat glass permits viewing of the pendulum rod. Since it was intended to be visible, the rod was gold leafed. An opening of distinctive pattern in the door glass makes it possible to view the oscillation of the bob.

The dial is painted on relatively heavy sheet steel. It bears the inscription *E. Howard & Co.* and below that *Boston.*

Since the Howard No.1 was simply too large for many offices, the company introduced the No.2 model, which was somewhat smaller, measuring 44" high. This clock became the second in a series of identical design. The No.3 was 38" tall, the No.4, 32" and the No.5, 29"

The smaller sizes were purchased for use in offices and homes, often as wedding presents.

Howard was one of very few manufacturers to make various sizes of the same design.

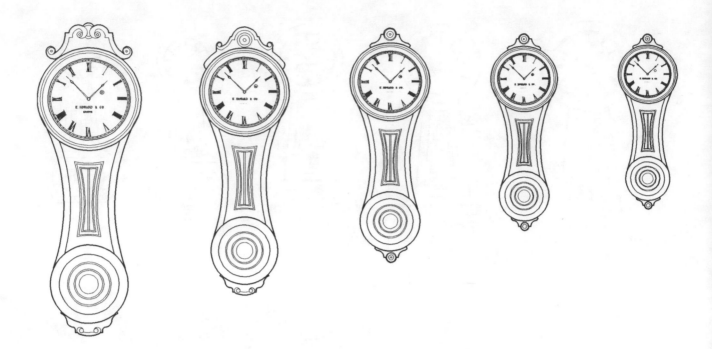

Figure 85   E. Howard & Co. Regulators Nos. 6 through 10
ca. 1874

Using another original and unique design, E. Howard developed a line of regulators numbered from 7 through 10. This is a continuation of the numbering system applied to the box-bottom design shown in Figure 84.

The largest, No.7, measures 58" high. This is eight inches longer than the No.1. The smallest, No. 10, is 33" high, four inches taller than the No.5. All are driven by a heavy lead weight.

Unlike the lower numbered series, the clocks in this one are not truly identical. The top splats of Nos. 6 and 7 are similar, but different in detail and are unlike the lower splats. Both are nicely carved.

Numbers 8, 9 and 10 are identical in design. The top splats, while slightly larger than the bottom ones, are identical in design. The circular design in the center is machine cut into the wood.

This series was equipped with the same time only movements as were used in the lower numbered series. They are of exceptional workmanship for the time and are of very high quality. They are characterized by heavy brass plates, finely machined, hardened and polished pivots, and precision cut wheel teeth.

The curved side, top and bottom pieces forming the case are sawn from solid wood, usually walnut, of very high grade.

The entire front is a door, hinged on the right side and having a push-button snap latch on the left. The solid wood circular segments forming the bezel around the dial and the round frame at the bottom. There are three pieces of glass, one over the dial, one in the throat section and one at the bottom.

The throat and bottom glasses are decorated with black paint and gold leaf. The gold leafed pendulum rod and distinctive Howard pendulum bob, with its engraved concentric circles, may be seen through clear openings in the glass.

This series was very popular and was manufactured well into the twentieth century. The smaller sizes were often presented as wedding gifts.

Figure 86 Ingraham "Ionic" Wall Clock
ca. 1908

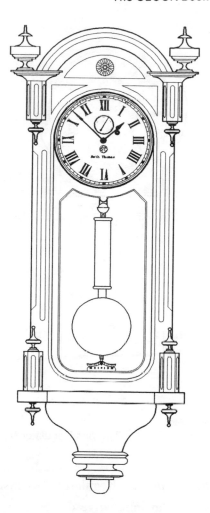

Figure 87 Seth Thomas Regulator No.6
ca. 1884

The *Ionic* design shown in Figure 86 was a new concept, developed in the 1890s by Ingraham. It was essentially an extension of the gallery clock, made by adding a round section at the bottom to accommodate a longer pendulum.

The bezel surrounding the dial, and that forming the lower round door, were both turned from wood. Eight sections were used, each with the grain running parallel to the edges. Originally all the pieces were of the same wood, either varnished or gold leafed. In the example shown, rosewood and a lighter wood, such as ash, were alternated.

The pendulum bob of earlier examples of this model were plain and the lower glass was decorated in black and gold. In this example, the lower glass is clear and an elaborate pendulum bob is visible.

Both the top and bottom doors are hinged at the right and are secured with a hook latch. The two round wood medallions on either side, between the top and bottom doors, are machined. The case is of pine, veneered with walnut or rosewood. The flat section between the top and bottom doors is veneered to match the woods used in the doors.

Adapted from designs of Vienna Regulator clocks that had become very popular in Europe, this model was intended for use in both offices and homes.

The movement is weight driven and essentially the same as that used in the Seth Thomas No.1 Regulator. The front of the case, mostly door, is made of solid wood, usually walnut. Indented designs are machined into the door and turned elements of walnut are added. Solid wood turned finials are provided at the top and bottom of the case.

Note the introduction of a beat scale attached to the backboard, below the pendulum.

The dial is of steel painted white, with black numerals and maker's trademark and name.

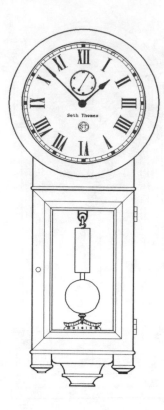

Figure 88   Seth Thomas Regulator No.2

The Seth Thomas Regulator No.2 shown in Figure 88 was an innovative design that achieved great popularity as an office clock. It was seen extensively in railroad stations and in banks, as well as other types of offices and public places.

This model was available in either Oak or Walnut. Both are weight driven. The bezel of both is solid wood.

The dial is of sheet steel, painted white, with black decoration. It boasts a seconds dial, or bit.

The door has a plain glass and is hinged at the right. It is secured by means of a rotating latch, operated through a hole in the left side of the door, by the winding key.

Behind the pendulum, mounted to the back board with small brass nails, is a beat scale. This was mostly decorative, but centering the end of the pendulum on the scale levelled the clock..

This design, with minor modifications,was made for many years by Seth Thomas.

DROP OCTAGON or SCHOOLHOUSE REGULATOR CLOCKS

Late in the 19th century, a clock design with an octagon shape surrounding the dial and having a box below the dial to enclose the pendulum was introduced.

This style was comparatively simple in construction and was relatively inexpensive.

The basic case was a simple pine box, rectangular in shape, except for the bottom. To this box, a pine construction in an octagon shape is attached to the upper portion. The pine is then veneered with oak or walnut and sometimes moldings are added. The dial and bezel are attached to this.

The bezel is of thin sheet brass formed into a molded shape. A single hinge is soldered to the bezel and a tab is soldered to it on the opposite side.. This tab fits through a slot cut in the octagon board and has a notch into which a rotating wood lever fits, to secure the bezel. A round glass fits inside the bezel and is secured with clips soldered to the inside of the bezel.

Dials are of tin plate (steel) painted white and finished with black numerals and other decoration. Later models used paper dials.

The 8-day movements are typical of those produced by Seth Thomas and other manufacturers at the time. They were usually available in time only or strike versions with hammer and coil gong to sound the hours and half hours.

While retaining the shape and proportions of the top intact, a number of variations were employed by various manufacturers, to give a different appearance to the case. Moldings of all conceivable shapes and sizes, made from the same wood as the veneer of the case, were employed.

Pendulum rods were almost always of wood, with a brass hook at the top to fit the suspension rod and an adjusting screw and nut below the bob. The brass bob has a round convex shape.

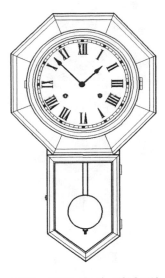

LONG   DROP With MOLDING

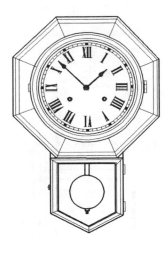

SHORT   DROP With MOLDING

LONG DROP ROUND EDGE

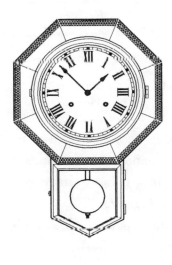

SHORT DROP PRESSED MOLDING

Figure 89   Drop Octagon or School House Regulator Basic Variations
ca. 1885-1920

Drop Octagon clocks came in two basic designs, *long drop*, about 32" high, and *short drop*, around 24" high. The word *drop* refers to the box at the bottom of the clock in which the pendulum bob may be seen. Dials are either 12" or 10". While all of those shown in Figure 89 have a pointed drop, some are square and some are rounded from front to back.

The bottom, or *drop* door is of solid hard wood, hinged and latched. It often is adorned with black and gold designs, but almost always has an opening of sufficient size so that the swinging pendulum bob can be observed. Elaborate bobs, even when they were very popular on other styles, were seldom used for drop octagon clocks.

Clocks of this type were often seen in small business establishments, like grocery and drug stores. Probably the most common location was in schools, where nearly every room had a drop octagon clock. For this reason, they have been tagged with the generic name, *Schoolhouse Regulator Clocks.* Some have *REGULATOR* on the glass.

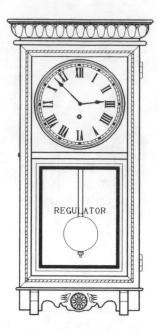

Figure 90 Dry Goods Store Regulator
ca. 1900

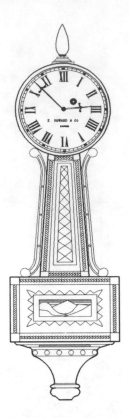

Figure 91 Howard Reproduction of Willard Banjo
ca. 1900

Because the style of clock shown in Figure 90 was frequently found in Dry Goods or General Merchandise stores, it has become known as the *Dry Goods Store Regulator.*

While the term "regulator" is, as we have noted, rather a misnomer, its inference of quality is most misplaced when applied to this model. Although the case is outwardly impressive, the time only movement is nearly always of the least expensive type. It keeps fairly good time, if carefully adjusted, but is far from a precision timepiece.

The box forming the basic case is of pine, with veneered sides. The usually figured cornice at the top, the door and the attached shelf-like base are all of solid wood, usually oak. Pressed designs are common for all decoration.

Measuring around three feet in height, they have dials usually 12" in diameter. Pendulum rods are of wood and the bobs are convex thin brass over lead or pot metal. The word *REGULATOR* is often prominently displayed on the lower glass.

Concurrently with the manufacture of clocks reflecting the unique tastes of the Victorian period, was the rather faithful reproduction of an original weight driven banjo made by the E. Howard Company of Boston.

As we indicated earlier, the Banjo design was manufactured in one form or another for nearly a hundred and fifty years.

The Howard versions were quite faithful *reproductions*, distinguishing them from *copies* or *imitations* of lesser quality made by others.

The clock shown in Figure 91 is taken from an original presentation banjo by Willard. The Brass bezel around the dial is of cast and polished brass, the side arms are of solid brass and all of the wood parts of the case front are gold leafed. Throat and door glass very closely simulate those of Willard clocks, featuring full colors and much gold leaf, hand applied.

Other makers, notably Waterbury, Sessions and Ingraham, also copied Willard banjos.

ENGLISH RAILROAD
STATION CLOCK
ca. 1890

WESTERN UNION
TELEGRAPH OFFICE CLOCK
ca. 1920

POSTAL TELEGRAPH
OFFICE CLOCK
ca. 1930

EASTERN AIRLINES
STATION CLOCK
ca. 1933

Figure 92 Round Commercial Wall Clocks
ca. 1890 - 1933

The railroads were among the first industries to find that accurate time was essential to safe and efficient operation. In England, a very fine type of clock movement was developed and used in railway stations by both company personnel and passengers. Shown on the left in Figure 92, this type featured a very rugged, yet precise spring driven fusee movement that ran for eight days. The *fusee* is a device that equalizes the force delivered to the movement by the spring as it unwinds.

The movement is housed in a simple box attached to the back of the large, round dial piece. This dial piece is of heavy hardwood, usually walnut, and supports the painted steel dial and heavy brass bezel with its round glass. The dials are from 10 to 12 inches in diameter. Some of these clocks were in railroad service for well over fifty years.

The *telegraph* was the fastest means of communication at this time. It was used extensively by railroads, from whose stations the general public could also send messages. Soon two major commercial telegraph organizations, Western Union and Postal Telegraph were organized. Around the time of World War I, they had offices in every city of any size in the United States.

One of the features of these offices was a large wall clock that told accurate time. Initially, like the railroads, a central office maintained a highly accurate weight driven clock. This clock was used at predetermined intervals to send a time signal to all stations on line. Based on this signal, local clocks were reset to the *official Western Union* or *Postal Telegraph* time. The second clock in Figure 92 is a spring driven one which was reset periodically by the local manager. It was not long before the signal itself energized an internal mechanism to simultaneously reset each clock down the line.

The third clock, a *Postal Telegraph* model, boasts on its dial face that it displays *Synchronous Electric Time*. This is a tribute to the technology that had been developed to insure the accuracy of electric power generators so that accurate time keeping could be based on the pulses of their current output. Telegraph clocks had metal and, later, *bakelite* plastic cases.

When the fledgling airline industry started in the 1930 era, there were few true airports. Most landing sites were simply fields in open country, with a small shack or *station*. The last clock in Figure 92 is a comparatively small standard model synchronous wall clock used by Eastern Airlines at its stations. Since airlines operated on 24-hour military time, a standard dial was modified by adding red numbers from 13 to 24 on an inner ring.

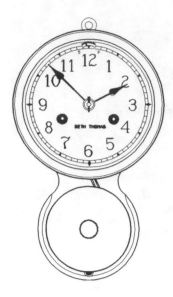

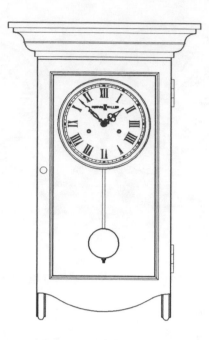

Figure 93   Seth Thomas Striking Ship's Clock
ca 1930

Figure 94   Howard Miller "Manchester" Wall Clock

Clocks used aboard ships of all kinds and commercial passenger, cargo and tow boats on the Inland Waterways of the United States use clocks striking the time in traditional ship's bell fashion.

In the days of sail, when it was necessary to have adequate manpower available at all times to tend to the handling of the ship, crews were divided in half, each called a *watch*, one *port* and one *starboard*. Each watch was on duty for a four hour period, when it was replaced by the other watch. For this reason, time at sea is told in divisions of the four hour watch.

Each half hour is marked by the sounding of a bell. For a watch starting at noon or midnight, at 12:30, one bell is sounded, indicating the first half hour of the watch has passed. At one o'clock, two strokes of the bell are sounded. At one-thirty there are two strokes, a slight pause and then one more stroke, indicating three bells. One bell is added every half hour. At two o'clock, (four bells) there are two strokes followed by a pause, then two more. At the end of the watch, four, eight, or twelve o'clock, four double strikes (eight bells) indicates the end of the four hour watch.

Even at the time of this writing, all sorts of case styles are made from and sold by current purveyors.

Clock companies that exist in this country today, except for an occasional low-volume operation, are not true clock manufacturers because they make neither the case nor the movement for the clocks that bear their name.

For a number of years, even when familiar traditional names like Seth Thomas appear on the dial of a clock, the movement and or case for that clock was most probably produced abroad, at one or more locations.

At this writing, nearly all mechanical clock movements are made in Germany. Quartz movements are usually produced in Germany, Switzerland, Japan, Korea or other oriental countries.

The clock shown in Figure 94 is an example of today's mechanical clock making. The movement was made in Germany. The case was probably made by an American furniture manufacturer. The movement was inserted by Howard Miller. In 1993, this clock was on sale for $269.00.

CHAPTER FOURTEEN

MANTEL, TABLE and ALARM CLOCKS

AMONG THE MOST POPULAR clocks ever in the American market are those we will look at in this chapter. Made during the period from the Victorian era of the 1890's to just before the beginning of World War II in 1939, they were produced during the heyday of the American clock industry.

Many millions of these clocks were made and millions of them were junked in favor of electric clocks, but millions remain in American homes as treasured heirlooms once owned by earlier members of the family.

FLAT TOP or BLACK Clocks

One of the styles of clocks in this category is based on clock cases made in France and Italy of various types of stone, ranging from marble in all colors to almost pure white alabaster to black onyx They are known as *Blacks or Flat Tops.*

The French, enamored of classical art and particularly sculptural representations, had combined marble, alabaster, or onyx with fire-gilt ormolu to produce very intricate and beautiful clock cases, in which the dial was so subordinated as to be almost indistinguishable.

All of these elaborate timepieces were essentially a simple box made of stone, in which the movement was housed. For practical, rather than aesthetic reasons, nearly all French mantle and table

clock movements are round. The dial and bezel are firmly attached to the movement and another bezel with a door, similar to, but simpler than the dial bezel is provided for the back. The bezels fit into large holes in the front and back of the case. Two brass strap arms attached to the front bezel have a bend at the end in which is a threaded hole. Long screws passed through holes in the rear bezel are screwed into these holes to secure the movement and both bezels to the case.

During the late 19th century, many of these stone case French clocks, complete with French made movements were imported into the United States. Cost was high because of losses due to damage to the brittle stone cases, their very heavy weight and damage to the movements by salt laden air during transport in the holds of ships.

. American manufacturers were not happy with this intrusion into their home market and set out to overcome it.

For a time, American manufacturers imported stone cases and added their own movements, dials, bezels, and other decorative hardware. This proved not to be the solution.

Producers in the American stone industry were found who contracted to make cases of marble, alabaster and slate, into which the clock manufacturers inserted movements. This arrangement was a fair stopgap measure, but was still comparatively expensive. Eventually a new class of clocks was

BASIC BLACK CASE

STRAIGHT LINE BLACK CASE

CURVED LINE BLACK CASE

Figure 95 Black or *Flat Top* Stone Clocks
ca. 1890

developed, based on the French style, but employing wood, iron and even *bakelite*, the first structurally strong and dimensionally stable plastic. Initially, cases made of wood painted black were made. Shortly thereafter, iron cases appeared.

Wood and iron cases resulted in lower costs and met with great favor among the buying public. Soon French clocks almost disappeared from the American market.

Because it is difficult to carve stone, so difficult as to be uneconomical for clock cases destined to be sold in a highly competitive market, designs were relatively simple.

All elements were made of flat slabs of stone about 3/8" thick. Edge molding was done on planing machines. Curves could be machine cut in the slabs and were used to a limited extent.

Stone for clock cases was sawed to the desired thickness from large blocks of quarried rough stone. The resulting slabs were than polished on one side. Individual pieces for each design of case were then sawed to shape. Large round holes were milled in the front and back pieces to accept the front and back bezels of the movement.

Intaglio, or shallow incised designs were machined into some of the front pieces and were then painted gold, silver or white.

Some cases employed stone of different colors and patterns, often combining colorful marble and black onyx.

There was an almost infinite variety of individual designs for these cases. Three representative ones

are illustrated in Figure 95, showing some basic design distinctions.

The case on the left and the elements of which it is constructed, are essentially rectangular. The only curves are in the molding of the edges of the top piece. This is the basic style and was made in the largest quantities by all manufacturers.

The second case, while still generally rectangular in appearance, has some relief from straight vertical and horizontal lines by the addition of a low rooflike top, providing molding not only at the top and rounding of the roof edges, but molding the pediment piece that rests on the base. The base itself has been cut out, with rounded corners. Feet are sometimes provided, as shown.

Another variation from the basic design is in the separate front side pieces, which are set back from the center piece. This adds significantly to the overall attractiveness of the case.

The case on the right shows the use of stone pieces cut into interesting curved shapes. The top splat is severely simple but, using the familiar swan neck design found in tall clocks, has a certain elegance of shape. It is decorated with a simple incised design.

The front side panels are intaglio decorated, like the straight line case. There was an infinite variety in these designs.

The bottom piece is shaped into a graceful curve, reminiscent of the Pillar and Scroll clock bases.

Any or all of these case types might have been made in France, Italy, or other European countries

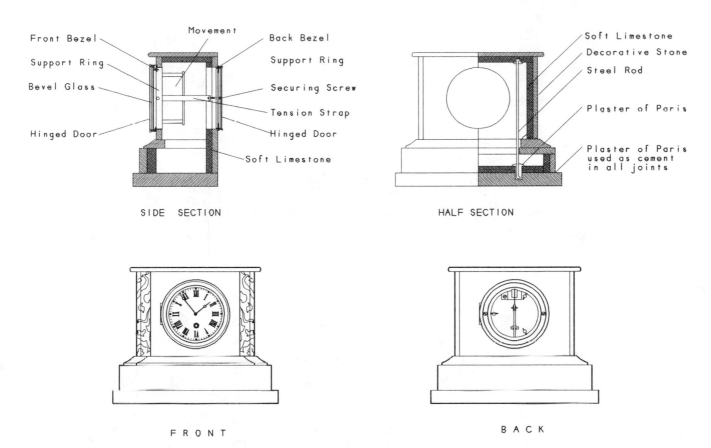

Figure 96 Stone Clock Case Construction

with suitable deposits of stone. They might also have been made in the United States. There is little obvious difference to distinguish one from the other.

Countless variations of these basic designs were generated. Because of their great weight, it is surprising that so many of them were sold. A number have survived and are true heirlooms in many American homes. Because of the brittleness of the stone, it is not uncommon to find broken corners and chipped edges. The surface polish of many has been damaged during misguided cleaning efforts.

STONE CASE CONSTRUCTION

The drawings in Figure 96 illustrate significant details of how stone cases are constructed. The front and back views of this case show the outward appearance of the case. This particular case uses strips of colorful marble on each side of the front.

The front bezel around the porcelain dial is of polished cast brass and is fitted with a beveled glass to protect the dial.

The rear bezel, although usually made of thin sheet brass, with decorative perforations, in this case carries a beveled glass that allows the movement and pendulum rod to be seen. The screw heads seen on either side secure the two bezels and movement to the case. Both the front and back bezels are hinged to allow setting of the hands, or movement of the pendulum rod.

The *Side Section* drawing is a cutaway view that shows how the front and back bezel support rings fit into circular holes in the stone slabs forming the front and back of the case. A brass tension strap attached to the front bezel support ring has a 90 degree bend at the back end with a threaded hole into which a long screw is threaded to secure the back bezel.

All elements of the case are flat slabs of stone. To provide additional structural stability, slabs of

LINTEL

POT METAL CAPITOL
Design Varies

COLUMN
Design, Material
and Finish Varies

POT METAL BASE
Design Varies

POT METAL FEET
Design Varies

MOLDED EDGE
Shape Varies

METAL DECORATION
Lion's Head and
Ring Common

SHELF - May be
Molded

BASE - Top Edge
May be Molded

Figure 97 Elements of Typical Wood *Black* or *Flat Top* Case

soft limestone back up the decorative stone. The elements between the front face and the base and the rounded edge of the top slab are shaped, or molded.

Plaster of Paris is used as a cementing agent at all joints, between the limestone and marble slabs and to secure the iron rods securing the top to the bottom.

Figure 97 is an example of a wood case in the *Black* or *Flat Top* style. The basic clock case is constructed of pine, using conventional cabinet making techniques, including nails and glue.

Before assembly, the final finish was applied to nearly all pieces forming the front, sides and top. For clocks with a plain black finish, the finish was a heavy asphaltum paint. For those with a simulated marble, or *Adamantine* finish the marbleized surface was of cellulose acetate, or *celluloid*. This was a thin film made by dropping various colors of liquid celluloid onto water, then gently stirring to mix them in a marble-like pattern. The resulting film

was then applied to the wood of the case.

This same technique, with modifications in blending the colors, was used to create simulated wood finishes that were also very popular.

Cellulose acetate (*celluloid*) is very soft and easily marred. It is also damaged by heat, first shriveling and then likely to burst into flame, under intense heat. It will be severely disfigured by solvents such as alcohol.

Because of its relative fragility, most of the surviving clock cases bearing adamantine finishes have scars or blemishes.

Most flat top cases are decorated with columns on either side of the dial. While two was common, there might be from one to four columns in each set. Columns are made of wood, painted to resemble marble, marbleized celluloid, or thin fluted sheet brass. Capitols and bases are of gilded pot metal and vary from rather plain to classic Greek orders.

Case feet are of gilded cast pot metal. The front ones are usually quite elaborate and, while similar at

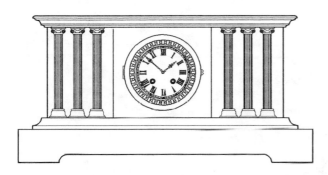
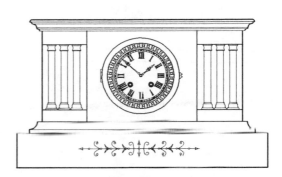

Figure 98 Basic Flat Top (*or Black*) Case Styles

first glance, exhibit great variety in detail. The rear feet are generally very simple supports. All of the feet have a flat, horizontal section with holes, through which nails secure them to the case bottom.

Often, decorative gilded medallions in the form of lions heads with a ring in the mouth, or just scroll designs, are attached by nails to the sides of the case.

IRON and BAKELITE Flat Top Cases

Toward the end of the period in which the flat top style was popular, some cases were made of thin cast iron and some of the first structural plastic, *Bakelite.* In outward appearance they were very similar to those made of wood. Comparatively few Cast Iron cases were made and even fewer Bakelite cases were produced.

Iron cases were little more than 1/8" thick in most areas and were an outstanding example of the iron founder's skills. Individual elements are fastened to each other by screws and nuts. Cast in fine sand molds, there were small pits in the castings. A heavy paint primer filled these imperfections and provided a smooth undercoat for the final finish, black enamel or asphaltum..

Figure 98 illustrates some basic style variations of Black or *Flat Top* clock cases. These and many more modifications are found in clocks made of any of the materials we have mentioned.

The clock at the upper left of Figure 98 is very much like early stone clocks. The bottom of the base is flat and has an incised decoration on its front. Such decorations in black clocks were usually filled with white paint, although a few were gold.

The cast brass bezel and dial are mounted on a rectangular surface that projects out from the case front. This was a common characteristic of black clock cases. Columns are mounted on either side. The end decorations in this case are scrolls. A cast metal scroll is attached to each side.

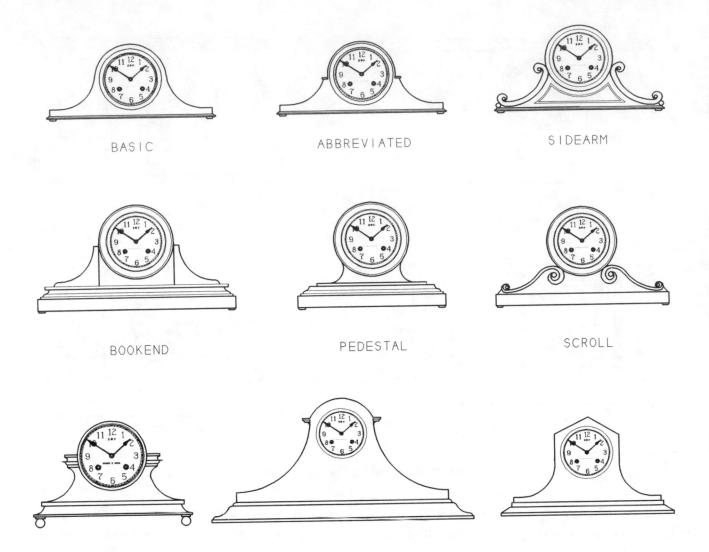

BASIC   ABBREVIATED   SIDEARM

BOOKEND   PEDESTAL   SCROLL

Figure 99 Tambour Case Style Variations

In the upper right of Figure 98 is a case similar to the first, but with lion's head decorations on either side, a cutout arch above the painted wood columns and with the base cut out to form feet. The bezel is a plain ring of thin sheet brass.

The clock at the lower left of Figure 98 is longer than the others, has three fluted brass columns on either side, and features elaborate Corinthian capitols. There are no decorative elements on the sides. Note the sharp square corners at the top of the base.

The last clock has three celluloid columns on either side of an elaborate bezel. It is unique in that the columns rest on a plain base at the bottom and have a similar rectangular piece at the top. There are no decorations on the sides.

TAMBOUR CASE CLOCKS

Sometimes referred to as *humpback or camelback* clocks, Tambour cases are defined by their wide bases and elevated, dominant dial. Figure 99 illustrates some of the many variations of this style.

By far the most commonly found shape today is the simply curved one shown at the upper left. The other styles are self-explanatory.

Tambour cases were made by nearly every manufacturer of clocks. Typically, the movement has stamped sheet metal feet attached to the front plate. Through holes in these feet, the movement is attached to the inside of the case front with wood screws. Bezels are formed of thin sheet brass with a single hinge and convex glass.

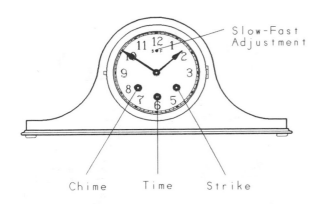

Figure 100 Chiming Tambour Clock

Figure 101 Howard Miller *Matthew* Tambour
ca. 1993

Figure 102 Howard Miller *Worthington* Tambour
ca. 1994

Most tambour clocks strike the hours and half hours on a coil gong attached to an iron post that is bolted to the bottom of the case. Some have one or two chime bars mounted on the base board. Two bars are used for a two-tone or *bim-bam* strike.

While not illustrated here, Westminster chiming movements were also installed in these cases. The chimes and the hour are struck on chime rods mounted in a cast iron base attached to the case bottom with screws.

Nearly all tambour cases are made of pine and are veneered, usually with mahogany. Moldings and scrolls are of solid wood, matching the veneer.

The Tambour design was popular for many years. Introduced around 1920, it was manufactured continuously right up to the present day. German makers exported many to this country. They are still being made today.

Tambour clocks with Westminster Chimes were quite popular. As it happens, the Tambour case style usually produces a very pleasing resonating tone when chimes are struck.

Usually, there are five bars on which the chimes and hour are struck. The Westminster Chime melody requires four notes, so four rods are provided for this. The hourly strike is struck on the fifth bar, which is lower in tone, plus one of the other bars. Occasionally, there are seven chime rods, three of which are used to sound the hours.

Chiming movements have three trains, one for the chime, one for time, and one for the strike. The

strike will not function unless the chime train has tolled the last portion of the Westminster melody at the hour. It then releases the strike train to sound the hour.

Some clocks have a lever in a slot on the dial that has a *Silent* position for eliminating chiming and striking.

Nearly all Tambour clocks may be adjusted from the front, by inserting the small end of a double ended key into the hole at the top of the dial and turning it toward either *S* or *F*. This will cause the clock to run slower or faster.

Only slight movement is necessary. A quarter turn at a time is recommended. The clock should be allowed to run for about 24 hours, then further adjustments made as necessary. Gain or loss of less than a minute a week is possible.

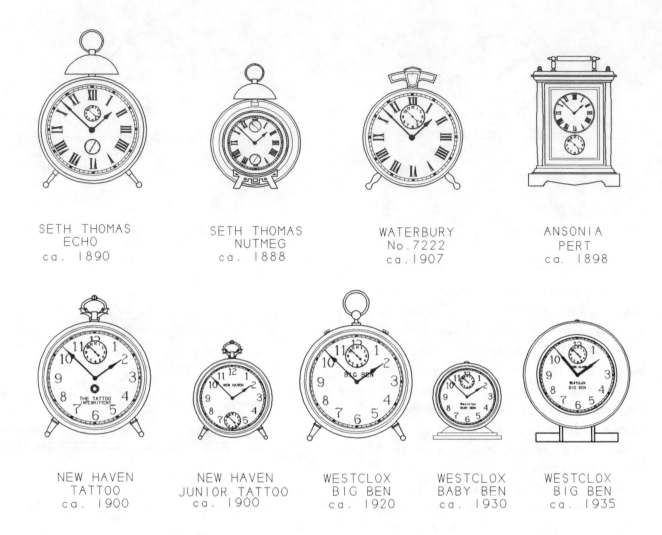

SETH THOMAS
ECHO
ca. 1890

SETH THOMAS
NUTMEG
ca. 1888

WATERBURY
No.7222
ca.1907

ANSONIA
PERT
ca. 1898

NEW HAVEN
TATTOO
ca. 1900

NEW HAVEN
JUNIOR TATTOO
ca. 1900

WESTCLOX
BIG BEN
ca. 1920

WESTCLOX
BABY BEN
ca. 1930

WESTCLOX
BIG BEN
ca. 1935

Figure 103   Representative Alarm Clocks
ca. 1888 - 1935

Attesting to the popularity of the Tambour style over a period of nearly a century, are these recent clocks, sold under the Howard Miller name. Both have German mechanical movements, although similar cases are equipped with battery operated Quartz movements.

A number of clock makers have used the tambour style over the years. While made for a brief time in Korea, most current tambour clocks have German mechanical movements in American-made cases.

Battery operated quartz movements with electronic Westminster chimes have been used in tambour cases in recent years. While they produce a recognizable melody, they do not yet approach the resonance and tone characteristic of mechanical movements striking chime bars.

ALARM CLOCKS

As we have noted, alarm attachments were added to weight driven clocks early in the nineteenth century and were available in Kitchen clocks during the entire period of their manufacture.

Around 1880, a new class of clocks, designed specifically for waking people in the morning, emerged. Alarm clock cases were originally made of thin brass, nickel plated. Later models were made of sheet steel, painted or nickel plated. Cases were little more than a housing for the movement and

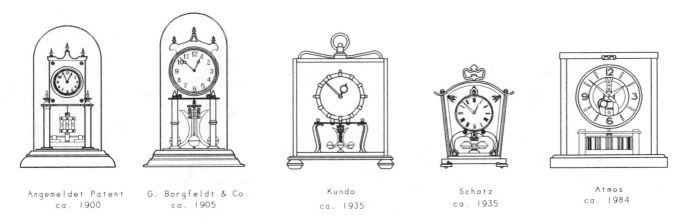

Angemeldet Patent
ca. 1900

G. Borgfeldt & Co.
ca. 1905

Kundo
ca. 1935

Schatz
ca. 1935

Atmos
ca. 1984

Figure 104 Rotary Pendulum (*400-Day or Anniversary*) Clocks
ca. 1900 - 1984

dial and were comparatively small. They fit nicely on a bed table, where they were viewed from close range.

Early mechanical alarm clocks and even some later ones, had one or two bells mounted on the top. Hammers striking these bells in rapid succession produced a loud ringing noise that woke even the soundest sleeper. They were equipped with a stop to shut off the alarm. Later models used the shell of the case as the alarm bell.

Designed to be easily moved from place to place, many have a ring or other device at the top that is used as a carrying handle.

Some, as the Ansonia *Pert* in Figure 103, copied the design of French Carriage Clocks.

Many alarm clocks have the numerals and hands painted with a luminescent paint that made them visible in the dark. This paint contained radioactive materials and was discontinued when the danger to workers exposed for long periods of time became known. Non-radioactive materials were substituted.

Dials are usually of paper, but some were plated metal. Time of alarm is usually indicated by a small hand and dial on the face of the clock dial.. Time and alarm were set using knobs in the back of the case.

A few early alarm clocks were equipped with seconds bits, a small dial and hand making one revolution a minute.

Almost all alarm clocks have a shutoff device to silence the alarm. This is either a button or a lever conveniently located..

ROTARY PENDULUM 400 DAY CLOCKS

Rotary pendulum clocks made in Germany began to appear in quantity in the United States around 1900. Sometimes called *Anniversary* clocks because they will run about 400 days on one winding and can thus be wound once a year, on an anniversary date, were very popular wedding gifts.

Their pendulums rotate slowly, back and forth and are fascinating to watch. In addition to the pendulum, these clocks are often characterized by a glass dome protecting the exposed highly polished brass movement.

All clocks of this type have a comparatively heavy pendulum bob assembly suspended on a very fine strip steel spring. The size, length and composition of this spring define the approximate rate of rotation of the bob. Finer adjustment is provided as part of the bob assembly. The earliest bobs of this type of clock were a solid brass disk with additional balance weights that could be moved in or out to finely adjust the rate of rotation. Later bobs were intricately contrived and included balls that could be adjusted in or out to adjust the rate.

Near the top of the suspension wire a tiny fork is attached. This fork straddles a small rod attached to the escapement anchor. As the bob is manually rotated to start the clock, the suspension wire is twisted so that the fork allows the anchor to move to release a tooth of the escape wheel. Power applied to the escape wheel by the main spring provides a slight push to the anchor and its pro

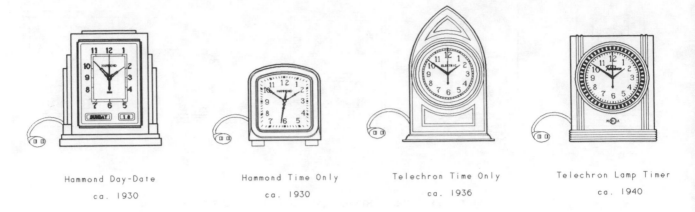

Hammond Day-Date
ca. 1930

Hammond Time Only
ca. 1930

Telechron Time Only
ca. 1936

Telechron Lamp Timer
ca. 1940

Figure 105 Synchronous Electric Table Clocks
ca. 1930 - 1940

jecting pin, which is then transferred through the fork to the suspension wire, giving it an impulse in the opposite direction from which it had last moved.

The suspension wire is supported by a split hooked block at the top. At the bottom is a similar block with a hook that supports the bob. This wire is extremely delicate and is easily twisted or broken. These are the most common causes of trouble in rotary pendulum clocks.

ELECTRIC TABLE CLOCKS

Synchronous electric clocks, featured small electric motors whose speed was synchronized with that of the generators at the electric power source. The run at a speed governed by the pulses or oscillations in alternating current.

The motor speed was reduced by a series of gears to a much slower output speed. The motor and all or most of this gear train were often housed in a sealed metal case. Second hands were common on electric clocks of all kinds, to not only indicate the passage of seconds, but to provide visible evidence that the clock was running.

Earlier synchronous movements are not self-starting. They require an impulse, in the form of a slight push on a lever on the back or bottom of the clock, to get them started. Later, synchronous motors were self starting and began running as

soon as power is supplied. This feature greatly simplified their use.

The first clock in Figure 105 was made by the Hammond Electric Clock Co. It is housed in a *bekelite* case and is found in both black and brown. I features windows that display the day and date. Manual resetting is required when months have less than 31 days. Time, day and date are set by means of knobs at the back of the case. There is no alarm.

The second clock, also made by Hammond is a small time-only table, desk, or boudoir model. It has a *bakelite* case, usually brown in color.

The third clock is a somewhat larger desk or table model made by the Telechron Company. It is time only. Its somewhat classical design is very different from other clocks of the period that usually reflect the public taste for *moderne* style. It has a second hand and setting knobs on the back.

The clock on the far right of Figure 105 is a special purpose clock designed to turn a lamp on or off, at preset intervals, in addition to telling the time.

An outlet on its back is used to plug in the lamp to be controlled. This outlet is switched on or off on a schedule set by the owner.

Around the perimeter of the dial are a series of tabs that can pulled out or pushed in. When a tab is pulled out, it is active and will turn the clock outlet *ON* or *OFF*. To turn the lamp on at 7:00 o'clock, the tab at that time on the dial is pulled out. To

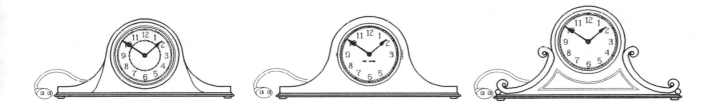

Figure 106 Synchronous Electric Tambour Clocks
ca. 1935

turn the lamp off at 10:00 o'clock, the tab at that hour is pulled out. The clock will then automatically turn the clock outlet *ON* at 7:00 and *OFF* at 10:00 o'clock.

More than one *ON-OFF* period may be designated. The first pin in a series will turn the outlet *ON*, the next will turn it *OFF*, the next will again turn it *ON* and the next will turn it *OFF*.

A toggle switch at the bottom of the clock, with *A* and *M* markings selects between *Automatic* control by the clock and *Manual* operation. By the owner.

When very small synchronous electric motors became available, clock manufacturers scrambled to utilize them as quickly as possible.

Demonstrating their eagerness to adopt this new technology, clock manufacturers first saw them simply as a source of power to replace springs. The earliest electric powered tambour clocks employed the same basic movements that had been used in tambour clocks for some years, except that electric motors replaced the main springs.

These motors are encased with a series of gears that greatly reduce the speed of the synchronous motor. The output shaft mounts a pinion gear that engages with the wheels of the mechanical movement to power it. There is usually a motor for the time train and a separate one for the chime or strike trains.

In some instances, the electric motors were attached to the movement and simply wound the springs of the mechanical movement, eliminating the need for manual winding.

Very soon, synchronous motors became available with gear trains that produced an output speed of one revolution per minute. When fitted to a simple set of gears, this drove the second, minute and hour hands of the clocks.

Established clock manufacturers purchased electric motors from firms who made them. Some motor manufacturers, notably Hammond and Telechron, entered the clock business, offering complete electric clocks for sale to the public.

Within a few years, electric clocks of all kinds came to dominate the market and soon mechanical clocks were considered obsolete.

The Tambour case style, however continued on and is currently available with either German mechanical movements, or battery operated quartz movements.

Figure 106 illustrates three of the many Tambour variations produced with electric movements. The basic plain design is shown in the middle, with two variations on either side.

ATMOS PERPETUAL CLOCKS

Made in Switzerland, these ingenious clocks have been manufactured in much the same form for over half a century. They are still being made in 1996. In theory, Atmos clocks, after the first winding will continue to run indefinitely, even for years.

A rather large aneroid bellows made of very thin metal contains a gas that expands and contracts with very minor changes in temperature of the air around it. This causes the bellows to move in or out. A chain attached to the front center of the bellows and in turn to a ratchet on the main spring arbor transmits the motion of the bellows to wind the spring, a very slight amount with each change of temperature. This keeps the spring wound and the clock functioning.

Since no manual winding is required, Atmos clocks approach the long -saught goal of *perpetual motion.* In point of fact, however, they aquire energy on an intermittent basis from variations in ambient temperature.

Atmos clocks are very finely made and all brass parts are usually electroplated with gold. The glass of the case is heavy and the edges are beveled and polished. In every respect, they are of the highest quality.

Over the years, these clocks have been given as anniversary, wedding or retirement gifts.

Figure 107   Representative *Atmos* Clock

CHAPTER FIFTEEN

TALL CLOCKS

(Grandfather and Grandmother)

IT IS SURPRISING HOW MANY American homes, even very modest ones, boast a Tall Clock. Until the famous poem *Grandfather's Clock,* clocks that stood on the floor and were from about five to more than eight feet In height were known collectively as *Tall* clocks. That poem, about the close relationship between an old man and his tall clock, caused nearly everyone to think of any Tall clock as a *Grandfather.*

It is probable that the stately quarter-hour bar chimes of most of these clocks, with their characteristic deep resonance, along with their impressive cases, is what makes them so popular today.

Today, clocks that are between five and six feet tall are generally referred to as *Grandmothers* while those over six feet are called *Grandfather.*

Most furniture stores and many specialized clock shops today sell Tall Clocks. Many are sold by mail order. Wood Tall clock case kits, consisting of precut wood parts and a German spring or weight driven movement, are extensively advertised and sold by mail.

Emperor Clock Co. of Fairhope, Alabama, was one of the first quantity marketers of comparatively inexpensive tall clocks in both Grandmother or Grandfather size. They sell kits as well as finished cases and completed clocks with imported movements. Other clock companies, often furniture manufacturers, have entered this market, making cases and installing imported movements.

Most were unable to operate successfully for any length of time.

Some enterprising do-it-yourselfers buy Tall clock kits, assemble them and install German movements, then offer them for sale. They often work from rural homes along major highways, where they advertise on billboards.

There are several companies selling Tall clocks with finer cases and movements. Among the oldest of these is the Howard Miller Co. of Zeeland, Michigan. They currently assemble and market a full line of high quality clocks of all kinds, from small mantel to large, elaborate Tall clocks. Retail prices of high quality tall clocks currently range from around $1000.00 to $3, 000. These clocks are to be found nationwide.

It is a common practice for marketers of clocks to buy solid wood cases from furniture manufacturers, based on competitive bids. Movements of very good to sometimes poor quality are purchased in Germany and installed in the cases. These movements may be spring driven, in the cheaper versions, or weight driven. Some early clocks by these companies had American made movements.

Weights are sometimes suspended on chains running on sprockets in the movement and are pulled up by a tab at one end of the chain, to wind the clock. No winding holes appear on the dial face.

In better quality clocks, the movements often have cables to support the weights. These cables are wrapped on drums in the movement. Each drum has a winding arbor and a matching hole appears in the dial face. Winding is accomplished with a key crank to turn the drum and raise the weight.

While less expensive Tall clocks usually chime the *Westminster* melody, more expensive ones usually allow the owner to select any one of three tunes, *Whittington, St. Michael or Westminster.*

Usually, chimes and hours are struck by hammers activated by separated trains in the movement, striking tuned rods. These rods are screwed into iron mounting blocks that are attached to the case. The rods are usually oriented in a vertical or near vertical plane.

Chime hammers are selectively lifted and dropped by lobes on a rotating drum powered by the chime train engaging extensions on each hammer in the prescribed order.

Each of the melodies has four parts. At quarter past the hour, the first part of the melody plays. At half past the hour, an additional part of equal length is added. Other segments are added at the three quarter and hour points. In this way, a recognizable tune indicates which quarter hour is being chimed.

The simplest of these melodies, the *Westminster,* uses only four notes. In the least expensive movements, only four rods are provided to generate the chime. At the hour, two of the rods are struck simultaneously to toll the number of the hour.

To the basic four rod set, an additional bar or bars may be added to enable a deeper, more melodic strike sound. The strike train, at the hour, activates a lever that lifts and drops one or more of the chime hammers to sound the hour.

The *Whittington* and *St. Michael* chime melodies are more complex and require eight notes. Thus, eight rods are required. Most triple chime movements have a separate set of hammers that strike the hours on a separate set of four or more rods.

Tubular chimes are suspended on cords at the back of the case and are struck by hammers, similar to those used with rods.

Movements may be stamped on the back plate with the name of the German manufacturer, and may have a legend something like *Made in Germany*

for .... Clock Company. If the movement is made in the United States, that designation will be shown.

Since those individually made by hand in colonial times, tall clocks have been produced by nearly every clock maker and most mass production manufacturers of clocks. Since very few of the hand-made variety were produced, and most of those are in museums or private collections, they are not often found in ordinary homes.

Even those made by mass-production manufacturers were comparatively expensive produced only in limited quantities, they are scarce and are highly prized by collectors. A number of these, designed for use in banks, clubs, mansions and other places with very high ceilings, were more than eight feet tall and would not fit in most homes today.

Some of the finest mass produced Tall clocks were made by the Herschede Hall Clock Company of Cincinnati, Ohio. Their top line clocks featured tubular chimes of special bronze or brass alloy that produced exceptionally full and resonant tone. No longer in business, Herschede clocks are highly prized by collectors. For most of its existence, Herschede manufactured its own high quality movements. Later, it purchased them from others.

Some enterprising importers, who capitalized on the low cost output of the short lived Korean clock industry and sold millions of their American clock replicas, continued to sell clocks with cases made in Korea and movements made in Germany. Their Tall Clocks are similar to those of other contemporary clock companies and are similarly priced.

Most of the better quality Tall Clocks currently available at retail outlets are designed so that their movements may be serviced with reasonable ease. Easily removable panels on either side of the hood give access to the sides of the movement and the hands and dial can be removed to expose the front of the movement.

Clocks of lesser quality have access to the movement only via a removable panel at the rear of the hood. To service the movement, the case must be moved so that the rear is accessible and the movement must be removed from the case. This is difficult, time consuming and expensive.

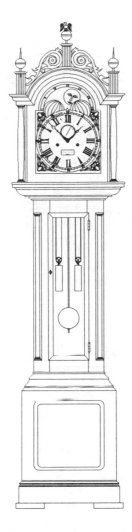

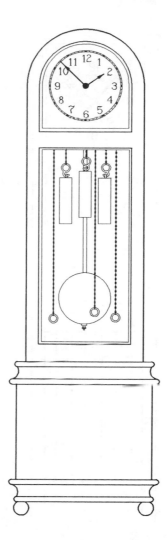

Figure 108   E. Howard Tall Clock
ca. 1890

Figure 109   German Tall Clock
ca. 1920

The Howard Company, while noted for its wall clocks, also produced other styles, including Tall clocks. The one shown in Figure 107 rather faithfully follows the traditional style and proportions of late 18th century clock makers. In place of the solid waist door of the earlier clocks, Howard used a door with a glass panel, exposing the weights and pendulum to view. The weights were of lead with polished brass shells.

The dial of this clock is of silvered brass with black enamel numerals. It boasts a seconds bit and a separate engraved name plate, inscribed with *E. Howard, Boston.* It has a moving moon phase dial with numerals indicating the 29½ day moon cycle.

Hours and half hours are struck on a large coil gong.

The German clock industry continued to strive to penetrate the American market and in the 1920s met with some success. The very plain, boxy style adopted by German case makers for wall, mantel and tall clocks appealed to the American tastes of the *Roaring Twenties*.

The clock shown in Figure 108 is representative. It has three trains and chimes Westminster quarter hours and strikes the hours. Other clocks, similar in appearance, had two trains and only struck the hours and half hours, often on a large coil gong. Still others, known as *bim-bam* strikers, have a two tone strike at each hour. Typically, the tone of all chime and strike systems is very resonant.

Movements of these clocks are large, heavy and well made.

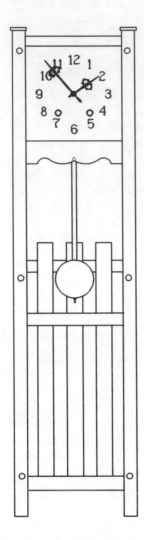

Figure 110   New Haven Mission Style Tall Clock
ca. 1920

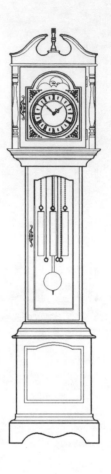

Figure 111   Emperor Grandmother Tall Clock
ca. 1976

Usually made of dark oak, Tall clocks in the mission style could hardly be said to have cases. The movement is supported on a scaffold-like framework of flat, often rough boards. This appears more like the work of a carpenter than a cabinet maker.

The clock in Figure 109 is representative. Vertical slats in front are shorter than those in the back, so that the view of the pendulum is unobstructed. Horizontal slats attached to the corner posts support the vertical pieces.

The dial is a single thin piece of rough-finished oak to which are applied cast brass numerals.

The 8-day movement is typical of those commonly used in all types of clocks of this period.

Hours and half hours are struck on a coil gong.

One of the clock makers to capitalize on the burgeoning *do-it-yourself* market of the seventies was the Emperor Clock Company of Fairhope, Georgia. Advertising in magazines such as *Popular Mechanics* and *Popular Science*, it offered kits of clock case parts to be assembled and finished by the buyer. It also supplied German movements. Finished clocks with movements installed were also available.

Emperor clocks are still available at this writing. These cases, in limited styles and of less than superior quality, are satisfactory time keepers and make it possible for many people to own an affordable Tall clock.

The *Grandmother* size, shown in Figure 111 is the most popular Emperor model.

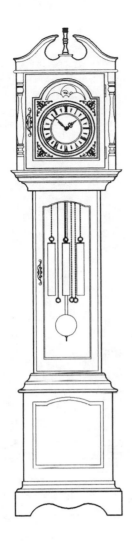

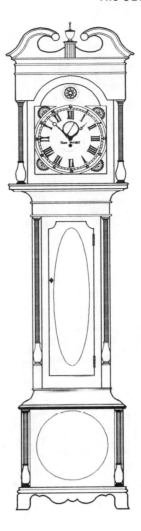

Figure 112 Emperor Grandfather Style Tall Clock
ca.1980

Figure 113 *Thomas Jefferson* Tall Clock
by Franklin Mint   ca. 1986

The Grandfather Tall clock shown in Figure 112 is almost identical the Grandmother in Figure 111, except that it is taller.

The 8-day German movements supplied by Emperor are of various types. Some are equipped with triple chime mechanisms that enable the owner to select Whittington, St. Michael or Westminster melodies. Others have only Westminster Chimes.

Some have moving moon dials above the regular dial, while others simply have a globe with the words *Tempus Fugit* (Time Flies) inscribed on it.

Essentially all Emperor-supplied movements are chain-driven. The clock is wound by pulling the end of the chain opposite the weight, to raise the weight.

An elegant and expensive Tall clock, designated as the *Thomas Jefferson*, was offered by the Franklin Mint through advertising in slick publications, such as *National Geographic* and by direct mail.

This clock, unlike other contemporary Tall clocks, employs beautifully selected and matched walnut burl veneers to produce a very authentic looking replica of an eighteenth century original.

While the single winding hole in the dial implies a time-only movement like the original, this clock is equipped with a German chain drive three-weight chiming movement.

The dial is of wood, painted white with gesso paint and gold leaf decoration and black numerals.

When offered for sale, on a one-time basis, this clock sold for $3,500.00.

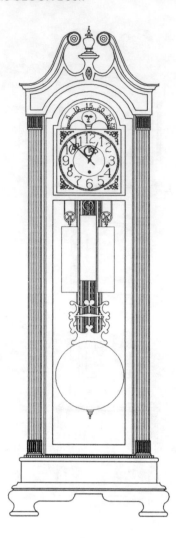

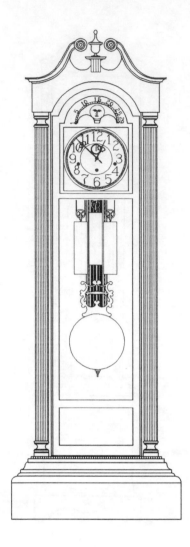

Figure 114 Howard Miller *Regency* Tall Clock
ca. 1992

Figure 115 Howard Miller *Chelmsford* Tall Clock
ca. 1992

Using a combination of solid and veneer walnut, this clock features large polished brass weights and very large lyre pendulum as major elements of its design.

The burl walnut inlay designs in the broken arch top are book matched for a balanced appearance. A glazed door forms a major part of the front of the case. On either side are finely fluted columns with polished brass fittings at top and bottom.

The German movement is equipped with a triple chime mechanism. A lever in a slot in the dial can be moved to select between Whittington, St. Michael or Westminster chime melodies. Chimes are sounded on eight long rods, while the hours are struck by hammers hitting five rods in unison. It was on sale in 1992 for $2,299.00

Similar in many respects to the *Regency* model shown in Figure 114. This clock differs in a number of ways. Most significantly, it is made of solid cherry and has no veneering.

The triple chime movement is similar but of lesser quality than that in the *Regency.*

The broken arch top is significantly shallower and the side columns have simple turned wood caps and bases, rather than polished brass.

The dial is simpler, with no silvering and the moving moon dial is also less elaborate. The door is divided into three segments, with the lower one being of wood, not glass.

The bottom of the case is simply rectangular, without the intricately cut molding of the *Regency.*

In 1992 it was on sale for $1,099.00.

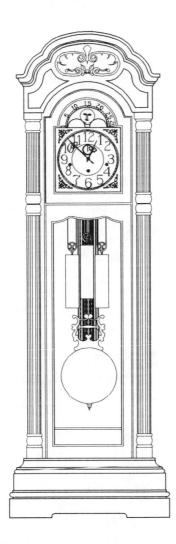

Figure 116 Howard Miller *Emden* Tall Clock
ca. 1992

Figure 117 Clocks Ltd. *Defree* Tall Clock
ca. 1994

This is a Tall clock without a broken arch top. It is of solid oak, with no veneer. The scalloped and incised top is massive in appearance.

The case features a small door over the dial and a larger one below, in front of the ornate lyre pendulum. Two piece fluted columns on either side of each door have simply turned caps and bases.

A mirror is positioned behind the pendulum on the inside back of the case.

The cable driven movement has only Westminster chiming. The lever in a slot on the right side of the dial allows the owner to select whether the chime is active or silent.

The dial, with seconds bit, is top of the line and features a moving moon dial.

Sale price of this clock in 1992 was $1,299.00.

One of the most ornate Tall clocks available in recent years is this one, sold by Clocks Ltd., of Wheeling, Illinois. It was made in either solid oak or walnut and was priced at $3,700.00.

In addition to elaborate decorative carving, including ball and paw front feet, this clock features a simulated temperature compensating mercury pendulum. Four cut glass tubes have nickel plated metal inserts to look like mercury.

The triple chime German movement is cable driven and is similar to, if not identical to those used by Howard Miller and others.

The dial, with seconds bit and moon dial is also of the same style and type used by other clock merchants. As with other cases of solid wood, stains are used to blend or disguise grain patterns.

CHAPTER SIXTEEN

CALENDAR CLOCKS

Mechanisms to enable a clock to show the current date, in addition to the time, became popular before the Civil War. They were available in kitchen and other shelf clocks and in wall clocks at a somewhat higher price than the non-calendar versions..

Known as *simple calendars,* these clocks have 31 numerals to indicate the date located outside of the time track on the dial. A long third hand rotates in a clockwise direction, advancing one numeral each day. When a month has less than 31 days, it is necessary to manually advance the hand to 1 at the beginning of the succeeding month.

The calendar hand is activated by a lever being lifted by a pin on the hour wheel to advance it one day in each twenty-four hour period. No separate source of power is required. The main spring powering the time train provides the energy necessary to move the hand.

In the late 1900's, an interesting form of digital clock showing the date was developed. It had 31 small cards, each with a number, that were loosely mounted on a shaft that rotated once in thirty one days. A stop held the top of each card, as the shaft slowly rotated, allowing one card to drop each day. In this way, the current date was displayed.

While this digital principle was used by several makers, it found only limited acceptance and few examples have survived.

Around 1860 and later, several mechanisms that made it possible to show not only the date, but the month and day of the week appeared.

Called *Day-Date* calendars, they also have to be manually advanced at the end of a 30 day month.

These clocks usually have a separate calendar dial, located below the time dial. The day and month are printed on paper strips pasted to a rotating drum. This drum is rotated by a system of levers and gears activated by a rod attached to the movement. This rod is activated once a day. The current day and month are seen through rectangular openings in the dial face. The date is shown by a hand pointing to a number on the dial.

Later, *Perpetual Calendar* mechanisms were developed that automatically compensated for the length of the month.

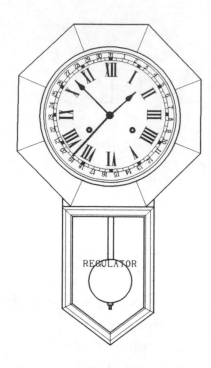

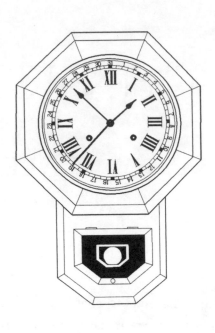

Figure 118 Long Drop Octagon Calendar Wall Clock
ca. 1890

Figure 119 Short Drop Octagon Calendar Clock
ca/ 1900

Nearly all clock manufacturers offered clocks indicating the date. The Drop Octagon or *Schoolhouse Calendar Regulator* was very popular for businesses as well as for schools.

The addition of a calendar indication made this type of clock an aid to teaching. In addition to telling the time, in terms of hours and minutes, it provided an object lesson in the counting of days in a calendar month. Since the date hand had to be set forward at the end of months with less than 31 days, it emphasized that months are of varying length.

The clocks shown in Figures 118 and 119 strike the hours and half hours, as indicated by the two winding holes in the dial. Most manufacturers offered time only versions, as well. These clocks were of eight days duration and had to be wound every week.

This Short Drop Octagon or Schoolhouse Regulator clock is typical of those made by many manufacturers. They were available in Oak or walnut in the wide variety of styles discussed in Chapter thirteen.

The short drop style simply has a shorter box at the bottom and a shorter pendulum. It differs from the long drop style in that the bottom door is hinged at the top, rather than the side.

While the Long Drop version often has the word *REGULATOR* in gold lettering on the door glass, the glass in the door of short drop clocks usually has a stenciled or transfer design. This design usually has an opening in it so that the pendulum is visible.

The calendar hand indicating the date is frequently painted red, instead of black.

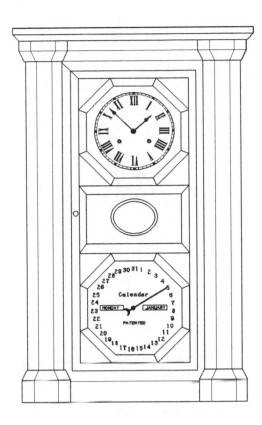

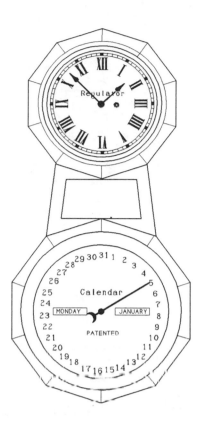

Figure 120 Seth Thomas Weight Calendar Clock
ca. 1864

Figure 121 Seth Thomas Office Calendar No.1
Ca. 1875

In 1864, the Seth Thomas Clock Co. acquired from the Mix brothers the rights to patents for calendar movements that indicated not only the day of the month, but the day of the week and the name of the current month.

The separate calendar movement is mounted below the regular time movement, which activates it, by means of an intermittently lifted and dropped lever.

Day of the week is shown in a slot to the left of the calendar dial, while the month is shown on the right. The date is indicated by a hand pointing to a number on the outer rim of the dial. This mechanism was used in many styles of clocks made by Seth Thomas and was soon imitated by other clock makers.

The case of the clock shown in Figure 119 is of rosewood veneer.

The clock in Figure 121 is an interesting example, notable for the fact that the time dial is substantially smaller than the calendar dial.

Wanting to make a smaller clock, while offering the day-date feature, Seth Thomas developed this unique case. Using a standard spring driven movement, with short pendulum and a smaller dial, was no problem, since these were routinely used in various shelf and wall clocks.

Rather than scale down the calendar movement regularly being produced, the company hit on the idea of making the bottom of the clock larger to accommodate the standard movement, dial and hand.

The case features decagonal bezels for both dials. The case is made of pine and is finished in veneered rosewood.

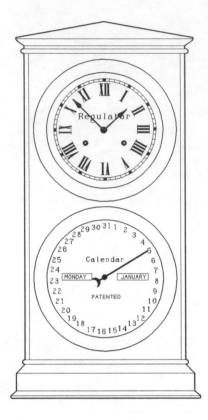

Figure 122 Seth Thomas Office Calendar No.2
Ca. 1875

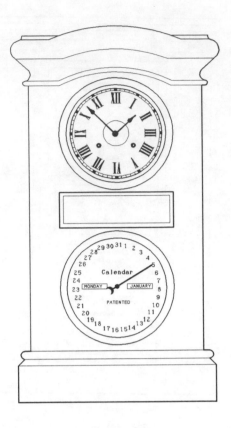

Figure 123 Seth Thomas Parlor Calendar No.1
ca. 1880

The Seth Thomas Calendar No.2 is a shelf clock, with smaller dials than previous calendar clocks. Both upper and low dials are the same size.

In addition to the calendar feature, this clock also strikes the hours and half hours.

The bezels for the time dial and the calendar dial are of walnut to match the case veneer. As are the moldings. The basic case is made of pine.

A new improved calendar mechanism, developed by Randal T. Andrews, an employee of Seth Thomas, was patented on February 15, 1876. This mechanism was used in this clock.

The new calendar movement made the earlier Mix Patent movements obsolete. Seth Thomas made a wide variety of clock cases in which this calendar mechanism was used.

This weight driven calendar clock also used the new Andrews patent calendar movement.

The pine case is veneered in rosewood, as are the bezels of both dials and the compound curved molding at the top.

Veneering moldings with complex compound curves such as those found on this clock is all but a lost art. Rosewood veneer is very brittle and making it conform to small radii while hot glue sets, especially in a production environment was a great accomplishment.

This feature is found on many clocks of the period, many of which have survived in remarkably good condition.

The Andrews patent calendar movement was used by Seth Thomas in a very wide variety of case styles.

Figure 124 Seth Thomas Calendar Weight Driven Column & Cornice Clock ca. 1860

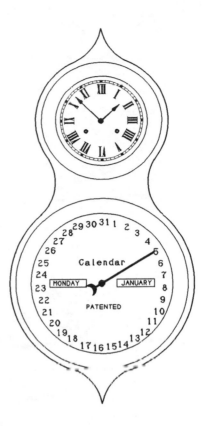

Figure 125 Seth Thomas Office Calendar No.1 ca. 1863

Among the earliest clocks to use a day-date calendar mechanism was this adaptation by Seth Thomas.

A then standard 8-day weight driven Column and Cornice clock was simply modified by the addition of the calendar mechanism, dial and hand.

Since the case of this style was long, simply to accommodate the long fall of the weights necessary to run a full eight days, there was ample space for the calendar movement near the bottom of the case.

The bottom tablet was simply replaced by a clear glass so that the calendar dial would be visible.

Similar adaptations of other case styles with weight driven eight day movements were not uncommon.

The early day-date calendar wall clock in Figure 125, known as the *Peanut* because of its shape, is similar to Figure 121 in that the upper, or time dial is smaller (5") than the calendar dial (7").

Like that model, it is probable that the case design of this model was the result of a desire to use time and calendar movements then in production. The calendar movement is a Mix patent type..

The case and wood bezels are of pine, veneered in walnut or rosewood.

While designated as an *Office* Calendar clock, this style found favor in many homes and some places of business.

It is interesting to note that some large wall clocks, notably the Seth Thomas Office Calendar No.4, had *larger* time dials.

Figure 126   Ithaca No.3½ Parlor Calendar Clock
ca. 1883

Figure 127   Seth Thomas Office Calendar No.8
ca. 1864

In 1865, a patent for a *perpetual* calendar clock mechanism was granted to Henry B. Horton of Ithaca, New York. He tried to license this invention to existing clock manufacturers, without success. With the backing of local investors, he started the Ithaca Calendar Clock Co. The company, making only calendar clocks was very successful, until it was forced into bankruptcy in about 1920.

The *perpetual* calendar mechanism automatically corrected for months with less than 31 days.

Case styles varied from severely plain to quite ornate, as illustrated in Figure 125. This model featured carved walnut and *ebonized* (black) columns.

The dials are printed, the time dial in black on paper, the calendar dial in silver on glass.

The Seth Thomas Office Calendar No.8 shown in Figure 127 is a rather large example. It measures 5 ½ feet tall. Both dials are 14"

Designed for use in public gathering places, such as large offices, banks and public buildings, such clocks are not often found in homes, except those of clock collectors.

It is interesting to note that, for a larger calendar dial, with larger date numerals and larger type on the day and month reels, it was necessary to modify the calendar movement. Larger and wider spaced drums were required for the day and month.

Some wall mounted calendar clocks, like other office clocks were nearly as large as tall clocks.

Other manufacturers made very large office clocks, as well as smaller models.

CHAPTER SEVENTEEN

CUCKOO CLOCKS

CUCKOO CLOCKS FASCINATE young and old today, as they have for more than a hundred years. Their combination of time-keeping, interesting animation, sound and carved cases provide interest in a great many homes.

The Black Forest (*Schwartzwald*) of Germany with its excellent timber resources has long been the center of a highly developed wood carving industry. Its carvers are recognized around the world for their artistry. Clock making was a natural development and was carried on in its early days as a cottage industry. Most of the work was done in private homes, on a somewhat specialized basis.

Wood carvers made the decorative shields that form the front and top of the case. Brass founders cast the wheels and plates of the movement and machinists finished them. Others made dials, hands, pendulums, weights and chains.

As clock making methods improved in other parts of the world, clock makers of the Black Forest followed suit and adopted mass production factory methods, becoming true manufacturers. Many cost cutting steps were taken, including the use of formed sheet steel and plastic parts. Quality of the movement suffered. In addition, carving quality deteriorated, especially after World War II.

While cuckoo clocks were the major output of Black Forest clock makers, they also made other types of clocks, notably the picture frame type. These clocks often had a glass dial covered by a rectangular molded frame with a clear glass pane.

The name *cuckoo clock* is commonly used to designate clocks of various kinds all of which feature decorative carving of a shield and top piece. Under this definition, some examples have carved representations of cuckoo birds as part of the shield decoration.

Others may have different animals and birds, notably foxes, rabbits, deer, quail, pheasants and eagles. Many have a door or doors that open at the hour and half hour to reveal a carved bird that bobs as the hours are struck on a gong and cuckoo whistles are activated.

Some cuckoo clocks include music box movements that play familiar tunes on the hour and half hour. In addition to the music, some have a rotating disc on which tiny dancers twirl.

Clock makers outside Germany intermittently tried to capitalize on the success of the cuckoo by adapting the design, notably in Japan and the United States. The *American Cuckoo Clock Co.* and the Lux Clock Company made cuckoo clocks in which the carving was replaced by molded shields made of a mixture of sawdust and molten rosin.

True Black Forest Cuckoo clocks have been made in a wide range of sizes, from miniatures measuring about 6" high to some well over four feet tall. Especially the larger ones feature very intricate and detailed high quality carving. Some of these almost complete obscure the clock dial.

One measure of the quality of cuckoo clocks is the quality of the carving. The best carving is deep and truly three-dimensional. Detail is precise and carefully executed. Outlines are clean and there is an absence of saw marks.

While occasional examples of oak, cherry and walnut cases are found, most cuckoo carvings are done in European lime or what we know as bass wood. The latter is almost free of grain and, when very sharp tools are used, may be carved into very intricate detail. It is later stained to simulate dark walnut.

Typical cuckoo clock cases are made of thin pine, often covered with hard wood veneer and are rectangular in shape with a pitched roof top. A carved piece, called a *shield* fits underneath the roof and extends below the bottom of the case. It is usually attached with small nails.

The clock dial, until fairly recently made of thin turned wood with cutout celluloid numerals, is attached to the case front with tiny nails.

A carved top piece is attached to the front edge of the case roof top, usually by means of small staples in its back, through which a wire hook attached to the roof top by a nail secures it.

The top piece is relatively delicate and easily damaged, so it is intended to be removed for moving or shipping. For this reason, it is not uncommon to find clocks missing the top piece.

The movements of the earliest cuckoo clocks had cast brass wheels, or gears, and other parts. The front and back arbor pivots were supported in holes in strips of wood running between solid wood top and bottom pieces. Later, cast brass front and back plates replaced the wood elements. Eventually, stamped sheet brass was used for front and back plates, wheels and levers.

The bellows, which are lifted and dropped by cams and levers, originally were made of very thin sheets of leather. In recent times, leather has been replaced with a synthetic fabric.

Cuckoo clocks are most often powered by weights suspended on link chains made of brass or steel. The chains run over a toothed sprocket in the movement that is fitted with a ratchet. When the free end of the chain is pulled down, a pawl rides over the ratchet teeth and the weight is raised. When the free end of the chain is released, the pawl engages and the weight applies power to the gear train.

Some cuckoo clocks, especially miniatures, have only a single weight to power the time train. There is no strike or cuckoo whistle.

When a clock has a cuckoo whistle, a second weight powers the strike train to activate the whistles and the hammer striking a gong mounted on the back of the case. It also opens a door in the top of the case front and moves a carved bird into position, where it bobs at each strike. In some cases, the second weight activates a music movement, or other animated devices.

A third weight may be present. Usually, it will operate a train activating a quail call, *bob white*, at the quarter hours.

Some cuckoo clocks run for 30 hours, while others run a full eight days. Pine cone shaped iron weights are used for both. Often the 8-day weights are larger and bulkier.

Figure 128 8-Day Cuckoo with Quail Call
ca. 1890

Figure 129 30-Hour Inlaid Front Cuckoo
ca. 1890

The clock in Figure 128 has three rather large weights. The left weight provides power for opening the door on the left, operating the quail call bellows and rocking the quail as its call is sounded.. At the hour, it also activates the strike train.

The center weight powers the time train that, in turn activates the quail door and bellows and rocks the quail that appears when the door opens

The weight on the right powers the cuckoo and strike train that opens the door on the right, makes the cuckoo bob up and down, operates the cuckoo call bellows and the strike hammer.

Made about 1895, the shield and top piece of this clock are deeply carved and well molded. Grapes and grape leaves form the motif for the design. The usual tree limbs appear as background and vine stems connect the leaves

Reflecting the tastes of the Victorian period, this style, featuring geometric inlayed wood in place of the traditional tree limbs and branches. Leaves and vines complete the design. At the base of the inlaid vertical shield pieces are turned wood finials. Squares of wood with turned centers also appear at the intersection of the vertical and horizontal inlaid pieces. The pendulum bob is also turned wood in a simple circular shape.

The string of leaves at the top is placed on top of the roof of the case, rather than in front of it as in

This is a simple 30-hour, two weight clock, with cuckoo whistles and gong strike. The door at the top of the case opens and a carved cuckoo bird appears and bobs up and down as the gong strikes and the whistles make the familiar cuckoo call counting the hours

Figure 130   Miniature 30-Hour Cuckoo
ca. 1900

.MINIATURE CUCKOO CLOCKS

Miniature cuckoo clocks, measuring about 6" in height, have appeared from time to time.

They nearly always have a single weight, tell time only and have no strike mechanism and therefore no cuckoo call or gong to sound the hours. A cuckoo is often featured in the top piece and in all other respects it resembles the conventional cuckoo clock design.

The weight, of conventional pine cone design, is much smaller than those used for larger clocks. The pendulum is usually a simple wire with a hook at the top to engage a similar hook at the end of the movement crutch. The bob is a simple round, flat wood turning, with a hole through which the pendulum wire passes.

There is no threaded nut to adjust the bob. Friction alone is depended upon to hold it in place. Precise adjustment is difficult, so the time keeping ability of these clocks is often rather poor.

The quality of carving varies from excellent, as in the example shown in Figure 130, to very poor. When the carving is of high quality, the case can be a true work of art.

Figure 131   30 Hour Cuckoo-Quail Call Clock
ca. 1910

This 3-weight clock, in addition to the time and cuckoo-strike trains, has a third train. It also has two doors at the top of the case. One for the cuckoo bird and the other for a quail.

At the quarter hours, the quail train is activated, the right door is opened and the quail bird appears. At the first quarter hour, the quail call, two short high pitched whistles, along with a gong strike is sounded. At the half hour, this call sounds twice, at the three-quarter hour three times and at the hour, four times. Following this, the cuckoo is activated and the hours counted.

A maple leave motif is used for the shield and top piece of this clock. In addition to the usual cuckoo at the top, a second one appears on a nest at the bottom of the shield. This is only one of many variations found in cuckoo clocks.

Figure 132 Spring Driven Mantel Cuckoo
ca. 1915

Figure 133 *Germany* 30-Hour Cuckoo Clock
ca. 1920

Easily identified as a cuckoo clock, this table or mantel clock uses springs rather than weights for power. It is key wound.

In other respects it is identical in operation to weight driven clocks. It has a time train and a strike train. A carved cuckoo bird appears in an opening at the top of the case, but there is no door. At the hour and half hour, the bird moves forward and bobs up and down with each strike. Whistles, as in other cuckoo clocks, produce a cuckoo call and a gong on the back board is struck for each hour.

The shield and top piece of this clock use the grape vine motif and the cuckoo at the top is engaged in eating from a bunch of grapes. As a free standing clock, a base is provided for support. This base is decorated with carving in keeping with the rest of the case.

In the example shown, the carving is of very high quality. Incising is deep and the farms are well molded. The case is nicely finished.

Following World War I, when shipment of cuckoo clocks to the United States was resumed, it was required that the source be indicated. The work *Germany* appears on the dial of this clock.

The design of the shield and top piece of this clock are much less intricate than most of those of earlier origin. While the case is about the same size, fewer leaves appear and they are larger and less deeply carved than most of those made before this time. This was part of an effort to reduce costs.

Following World War II further cost cutting steps were taken. The shield and top piece were made from thinner wood and the carving shallower and of lesser quality. Hundreds of thousands of American service men stationed in Germany purchased cuckoo clocks as souvenirs.

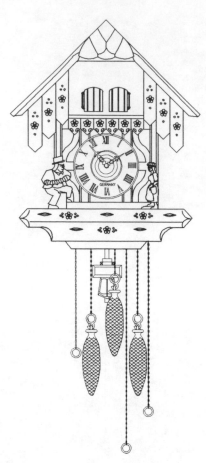

Figure 134 Painted Musical Cuckoo Clock
ca. 1980

While most cuckoo clocks adhere to traditional bird and leaf decorative designs, other more colorful styles have appeared from time to time. The example in Figure 134 is a fairly recent example.

This three-weight clock has time, conventional cuckoo call and strike trains, as well as a third train that operates a musical movement. Following the strike and cuckoo call at the hour and half hour, the right door opens and the figure of a man bobs up and down as a tune is played on a musical movement.

The colorful case is made up of several elements. The roof is decorated with a sloping front piece at the ridge and three decorated tabs under the eaves on either side.

The entire case is painted and hand painted decoration is applied to the tabs and the cross pieces at the bottom of the front. Three dimensional figures appear on the base at either side of the dial.

Similar clocks are available in 1994.

CHAPTER EIGHTEEN

VIENNA REGULATOR CLOCKS

VERY POPULAR IN EUROPE during the nineteenth century, a style of clocks made in Vienna, Austria were sold in some quantities in America. Clocks of this type have come to be known as *Vienna Regulators.* Their influence on The wall clock styles of American manufacturers is apparent.

Paralleling the clock making industry in the United States, the earliest Vienna Regulators made around 1700 were hand made by journeyman clock makers with the help of their apprentices. They were generally of very fine workmanship. The movements were usually smaller than those made in the United States, with heavier plates and finer pivots. In general, the workmanship was superior. This continued, even after mass production manufacturing methods were adopted.

Individually crafted Vienna Regulator clocks vary in size from large ones with full seconds beat pendulums, to miniatures. Some of the finest of the large clocks had running times of from two weeks to a full year on one winding. Most were of eight day duration. The cases of such clocks were usually of the *Lanterndluhr* style, see Figure 137.

Some are single weight driven, time only. Others have two weights and chime on bars or coil gongs. A few have three weights and have a *grande sonnerie* quarter hour chiming system. In this system, at each quarter hour, the number of the previous hour is struck, followed by a single strike for each quarter hour past the hour. This was sometimes done on a separate gong with a tone different from that used for the regular hour strike.

A common characteristic of Vienna clocks is that the movements are supported on metal brackets attached to the back board of the case and are easily removable. The pendulum hangs on a suspension spring mounted on the back board. The pendulum rod has a vertical slot into which a pin on the movement crutch fits to transmit impules to the pendulum. The gong is also attached to the back board.

Dials are nearly always of porcelain and numerals and time track are finely delineated.

As with American clocks, there were many manufacturers of Vienna Regulators and an infinite number of case designs.

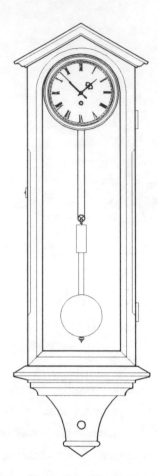

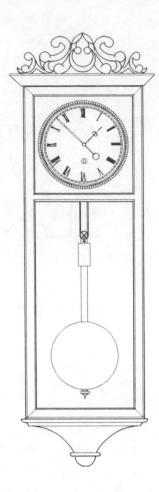

Figure 135   Early Single Weight Vienna Regulator
ca. 1820

Figure 136   Straight Line Vienna Regulator
ca. 1825

This is an early example of the Vienna Regulator style. It is time only, with a single weight. The dial is of porcelain with a cast brass bezel attached to it. The dial is attached to the movement that is attached to wooden brackets secured to the back board.

A comparatively small weight provides power for eight day running time. It is supported on a compound brass pulley. The orginal suspension cord is cat gut.

The case is of solid pine finished with a paint wash. The inside edges of the door are nicely molded and the outer door edges are partially bevelled. The pediment base has fine simple molding.

The hands are delicately cut and finely finished and blued.

The single weight, time only eight day clock shown in Figure 136 is typical of the elegant simplicity of early Vienna Regulator cases.

Elegantly proportioned, it has a carved splat at the top and nicely veneered door front.

The large dial has a finely detailed cast bezel and is of high quality porcelain. The very finely cut hands are nicely blued.

The high quality movement is mostly hand made and is supported on cast iron brackets. It is secured by means of knurled thumb screws.

This case as were most Vienna clocks, was of pine with veneered exterior surfaces. Walnut veneer was common, along with mahogany and ebony used in edge banding.

The cabinetry and hardware of these clocks is of the highest quality.

Figure 137   Vienna *Lanterndluhr* Clock
ca. 1840

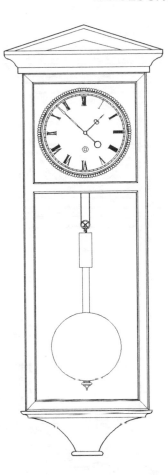

Figure 138   Straight Line Vienna Regulator Clock
ca. 1840

Considered by many to be the most beautiful clock case ever designed, because of its elegant proportions and simplicity of design, the *Lanterndluhr* style case housed some of the finest Vienna movements.

The example in Figure 137 features carefully selected and matched walnut crotch veneer with cross banding for the top door, the throat piece and the bottom door. Solid wood elements, including molding are made of walnut.

The movement is of 30 days duration and has time, strike and *grande sonnerie* quarter hour chiming.

The large porcelain dial is surrounded with an intricately designed polished cast brass bezel.

There were many variations of this basic design which was used by most Viennese clock makers.

Among the simplest and most pleasing of classic Vienna case designs, the one illustrated in Figure 138 was used by many clock makers. Cases for Vienna clocks were usually made by skilled cabinet makers who supplied them to the movement manufacturers. Dials and hands were also produced by specialty houses and sold to the clock manufacturer.

Assembly of all elements was done by a company whose name sometimes appeared on the dial and often on the movement. This entity was considered to be the maker of the clock.

The basic straight line case later evolved into more ornate designs of the Victorian or *Biedermeier* period.

There was little significant change in the design of movements during this time.

Figure 139 Round Top Vienna Regulator Clock
ca. 1850

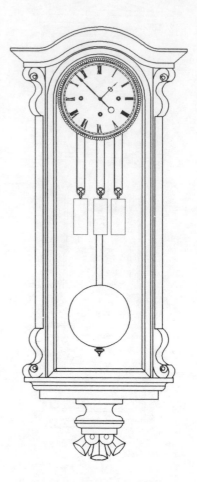

Figure 140 *Biedermeier* Vienna Regulator Clock
ca. 1850

Essentially a straight line case, but with a rounded and carved top, this fine time only clock has a running time of 8 days. It is unusual in that it has two separate glasses. Solid wood molding separates the hood from the lower door. Both are veneered with satin banding.

The large porcelain dial is surrounded by an intricate cast brass and machine turned bezel. The hands are of hardened and tempered blued steel and are very delicate in appearance.

As with most Viennese clocks, the pendulum is of wood. The bob is made of polished convex shaped sheet brass on both faces. A threaded steel rod is attached to the bottom of the pendulum with a nut below the bob for adjusting the rate.

Vienna Regulator clocks can be adjusted to keep very accurate time.

Retaining much the same proportions as the straight line style, this clock reflects the beginnings of more highly decorated designs. The top of the case features a curved molding. The top of the door is rounded to match.

Side columns set at an angle have been added and feature scrolled and carved top and bottom. The bottom is made up of simple moldings, except for the rather elaborate carved finial.

Not veneered, this example is made up of solid woods, painted, then dry brushed with a lighter color to simulate hard wood graining.

The dial is still of porcelain, with a finely made polished cast brass bezel. The three weights indicate that movement is time and strike with *grande sonnerie* quarter hour chiming. The pendulum rod is of wood painted black.

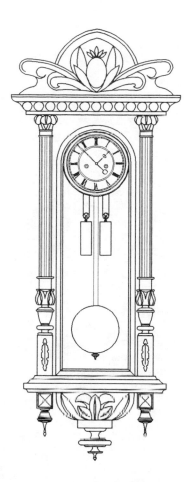

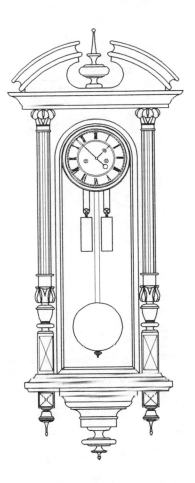

Figure 141 Half Column *Biedermeier* Vienna Regulator
ca. 1880

Figure 142 Half Column *Biedermeier* Vienna Regulator
ca. 1890

In keeping with the Victorian taste for more elaborate furniture decoration, often incorporating classical Greek architectural details, is this clock made by Gustav Becker, a major clock maker of the time. It features fluted half columns with turned and carved top and bottom details. The columns are attached to the door.

The inner edge of the door is molded and it carries a full length glass.

The top splat is also carved, as is the bottom piece. An elaborate three dimensional molding surrounds the top. Nicely turned finials are on either side at the bottom, plus a larger finial at the bottom center.

This is a two weight clock, with time and strike trains. Hours and half hours are struck on a coil gong. The dial is porcelain, the hands delicate.

In many ways similar to the clock in Figure 141, this is an example of the many variations of a basic design that were developed over the years by different manufacturers.

The door, with its fluted and carved columns is essentially identical, as are the bottom corner blocks and finials. The top and bottom decoration, however is markedly different. As is demonstrated here, a great many variations were achieved by using various combinations of stock molding and different finial designs.

Primarily for convenience and to avoid damage in shipping, the top piece was positioned by two dowels fitting in holes in the case top. It was easy to remove and replace. This also made it easy to change the overall appearance of the clock by simply changing the design of the top.

Figure 143 Spring Powered Vienna Regulator
ca. 1890

Figure 144   R&A Vienna Regulator
ca. 1890

As a measure and to reduce costs, particularly on overseas shipments, traditional weights were replaced by springs in some models. These clocks usually featured a brass pendulum bob with a porcelain insert bearing the letters *R* and *A* with a two headed vertical arrow between them. These letters stand for *Retard* and *Advance*. Presumably, the arrow indicates that moving the bob down retards the movement and raising it increases the rate, making it run faster. They are commonly referred to as *R and A* Vienna Regulators.

While retaining many of the traditional Vienna Regulator case features, the proportions were changed, because of the shorter pendulumand the dial was usually smaller. Running time is 8 days.

Porcelain dials were used, many of the two piece type with a brass ring joining them.

Since the tops and finials of Vienna Regulator Clocks were easily separable from the case, many have been lost or misplaced. It is not uncommon to see them displayed without the top or finials, as shown in Figure 144.

Some collectors believe that R & A Vienna clocks were sometimes sold by the manufacturer without tops, at a reduced price.

As with many old things, some Vienna clock tops of both weight and spring driven types were separated when they were thought to be out of date and were relegated to the attic. Unfortunately, many have never been recovered.

Even without the top piece, or without finials such clocks are eminently presentable and are displayed with pride in many homes today. They are excellent time keepers.

BIBLIOGRAPHY

The following list contains books I have found to be helpful in pursuing information about a wide variety of clocks. Most are somewhat general in nature, while others deal with a more narrowly defined type. I have found all of them to be interesting and of value in broadening my knowledge of clocks.

Some titles may be available at your local library. Many of them are available for loan to members of the National Association of Watch and Clock Collectors. Most are obtainable from one of the horological book sellers listed on page 181.

TITLE	AUTHOR	PUBLISHER
American Clock, The	Distin and Bishop	E. P. Dutton & Co.
American Clocks, A Treasury of	Brooks Palmer	The Macmillan Company
American Clocks & Clock-Makers	Carl W. Dreppard	Charles T. Branford Company
American Clocks, 19th Century	H. G. Harris	Emmerson Books, Inc.
American Clocks, Collector's Guide to	Anita Schorsch	Warner Books
Americana, Horology	Lester Dworetsky	Horology Americana, Inc.
Americana Auction Brochure, May 21, 1985		Richard A. Bourne Auctioneers
American Clocks & Watches, 200 Years of	Chris Bailey	Prentice Hall
Antique American Clocks & Watches	Richard Thomson	D. Van Nostrand Company, Inc.
Robert Dickstein		
Book of American Clocks, The	Brooks Palmer	The Macmillan Company
Calendar Clocks	Andrew Hays Miller	Antiquitat Publishers
	Dalia Maria Miller	
Clocks (The Cooper-Hewitt Museum Collection)	Douglas H. Shaffer	Smithsonian Institution
Clocks	Simon Fleet	Octopus Books
Clocks	Cedric Jagger	Crescent Books
Clocks and their Value	Donald de Carle	Anchor Press Ltd.
Clocks & Watches	Willsberger, Johann	The Dial Press
Clocks and Watches	G. H. Baillie	Scolar Press
Clocks and Watches	Eric Bruton	Hamlyn Publishing Group
Clocks and Watches, The History of	Eric Bruton	Rizzoli International Publications Inc.
Clocks, In Quest of	Kenneth Ullyett	Barrie & Rockliff
Clocks, The Country Life Book of	Edward T. Joy	Country Life Ltd.
Clocks, Watches and Chronometers	Abraham Rees	Charles F. Tuttle Company
Clockwork Universe, The	Maurice Mayr	Neale Watson Academic Publications
Cuckoo Clock, The Black Forest	Karl Kochman	Antique Clocks Publishing
Dictionary of Clocks and Watches	Eric Bruton	Bonanza Books
Electric Horology, 150 Years of	Elmer C. Crum &	NAWCC Chapter #125, Midwest
	William F. Keller	Horology Group
European Clocks	E. J. Tyler	Wardlock & Company Ltd.
French Clocks	Winthrop Edy	Studio Vista
Four Hundred Day Clock Repair Guide	Charles Terwilliger	The Horolovar Company
Horology, Treatise on Modern	Claudius Saunier	Charles T. Branford Company

HOROLOGICAL BOOK DEALERS

In addition to the firms listed below, books on horological subjects may be stocked by local book stores. If still in print, most book stores will be happy to order them for you. Ask them to check the current listing of *Books in Print*. Many major museum book stores also carry books of horological interest.

Adams Brown Co.	26 N Main Street	Cranbury	NJ	08512
Arlington Book Co.	2706 Elsmore Street	Fairfax	VA	22031
Discount Books	132 Ashurst Lane	Bristol	TN	37620
S. LaRose, Inc.	3223 Yanceyville Street	Greensboro	SC	48154
Merritt's Antiques	R. D. #2	Douglasville	PA	19518
NAWCC Museum	514 Poplar Street	Columbia	PA	17512
Scanlon American Reprints	1112 Ulrich Avenue	Modesto	CA	95350
The Time Museum Bookshop	7801 East State Street	Rockford	IL	61125
Trantiques Book Co.	3303 Edgemont Avenue	Brookhaven	PA	19015
U.S. Books	7707 Kiva Drive	Austin	TX	78749